YOUNG WISDEN

A NEW FAN'S GUIDE TO CRICKET

TIM DE LISLE
AND LAWRENCE BOOTH

WISDEN

First published in the 2007 by A & C Black Publishers Ltd
This edition published 2011 by John Wisden & Co
An imprint of A & C Black Publishers Ltd
36 Soho Square, London W1D 3QY
www.wisden.com
www.acblack.com

ISBN-13: 978 1 4081 2463 5

A CIP catalogue record for this book is available from the
British Library.

Commissioned by Charlotte Atyeo
Designed and typeset by Nigel Davies
Pre-press production by James Bunce

Cover photographs © Getty Images

All photographs © Getty Images except for: pages 22, 23, 38,
41 and 110 © Nigel Davies; page 115 © Billy Bowden;
page 125 © Crazy Catch.

This book is produced using paper that is made from wood
grown in managed, sustainable forests. It is natural, renewable
and recyclable. The logging and manufacturing processes
conform to the environmental regulations of the country of origin.

Printed and bound in China by C&C Offset Printing Inc. Ltd

CONTENTS

THE AIM OF THE GAME

The object of the game is to score more runs than the other side – but you also need to bowl them out. So the currency of cricket is runs and wickets.

Runs

A run is what you get when you and your partner each run to the opposite end of the pitch before the fielders can get the ball to the stumps. You get more runs for a better shot (or, sometimes, a lucky one): if you steer the ball away from the fielders, you get two or three, and if the ball reaches the boundary, you get four. If it flies over the boundary without touching the ground, you get six. A good team will score plenty of fours, but also loads of ones and twos. **Running between the wickets** is a vital skill. Australia may have lost their aura but they still do it better than everyone else.

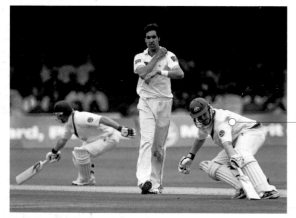

◄ Run 'em up!
Australia's Tim Paine left and Steven Smith push hard during the first Test between Pakistan and Australia at Lord's in 2010. Umar Gul looks on.

Wickets

There's a famous **tea towel**, often found in Christmas stockings, which explains how cricket works. "You have two sides, one out in the field and one in," it begins. "Each man that's in the side that's in goes out, and when he's out he comes in and the next man goes in until he's out. When they are all out, the side that's out comes in and the side that's been in goes out and tries to get those coming in, out …" Quite fun but not very helpful.

The tea towel is right to concentrate on the business of being out. It's the key to cricket. When a wicket falls, the game moves forward. There are a surprising number of ways of getting out – see page 8.

This is why bowling ultimately matters more than batting. If a team with great bowlers meets a team with great batsmen, the team with the bowlers will usually win. Australia's rise to the top in the 1990s came when one great bowler, Shane Warne, was joined by another, Glenn McGrath. Their batsmen were very good too, but not awesome. And when Warne and McGrath retired, after the 2006–07 Ashes, Australia looked distinctly mortal.

CRICKET
(as explained to a foreign visitor)

You have two sides, one out in the field and one in.

Each man that's in the side that's in goes out, and when he's out he comes in and the next man goes in until he's out.

When they are all out, the side that's out comes in and the side that's been in goes out and tries to get those coming in, out.

Sometimes you get men still in and not out.

When both sides have been in and out including the not-outs

That's the end of the game!

HOWZAT!

One innings or two?

Each team has the same number of innings – ie goes at batting. In a one-day match, they have one innings each. In a match of three or four days, known as first-class, they have two innings each. Same in a Test match, which takes five days. In an 11-a-side match, an innings consists of 10 wickets.

Why 10 wickets, not 11?

Because batsmen have to bat together. The team's innings ends when the last pair are parted, with one of them left not out. So batting always happens in partnerships. This is vital. When you bat yourself, you may feel very much alone – but there's always someone at the other end, and it helps to think about them too.

So what wins matches?

Good question. There's a saying: bowlers win matches. Which is true. There's another saying: catches win matches. Which is also true (and more catchy). But there's a third thing that wins matches: partnerships. A low-scoring match, especially, can be won by one big partnership. So when two batsmen get a start, they must make the best of it.

A classic example was the Lord's Test between England and Pakistan in 2010. The match would later become infamous after two Pakistani bowlers were accused by a Sunday tabloid of bowling no-balls for money.

But before that, it was famous for a record-breaking partnership between Jonathan Trott and Stuart Broad.

England had been reeling at 102 for 7 in perfect conditions for swing bowling when the pair came together shortly after lunch on the second day. But Trott, a South African-born batsman with almost inhuman powers of concentration, and Broad – whose previous best score in Tests had been 76 – calmly played themselves in as the ball lost its shine.

Amazingly, Trott and Broad were not parted until four overs before lunch on day four, by which time Pakistan had lost the will to live, and the batsmen had added 332, a record for the eighth wicket for any country in a Test match. Trott made 184, and Broad 169 – only four runs short of equalling the highest score by a No 9, made by New Zealand's wicketkeeper Ian Smith against India in 1990. It was the kind of performance statisticians dream about.

England's nine other wickets managed just 114 together, and Pakistan were just as bad. They scored 74 and 147 to go down to their heaviest-ever defeat: an innings and 225 runs, which meant England didn't need to bat again. When a Test match goes wrong, it can go really wrong.

England v Pakistan, 4th Test, Lord's, August 26–29, 2010. England 446; Pakistan 74 and 147. England won by an innings and 225 runs

	IJL Trott	SCJ Broad
runs	184	169
balls	383	297
fours	19	18
sixes	0	1

THE 11 WAYS OF BEING OUT

Being out is the most miserable moment in cricket for the batsman: it has even been described as a little death. And there are a surprising number of ways to perish. They fall into three groups…

THE BiG THREE

Bowled

For a batsman, it's the worst sound in the world – shrill, chilling and horribly final. You play a shot, the ball somehow passes your bat and clink! You're gone. While the fielding side gather for a noisy group celebration, you set off in silence on a long, lonely walk.

Being bowled is the simplest dismissal. You missed a straight one – or maybe edged it (known as "played on"), because if the ball touches your bat, pad or body on the way, it still says "bowled" in the scorebook. The only thing that can save you is if the umpire calls "no-ball!" Or if the stumps are brushed so faintly that the bails stay on. Don't bank on it.

Caught

This is the most likely way for a good player to be out. More than half of all Test dismissals are catches. Ricky Ponting has been caught 131 times in Tests, and dismissed in other ways 93 times – lbw 41, bowled 31, run out 14, and stumped seven.

Catches win matches, and sometimes start arguments. There are two common bones of contention: did the bat or glove touch the ball, and was the catch taken cleanly? The definition of a fair catch is quite fiddly. Here are the crucial bits:

The fielder CAN...
- touch the ground with his hand, as long as the ball doesn't touch the ground too.
- lean over the boundary, as long as he doesn't touch it or the ground beyond it. (This is rough on the batsman, who was just thinking he had hit a six.)
- catch the ball via another fielder (or an umpire).
- hug the ball to his body: hands are not strictly necessary.
- catch the ball by accident in his clothes, or, if he is keeping wicket, in his pads.

The fielder CAN'T...
- catch the ball in his cap or helmet, or via one of his team-mates'.
- lose control of the ball while still on the move. "The act of making the catch," says Law 30, rather solemnly, "shall start from the time when a fielder first handles the ball and shall end when a fielder obtains complete control both over the ball and over his own movement."

LBW

Leg before wicket is the thing that stops you saving your skin with your pad. If the fielding side **appeal**, and the umpire feels sure the ball was going to hit the stumps, you're out, as long as:

- the ball didn't pitch outside leg stump (this is to stop boring defensive medium-pace bowling from round the wicket).
- you didn't play a shot if it hit you outside the line of off stump.
- you didn't hit it first with your bat or glove. This saves you from an lbw, even though it doesn't stop you being bowled.

Lbw is slightly more common than bowled: in Tests since 2000, there have been 2516 players bowled and 2601 lbw. Some of them shouldn't have been given out – though others should have. This is why we have Hawk-Eye, the tracking technology.

THE NEXT TWO

Stumped

You're not trying to run, but your stroke takes you out of your crease, you miss the ball, and the keeper **whips the bails off** before you can scramble back. Warning: you may look quite silly. On the other hand, dancing down the pitch to a slow bowler is a good way to play him, so you'll probably score lots of runs too.

The top stumping victims of all time are Wasim Akram, of Pakistan, and Australia's Ricky Ponting, with 21 in international cricket. The top nine have all captained their country. So much for leading by example.

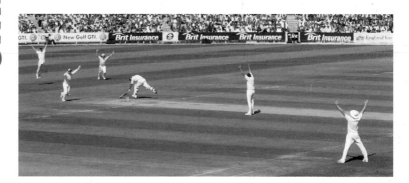

Run out

You think there's a run there, or your partner does, but it turns out there isn't, as the fielding side get the ball to the set of stumps you're running to before you arrive. You depart kicking yourself. Run-outs are traditionally accompanied by cries of "Yes! No! Wait! Sorry!" Mostly, it's not the decision to run that does for the batsman: it's the indecision, the moment of hesitation.

India's Rahul Dravid is currently the king of run-outs: he has fallen that way 51 times in international cricket. Next comes Marvan Atapattu of Sri Lanka, with 48, followed by Inzamam-ul-Haq, the magnificently slow-moving ex-captain of Pakistan, on 46. Ponting (again!) has been run out more times than anyone in Tests (14) – including two famous Ashes direct-hits: by England's sub fielder Gary Pratt at Trent Bridge in 2005, and Andrew Flintoff at The Oval four years later (see picture above).

A run-out doesn't count as a wicket to the bowler. It's also the only dismissal that allows you to score runs at the same time – if you are out going for, say, a third run, you get to keep the first two.

► **Run out**
Andrew Flintoff **far right** runs out Ricky Ponting at The Oval in 2009 with a direct hit from mid-on.

◄ **LBW**
South African wicketkeeper Mark Boucher appeals for an lbw decision against West Indies' Shivnarine Chanderpaul.

THE SiX WACKY ONES

Hit wicket

Back in 1975, the first World Cup final was held at Lord's. I was there, aged 12, with my dad, *writes Tim de Lisle*, and the atmosphere was electric. Dennis Lillee of Australia, a big, fierce, fast bowler, opened the bowling to Roy Fredericks of the West Indies, a small, stylish left-hander. At first Fredericks played quite carefully. Then Lillee tried a bouncer. Fredericks swivelled and played a perfect hook shot, right off his nose. It sailed over the boundary. Most of us didn't even notice that he had trodden on his stumps. He was out, hit wicket bowled Lillee, for only 7. It was quite a way to go – defeated by the force of his own rotation. At least he finished on the winning side.

Hit wicket – dislodging your own bails, whether with the bat or your body – is the most common of the wacky dismissals. There were 18 cases in Tests in the 2000s. The all-time champion is Denis Compton, a much-loved England batsman of the 1940s, famous for playing the sweep shot, which may explain why he hit his wicket five times – twice more than anyone else.

▲▶ **Hit wicket** Ian Botham above attempts to avoid a bouncer from Curtly Ambrose, but dislodges a bail while stumbling over his wicket playing for England v West Indies at The Oval, 1991. Denis Compton right falls on his wicket in the Trent Bridge Test against Australia in 1948.

Handled the ball

You're out handled the ball if you "wilfully" (ie deliberately) touch the ball, while it is in play, with a hand that is not holding the bat, unless you have the "consent" (agreement) of the other side. In practice, this means you can throw the ball back to the bowler if you've finished playing your shot and you're not running – although Australia's Andrew Hilditch was once given out at the non-striker's end after handling a wayward throw during an ill-tempered game against Pakistan in Perth. What you can't do is try to push the ball away as it heads towards your stumps. Seven men have been out this way in Test history, and the last three were Test captains – Graham Gooch and Michael Vaughan of England (though Vaughan wasn't captain at the time), and Steve Waugh of Australia. They all disappeared shaking their heads.

Obstructing the field

This is defined as "wilfully obstructing or distracting" the fielding side "by word or action". In practice, this means hitting the ball after it has been touched by a fielder – eg deliberately blocking a throw to save yourself being run out. And batsmen usually get away with it, because it is hard to prove the deliberate bit.

Only once has a Test batsman been given out this way: Len Hutton, one of England's all-time greats, against South Africa in 1951. He top-edged the ball, and then tried to stop it hitting the stumps with the bat, which is allowed, but in the process prevented the wicketkeeper, Russell Endean, from taking the catch, which isn't. Another time, Hutton was out hit wicket. Perhaps, like India's Mohinder Amarnath, he was trying to collect the set: Amarnath is the only player to have been out obstructing the field *and* handled the ball in one-day internationals. Careless.

Hit the ball twice

You're allowed to hit the ball twice if it looks like hitting the stumps. You can even kick it away. Otherwise, you're out if you deliberately take a second bite of the cherry. It just hasn't ever happened in an international.

▶ **Kick it** Paul Collingwood stops the ball from hitting his stumps.

Timed out

Technically, you can be out if you take three minutes to reach the middle at the start of your innings. In practice, this is often talked about but never happens at international level. It happened to AJ Harris of Nottinghamshire against the students of Durham in 2003 (he had a groin strain, and simply couldn't move fast enough), and it nearly happened to India's Sourav Ganguly in a Test at Cape Town in January 2007. Ganguly, who had sometimes been late for the toss when he was India's captain, took SIX minutes to appear, but got away with it as the delay was the result of a debate about whether Sachin Tendulkar was allowed to go in. He was padded up ready to go, but when the relevant wicket fell at 10.43am, the fourth umpire told Tendulkar he wasn't allowed in until 10.48, because he had spent some time off the field earlier. One of the on-field umpires, Daryl Harper, asked the South African captain, Graeme Smith, not to appeal for timed out, and he sportingly agreed. South Africa still had time to win the match by five wickets.

Retired out

If you are finding the game so easy it's boring, you can stop batting and let someone else have a go. In 2001, Bangladesh went to Sri Lanka as part of the short-lived Asian Test Championship. Bangladesh, playing only their fifth Test, were all out for 90, skittled by Murali. Two Sri Lankans, Marvan Atapattu and Mahela Jayawardene, made 201 and 150 respectively, and then lost the will to bat, so they went down as "retired out" – the only two such dismissals in Test history. It should really have said "retired bored". If they had retired hurt, claiming to have cramp, they would have gone down as not out and improved their average, so they get marks for honesty. And they still won by an innings.

Conclusion

Keep the ball down, cover your stumps, run without hesitation, and the only serious risk you're taking is being lbw. So if you take a big step forward, which makes most umpires reluctant to give you out, you will never be out at all. In theory.

THE 4 POSSIBLE RESULTS

When a match gets exciting, you hear the commentators say "all four results are possible here". What they mean is: one team can win, so can the other, it could be a draw, and it could be a tie.

Winning batting first

You make lots of runs, then bowl the other side out for fewer. This is how most captains prefer to do it. Bowlers often do better with a big score behind them – it's like a strong wind. And batting last, especially in a two-innings game, is mysteriously difficult. The pitch gets a bit uneven or cracked, and the weight of history bears down on the batsmen, who know that few big scores have been made batting fourth. Then again, batting second is often easier than batting first, because the pitch has flattened out. The pitch, you see, is crucial. More on that on page 16. The win is expressed as being "by X runs".

► **That's it!**
England batted first at The Oval in 2009, beat Australia by 197 runs and regained the Ashes. See the scorecard on page 14.

Winning batting second

Often easier at lower levels. You go in to bat knowing exactly how many you have to get. You may not even have to bat better than your opponents. In a one-day game, they might have made 220 for five from their 50 overs. As long as you get to 221 in your 50 overs, it doesn't matter if you have lost six, seven or even nine wickets. Bit unfair, isn't it? The win is expressed as "by X wickets" – X being the number you had left.

Whether batting first or second, a team can win by an innings. This means making more runs in one innings than your opponents do in two (completed) ones. If you bat first, you can ask your opponents to bat twice in a row – or "follow on" – if you have a big first-innings lead. In a Test, the lead has to be 200 runs; in a county or similar match, 150. The win is expressed as being "by an innings and X runs".

The draw

This is the one non-cricket lovers, especially Americans, find hard to understand. A game can go on for five whole days and not produce a winner? Bizarre, but true. If the side batting last doesn't reach its target, but isn't bowled out either, then the match is drawn. This can be very dull, or it can be exciting – if all four results were possible till the end. Draws used to happen a lot in Test cricket. Nowadays, thankfully, they are rarer, as batsmen are much more enterprising.

The tie

This is when the team batting last is all out with the total scores level. It is very rare in two-innings matches: out of the first 1973 Tests, only two were tied (see page 100). Ties are more common in shorter games: in one-day internationals, there were 23 in the first 3056 matches. But in Twenty20 internationals, the tie has been banned. Five of the first 191 games ended with the scores level, and the first three were decided by bowl-outs, with five players from each side bowling two deliveries at a set of unguarded stumps – a surprisingly tricky task. The two most recent ties have been settled by a one-over "eliminator", in which one team's best bowler sends down six balls to the other team's best batsmen. Traditionalists may object – but at least it ensures there's always a winner.

If the scores finish level in a two-innings match but the team batting last is not all out, that's technically not a tie. It is known as a draw with the scores level. The only time it has ever happened in Tests was in England's first meeting with Zimbabwe, at Bulawayo in 1996–97. The England coach, David Lloyd, was furious because the Zimbabweans had been allowed to get away with bowling deliberately wide. He famously said: "We flippin' murdered 'em." This had a grain of truth, but wasn't very gracious.

Winning batting first

Widest margin in a Test

England (903 for 7 declared) beat Australia (201 and 123) by an innings and 579 runs at The Oval, 1938.

Len Hutton left made 364, a new world record. Australia were missing two batsmen in each innings including their superstar, Don Bradman, who had broken his ankle in a freak accident – his foot got stuck in a foothold while he was bowling. But England's mammoth victory was not enough to win the Ashes: the series was drawn 1-1, so the Ashes remained with the holders, Australia.

Narrowest margin in a Test

West Indies (252 and 146) beat Australia (213 and 184) by one run at Adelaide, 1992–93.

The series hinged on that one run. If Australia had won the match, they would have taken an unbeatable 2-0 lead with one Test to go. As it was, West Indies pulled it back to 1-1 and went on to win the fifth Test and with it the series. It was almost the end of an era. Australia didn't lose another Test series at home until 2008–09, when Graeme Smith's South Africa beat them 2-1; West Indies haven't won anywhere other than Bangladesh and Zimbabwe since they won in New Zealand in 1994–95.

▼Narrow squeak Courtney Walsh celebrates the wicket of Craig McDermott to win the Adelaide Test of 1992–93.

HOW TO READ A SCORECARD

They're in the papers, on the web, on the telly, and in your hand if you go to a game. But they don't always explain themselves very well. Here's what they would say if they did, using a scorecard from one of England's most famous recent Tests.

Batting side

England are first because they batted first – and if you look at the **Toss** you'll see it was Andrew Strauss's choice. A simple decision to make, and – as it turned out – the correct one.

Batsmen

Traditionally shown with initials rather than first names. Often have numbers too, so an old-fashioned scoreboard might say "1" rather than "Strauss".

Balls faced

The number of balls a batsman faced can tell you lots at a glance. In England's first innings, most of the batsmen scored at a rate of a run every other ball, which suggested a healthy mix of defence and attack. In their second, Strauss played carefully to establish a platform, while Flintoff – in his final Test innings – and Swann had some fun. Clark's golden duck right near the end left Harmison on a hat-trick. He didn't succeed – but it didn't matter.

Number of bowlers

This tells you a lot about how a captain was thinking. England had the more balanced attack, because Flintoff batted at No 7, which meant their sixth bowler – Collingwood – was required for only one over all match. But Ponting, with just four frontline bowlers at his disposal, had to mix and match, using eight players in all and losing faith in Hilfenhaus in the second innings. What really hampered Australia, though, was their failure to pick Nathan Hauritz, a specialist offspinner, on a pitch which looked under-prepared to start with and took increasing amounts of turn as the game wore on. North did pretty well with his part-time offbreaks, but he managed only four wickets in the game to Swann's eight – a crucial difference. Harmison was underused in Australia's first innings, but with Broad bowling the spell of his life, that was a luxury England could afford.

Key men

The captain and wicketkeeper are identified by their own little symbols – usually an asterisk for the captain and a cross or dagger for the keeper.

Not out

At least one batsman is always left not out. In all four cases it was a tailender, which is as it should be. But in England's second innings, the No 11, Harmison, didn't get a bat. This was because Strauss **declared** which means he closed the innings before it was over. His logic? England were already 545 ahead – 127 more than any team had ever made batting last to win a Test.

Bowling figures

Usually four of them per bowler. In this order: overs, maidens (overs without a run conceded by the bowler), runs conceded, wickets taken. Hilfenhaus managed only one maiden in the second innings and went for nearly a run a ball – pretty expensive by Test standards.

5th Ashes Test
England v Australia
The Oval, August 20-23, 2009

England won by 197 runs. Five-Test series won by England 2-1

ENGLAND — 1st innings

Batsman	Dismissal	R	B	4/6
AJ Strauss*	c Haddin b Hilfenhaus	55	101	11/0
AN Cook	c Ponting b Siddle	10	12	2/0
IR Bell	b Siddle	72	137	10/0
PD Collingwood	c Hussey b Siddle	24	65	3/0
IJL Trott	run out Katich	41	81	5/0
MJ Prior†	c Watson b Johnson	18	33	2/0
A Flintoff	c Haddin b Johnson	7	19	1/0
SCJ Broad	c Ponting b Hilfenhaus	37	69	5/0
GP Swann	c Haddin b Siddle	18	28	2/0
JM Anderson	lbw b Hilfenhaus	0	6	0/0
SJ Harmison	not out	12	12	17/0
Extras	12 b 5 lb, 18 nb, 3 w	38		
Total	90.5 overs, 414 mins	332		

Fall of wickets
1-12, 2-114, 3-176, 4-181, 5-229, 6-247, 7-268, 8-307, 9-308

Bowling (1st)
Hilfenhaus 21.5-5-71-3, Siddle 21-6-75-4, Clark 14-5-41-0, Johnson 15-0-69-2, North 14-3-33-0, Watson 5-0-26-0

ENGLAND — 2nd innings

Batsman	Dismissal	R	B	4/6
AJ Strauss*	c Clarke b North	75	191	8/0
AN Cook	c Clarke b North	9	35	0/0
IR Bell	c Katich b Johnson	4	7	1/0
PD Collingwood	c Katich b Johnson	1	7	0/0
IJL Trott	c North b Clark	119	193	12/0
MJ Prior†	run out Katich	4	9	1/0
A Flintoff	c Siddle b North	22	18	4/0
SCJ Broad	c Ponting b North	29	35	5/0
GP Swann	c Haddin b Hilfenhaus	63	55	9/0
JM Anderson	not out	15	29	2/0
SJ Harmison	did not bat			
Extras	1 b, 15 lb, 9 nb, 7 w	32		
Total	95 overs, 408 mins	373-9 decl		

Fall of wickets (2nd)
1-27, 2-34, 3-39, 4-157, 5-168, 6-200, 7-243, 8-333, 9-373

Bowling
Hilfenhaus 11-1-58-1, Siddle 17-3-69-0, North 30-4-98-4, Johnson 17-1-60-2, Katich 5-2-9-0, Clark 12-2-43-1, Clarke 3-0-20-0

How out

That little b does a lot of work: it tells you who the bowler was. Bowlers get a credit for any of the common dismissals except a run-out – you can tell Flintoff removed Ponting with a direct hit because there's no second name (although you had to be watching to enjoy the drama of the moment). Even hit wicket counts to the bowler's tally. A b without a c means the batsman was bowled, either cleanly or played-on. A c means the batsman was caught, st stumped; lbw, as you know, means leg before wicket.

Extras

This could be really confusing. In the Extras line, b changes its meaning, from bowled to byes – runs taken when the ball hit neither bat nor pad (and the wicketkeeper couldn't gather it). There are four types of run that don't come off the bat and they are given in this order:

b   byes
lb leg-byes (ball went off the pad or, less often, the body)
nb no-balls (bowler overstepped or bowled third bouncer in same over; run awarded automatically and the ball must be bowled again)
w   wides (ball out of batsman's reach; punishments as per no-balls)

The greater discipline of England's attack was reflected in the number of extras conceded by both sides: 70 by Australia, only 27 by England.

Fours and sixes

Another media innovation, and a good one. Unusually, not a single six was hit all game, partly because The Oval is the largest playing area in England, partly because the tension of the game may have persuaded the batsmen to take fewer risks. But the fours column tells its own story. Swann, for example, hit one more four than Strauss in England's second innings, despite facing 136 fewer deliveries: two very different knocks for two very different situations.

Umpires

The two on-field umpires are given first. They have to be from countries other than those playing, so there's Asad Rauf from Pakistan and Billy Bowden from New Zealand. After the semi-colon you get the third or TV umpire, Peter Hartley. He can be local (and is – he's English). His job is to sit in the stand with a TV monitor and rule on tight run-outs and stumpings whenever his two colleagues make the telly sign. And if both sides have agreed to use the relatively new Umpire Review Decision System – which they didn't in this series – he may also have to adjudicate on lbws or questionable catches if the players decide to challenge an on-field decision. The match referee – Sri Lanka's Ranjan Madugalle – is the umpires' boss.

Fall of wickets

The number of runs the batting side had when each wicket fell. You can use this to trace the partnerships – which win matches, remember. For England, two partnerships stood out, and they both involved Strauss: 102 in the first innings for the second wicket (ie after one wicket had gone down) with Bell; and 118 in the second for the fourth wicket with Trott (much-needed after three wickets had fallen for only 12 runs). Australia managed one century partnership (127 for the third wicket between Ponting and Hussey in the second innings), but they could have done with something similar first time round. After Watson and Katich put on 73 for the first wicket, all ten wickets fell for 87. Ouch.

Overs per innings

The typical Test innings lasts 100 overs, with the fielding side getting a new ball after 80. It's easy to see where Australia lost the Ashes: their first innings lasted about half as long as it should have done because Broad found his length and rhythm on the third afternoon. Equally, the Australian bowlers allowed England to score too quickly all match, especially in the second innings, where they conceded 3.92 runs per over – the kind of rate at which Australia themselves used to score on a regular basis when they were the No 1 team in the world.

AUSTRALIA

Batsman			R	B	4/6
SR Watson	lbw	b Broad	34	65	7/0
SM Katich	c Cook	b Swann	50	107	7/0
RT Ponting*		b Broad	8	15	1/0
MEK Hussey	lbw	b Broad	0	3	0/0
MJ Clarke	c Trott	b Broad	3	7	0/0
MJ North	lbw	b Swann	8	17	1/0
BJ Haddin†	c Prior	b Broad	1	9	0/0
MG Johnson	not out		11	24	2/0
PM Siddle		b Swann	26	33	5/0
SR Clark	c Cook	b Swann	6	8	1/0
BW Hilfenhaus		b Flintoff	6	21	1/0
Extras	1 b, 5 lb, 1 nb		7		
Total	52.5 overs, 226 mins		160		

Fall of wickets 1-73, 2-85, 3-89, 4-93, 5-108, 6-109, 7-111, 8-131, 9-143

Dismissal		R	B	4/6
lbw	b Broad	40	81	6/0
lbw	b Swann	43	68	7/0
run out Flintoff		66	103	10/0
c Cook	b Swann	121	263	14/0
run out Strauss		0	4	0/0
st Prior	b Swann	10	24	2/0
c Strauss	b Swann	34	49	6/0
c Collingwood	b Harmison	0	5	0/0
c Flintoff	b Harmison	10	14	1/0
c Cook	b Harmison	0	1	0/0
not out		4	8	1/0
Extras 7 b, 7 lb, 6 nb		20		
Total 102.2 overs, 431 mins		348		

Fall of wickets 1-86, 2-90, 3-217, 4-220, 5-236, 6-327, 7-327, 8-343, 9-343

Bowling

(1st) Anderson 9-2-29-0, Flintoff 13.5-4-35-1, Swann 14-3-33-4, Harmison 4-1-15-0, Broad 12-1-37-5

(2nd) Anderson 12-2-46-0, Flintoff 11-1-42-0, Harmison 16-5-54-3, Swann 20.2-8-120-4, Broad 22-4-71-1, Collingwood 1-0-1-0

Toss	England
Umpires	Asad Rauf (Pakistan), BF Bowden (New Zealand); PJ Hartley
Match Referee	RS Madugalle (SL)
Test debut	IJL Trott
Man of the Match	SCJ Broad

PITCH, TOSS AND WEATHER

It's not all about runs and wickets.
The earth, the air and the toss of
a coin make a big difference too.

Batsmen and bowlers bicker about which of them really rules the game. In fact, neither lot does. It's the pitch.

The pitch dictates what a good score is. You can see this by looking at the scores through a Test series. In one Test, both teams may make 500, and the game peters out into a draw. In the next, both may struggle to reach 300, and the game is over in three or four days. The difference is in the conditions. It's in the lap of the gods – and the groundsman.

A good pitch … but who for?

A good pitch for batting is flat, hard, dry and light-brown. Flat means the bounce will be even. Hard means the ball will come onto the bat and ping off it.

Dry and brown mean the ball won't sink into the surface and move off the seam.

A good pitch for bowling has a touch of greenness or damp or both, which gives sideways movement. Or, it's dry, but has cracks, which will open up as the game goes on, producing some uneven bounce. If it's very dry, there will be turn for the spinners and sometimes reverse swing for the fast bowlers.

A good pitch for cricket will help the bowlers and the batsmen at different times. It will be bouncy throughout. It will have a touch of moisture early on to help the seamers; then it will dry out and help the batsmen for a couple of days; then it will start cracking or roughing up, giving help to the spinner and the reverse swinger.

▶ **Heads or tails?**
Andrew Strauss tosses the coin at the start of the 2009 Ashes in Cardiff. Ricky Ponting called correctly and batted – and England ended up holding on for a nail-biting draw.

It's a toss-up

Some matches are decided in a single moment, by a curious little event which happens before 20 of the 22 players even take the field: the toss. The home captain flips a coin, the away captain calls heads or tails, and the winner has the choice of batting first or second.

The toss itself is pure luck, a 50-50 chance, but the choice is judgment. Again, this depends on the pitch. Normally, the winning captain bats first. There's a quote about this from Colin Cowdrey, who captained England in the 1960s and ended up being made a Lord. "Nine times out of ten," he said, "you should automatically bat first. The other time, you should think about fielding, then bat." He was as good as his word: as England captain, he won the toss in 17 Tests and batted every time.

But that was the 1960s, when most captains were cautious.

These days they are bolder. England won the toss and fielded 75 times in their first 133 years in Test cricket (1877–2010), and 45 of those 75 came in the last 30 years. Lately bowling first has led to more wins than losses, but when it doesn't, it can be a big blow. ■ ■ ■ ■ ■ ■ ■ ■ ■ ■ ■ ■ ■ ■ ■ ■ ■ ■

Sometimes the captain's choice is really tricky. "A good toss to lose," say the commentators – because it's a 50-50 decision and the team winning the toss is expected to do well. But that expectation isn't entirely logical. Several Test teams actually do better when losing the toss. In the 10 years to October 2010, England, India and Pakistan all won more of their matches when losing the toss than when winning it. Australia, South Africa and Sri Lanka did better when winning the toss, and with New Zealand and West Indies it made no difference. So perhaps it's less crucial than we think.

When bowling first goes wrong, it can go very wrong. Just look at two recent Ashes series. The 2002–03 Ashes began with Nasser Hussain of England putting Australia in to bat on a belting pitch at Brisbane. Australia strolled to 364 for two on the first day and England never recovered, losing 4-1. The Ashes series of 2005 hinged on the toss for the second Test, when Ricky Ponting , already 1-0 up, opted to bowl first. England responded by slamming 400 in a day, won the match by a heart-stopping two runs, and went on to a famous series victory.

Some like it hot ... some don't

The weather can play a big part. Sometimes one side bats in blazing sunshine, while the other bats under thick cloud. Here's why it matters:

WEATHER	WHO LIKES IT	WHY
HOT AND SUNNY	batsmen >>>	good visibility, little swing, bowlers tire
	spinners >>>	pitch dries out, takes turn
	spectators >>>	good visibility, chance to get tan (don't forget the sunscreen)
CLOUD COVER	seamers >>>	ball usually swings, pitch retains moisture
HUMIDITY	seamers >>>	ditto
SHOWERS	seamers >>>	bowlers fresh, pitch damp, batsmen's concentration broken
... BUT SOMETIMES	batsmen >>>	if umpires slow to go off, ball gets wet and starts to resemble bar of soap; bowlers' run-ups treacherous
NON-STOP RAIN	lazy sods >>>	chance to put feet up
	injured players >>>	time to recover, don't miss anything
GENTLE BREEZE	fielding side >>>	cool, refreshing
HOWLING GALE	batsmen >>>	hard for bowlers to control the ball, and to repeat their action
FREEZING COLD	batsmen >>>	cold hands more likely to drop catches

ARMED ... AND EXTREMELY SAFE

Few games require more equipment than cricket. Even a player as good as Alastair Cook needs plenty of protection.

BAT

For a long time, bats looked like hockey sticks. Then overarm bowling came along, and they turned into planks with handles. Now they are more like clubs with springs. The England opener Alastair Cook has a deal with Gray-Nicolls, who started life making rackets in Cambridge for a sport called, well, rackets (a forerunner of squash) in the mid-19th century. Early customers included Ranjitsinhji, the Indian prince who played the sport at Cambridge University and went on to win 15 Test caps for England, and King Edward VII. They've been making cricket bats since 1876, and counted W.G. Grace among their posterboys: W.G. used a Gray-Nicolls to make 1000 runs in May in 1894. The company grows 90% of its own willow and calls its bats names like Nitro, Powerbow and Ignite. Cook uses an Oblivion, which is not believed to be a comment on the future of his Test career. But it doesn't matter what a bat is called. What matters is how it feels and how it plays.

made of willow, with Irish linen to bind the handle, and rubber to cover it; the handle itself is mainly made of cane

limits length 38 inches (965mm), width 4¼ inches (108mm); strangely, there is no limit on weight, but 2lbs 7oz or less is considered light for a grown man, 2lbs 8oz to 2lbs 10oz is medium, and 2lbs 11oz or more is heavy

price £40–£240

BATTING GLOVES

Once they had spikes. For a brief time in the mid-1970s they were flat, like little thigh pads for the hands. Now gloves nearly always have sausages. Even so, fingers get broken. Nasser Hussain, England captain from 1999 to 2003, got so many breaks he was known as Poppadom Fingers. Some top players have them customised: Hussain's predecessor Alec Stewart, after getting a few fractures in mid-Test career, wore a little plastic scabbard over the forefinger of his bottom hand, which seemed to work – he went on to become England's most capped player, appearing in 133 Tests. He was also famous for having the neatest corner of the dressing-room.

made of palm cotton, nylon or leather; sausages foam; panels may be suede or leather

limits practicality – need a flexible grip on the bat

price £8–£60

HELMET

Generations of cricketers batted in caps or even went bare-headed, but nasty accidents did happen occasionally and since the late 1970s, almost everyone (except Viv Richards) has worn one. England players used to be allowed white ones but now they have to wear navy blue ones, which match their caps.

made of shell ABS (acrylonitrile-butadiene-styrene) plastic lining foam visor titanium or steel strap nylon and lycra

limits nobody wants much weight on their head

price £37–£100

ARM GUARD & CHEST GUARD

Cook seems not to be wearing these. Many batsmen prefer not to, but a fast bowler may look a little bulkier as he potters out to bat against a fellow paceman.

made of high-density foam

limits length of forearm, volume of shirt **price** £7–£20

THIGH PAD

If you've ever been hit there, you'll want one. The Australian batsman Mark Waugh drew a stick figure on it every time he hit a first-class hundred. He had to keep using the same thigh pad, which outlived more than 30 bats before finally succumbing to old age. It helped him make 59 hundreds.

made of high-density foam

limits space in trousers

price £9–£28

PADS

The manufacturers call them leg-guards. Nobody else does, but cricketers are grateful for the broken legs they prevent. Tuck in the straps so they are less likely to nick the ball and make the umpire think you're out.

made of mainly foam and cane with some leather

limits practicality – need to be able to run

price £16–£80

FiND OUT ABOUT

the right bat size www.thecricketstore.net

bat-making salixcricketbats.com

ball-making read the article on www.espncricinfo.com/magazine

NOTE Prices may vary, as may the materials used

BALL

Red, shiny, hard and hand-stitched, a top-quality cricket ball is a beautiful thing – when new.

Eighty overs later, it will be pinkish, dull, soft and hideous. It takes cows, sheep, trees and dozens of human beings to make a cricket ball. The human beings and the sheep are alive; the other ingredients are dead. Most of the balls for Test matches are made by Dukes or Kookaburra. Dukes are used in England, have a proud seam and swing a lot. Kookaburra are used more elsewhere, especially in Australia, have a flatter seam and tend to swing only for the first hour.

made of people say leather, but actually the ball is made of at least four materials – the core is cork or a cork-rubber mixture, then there's a layer of wool string, then the leather skin, some more string (sometimes made of flax) to form the seam, and finally a layer of lacquer

limits weight 5½ oz to 5¾ oz (155.9g to 163g), circumference 8¹³⁄₁₆ inches to 9 inches (224mm to 229mm); seam 78 to 82 stitches

price £5–£65

BOX

You can't see it, but it's definitely there: no male cricketer over the age of 13 leaves home without one. Mostly, boxes get given more elaborate names by manufacturers who seem reluctant to face the simple truth of what they do. "Abdo guard" is a favourite. When leading batsmen get hit in the box, the commentators tend to resort to euphemism too. "And he's hit amidships!" is a favourite. "That's the most painful part of the anatomy," is another. One Test physio had no such qualms. A West Indian tail-ender, who might prefer not to be named, was hit in the box, and ended up in hospital. The physio helpfully explained to the press that the box hadn't quite been in the right place when it was struck – one testicle was inside, and one out. Seldom has a cricket story inspired so many sympathetic winces.

made of plastic **limits** only the size of your trousers, but no point wearing one that's too big **price** £2–£4

THE LAWS
AND THE MEN WHO ENFORCE THEM

Cricket is like school – there are a lot of rules. They are even called the Laws, as if they were made in Parliament. There are so many they take up almost 50 pages in *Wisden Cricketers' Almanack*. We don't have that many, so here are some of the main points.

THE UMPIRES

There are two of them, one at each end. The one whose end the bowling is from stands a few yards behind the stumps, enjoying the best view in the house. The other stands sideways on, 20 yards back, usually at square leg, sometimes at square cover if there is a fielder in the way. They are on the field for longer than anyone else.

The bowler's-end umpire is the busy one. He has to watch out for no-balls, then instantly switch his focus to the far end so he can make crucial decisions about lbws, edges to the keeper and bat-pad catches to the close fielders, as well as less vital ones about wides, byes and leg-byes. He also counts the number of balls in the over, usually by moving six pebbles across from one pocket to the other, and makes the majority of the signals. These are addressed to the scorers, of whom there are also two (cricket is like Noah's Ark: the animals come in two by two). The scorers raise a hand to show that they have seen the signal.

Out! | **No ball** (also spoken) | **Wide** | **Bye** | **Leg-bye** | **Four** | **Six** | **Refer to tv umpire**

15 UMPIRING SIGNALS as demonstrated by HUGO BLOGG, who at 12 years old is the youngest person to qualify as a

3 KEY LAWS

Bowl with a straight arm. If you straighten your elbow as you deliver the ball, you are not bowling – you're chucking, which gives you an unfair advantage. Quite a lot of bowlers do this occasionally as they strain for extra pace or bounce. Some observers, mostly in Australasia, think Muttiah Muralitharan does this all the time. Others agree with the game's bosses that his action is unusual but within the rules. The rules have been relaxed recently – bowlers are now allowed 15 degrees of flexion, as video evidence suggested that many of them were breaking the old rule.

Don't tamper with the ball. You can dry it, polish it and apply saliva or sweat to it. But you can't do anything else.

Don't distract or obstruct the batsman. Once the bowler runs in, the fielders can walk in, but they can't change position or do anything to put the batsman off.

6 KEY PIECES OF ETIQUETTE

Etiquette is a funny word which makes things sound rather … twiddly. But it just means accepted behaviour, which helps to make things happen. Here are some dos and don'ts.

All Do accept the umpire's decision – it may be wrong but he's not about to change it.

Fielding side Don't celebrate till the umpire's finger goes up.

Bowler Don't follow through close to the stumps.

All Don't run on the pitch.

Fielders Don't appeal for a catch if you're not sure about it.

Fielders Do applaud the batsmen when they reach 50 or 100, or get out for plenty.

6 TOP TEST UMPIRES

Simon Taufel Aus, 64 Tests Sideburns, five times ICC Umpire of the Year

Billy Bowden NZ, 64 Tests Crooked fore-finger, general eccentricity

Aleem Dar Pak, 60 Tests Solid judgment and calm way with players

Steve Davis Aus, 28 Tests Genial and unruffled, looks like your grandpa

Ian Gould Eng, 16 Tests Ex-England one-day keeper known as "Gunner"

Asad Rauf Pak, 31 Tests Laid-back and unfussy, does things at his own pace

4 KEY AREAS FOR THE UMPIRES

1 The weather

Should rain stop play? It's up to the umpires. At the first drop of drizzle, they play on. If the rain gets harder, they confer, and play on again, hoping the shower will pass. Then they confer again, or exchange a knowing glance, and remove the bails. Everyone trots back to the pavilion.

2 The light

The sky darkens, the light meters come out and often the light is offered to the batsmen – ie they are given the chance to come off. Test umpires tend to offer the light too readily, and batsmen tend to take it too readily. When play does continue in the gloom, the batsmen's eyes adjust amazingly well. It's actually the fielders who struggle, because they don't know when to expect the ball.

3 Intimidatory bowling

It means designed to frighten. A lot of pace bowling does this a bit. The umpires step in when it becomes a relentless bombardment.

4 Ball-tampering

The ball suddenly starts swinging again when it's old. This could be perfectly legal – the fielding side have polished one side, the other has been roughed up by the turf, and the bowlers have the skill to whip it in at the batsmen's toes. Or they may have worked on it illegally, by lifting the seam. The umpires have to decide. They can award five penalty runs against the fielding side – but the only umpire ever to do this, Darrell Hair, who penalised Pakistan in a Test in England in 2006, paid a heavy price. The Pakistanis refused to play on, so Hair ruled that they had forfeited the match. He was technically right, but inflexible and undiplomatic. He stood in only two more Test matches before retiring.

THE SPIRIT OF CRICKET

For more than 200 years, the spirit of the game was something talked about but not written down. Then, in 2000, the guardians of the laws – MCC – put it on paper and attached it to the laws as a preamble. The full text can be found at **www.lords.org** but it's a bit long-winded, so here are the main points:

Cricket is a game with a special appeal. It should be played not only within its Laws but also within the spirit of the game – fair play, basically. If you abuse this spirit, you damage the game. The umpires are the sole judges of fair and unfair play, but it's up to the captains to make sure their players keep to the spirit. If a player behaves badly, the umpire concerned should report him to the other umpire and to his captain, and tell the captain to do something about it.

The spirit of the game means respecting:

- your opponents
- your captain
- the authority of the umpire
- the game's traditional values.

It is against the spirit:

- to dispute the umpire's decision by word, action or gesture
- to swear at an opponent or umpire
- to go in for any cheating or sharp practice, such as:
  - to appeal knowing that the batsman is not out
  - to advance aggressively towards the umpire when appealing
  - to try and distract an opponent, either verbally or with persistent clapping or unnecessary noise disguised as motivation of your own side.

There is no place for any act of violence on a cricket field.

Captains and umpires set the tone for the match, but every player is expected to contribute.

FIND OUT MORE

The full Laws of Cricket can be found:
- in *Wisden Cricketers' Almanack*
- in the Lord's shop, as a **booklet** to buy (£2.50)
- online, at **www.lords.org**

The leading book on how to apply and interpret the Laws is Tom Smith's *New Cricket Umpiring and Scoring* (Weidenfeld, 2004, £9.99).

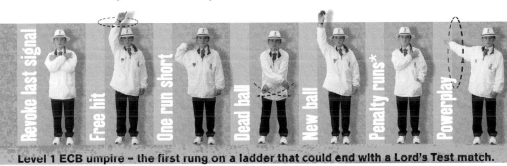

Revoke last signal | Free hit | One run short | Dead ball | New ball | Penalty runs* | Powerplay

Level 1 ECB umpire – the first rung on a ladder that could end with a Lord's Test match.

*PENALTY RUNS Right arm resting on left shoulder – five runs to fielding side
Right arm tapping left shoulder – five runs to batting side

7 DODGY PRACTICES CRICKETERS GO IN FOR

Claiming catches when they're not sure the ball has carried.

Time-wasting when playing for a draw.

Taking the light when they're in no danger.

Rubbing their arm to trick the umpire when the ball has actually flicked the glove.

Selective walking when they have edged the ball to the keeper. Walking means giving yourself out without waiting for the umpire's decision. Some think it's honourable; others think it's crazy. But the important thing isn't whether you walk – it's whether you are consistent about it. By walking most of the time, you may con the umpire into giving you not out when you actually edged it.

Moving or running after being struck on the pad to distract the umpire and get away with an lbw. A trick beloved of old pros.

Sledging – talking to or about the batsman in a way you hope will help get him out. It's clearly against the spirit of the game, so it shouldn't be tolerated. Any winning team, from Australia to St Cake's 2nds, would be more impressive if they didn't sledge. Often it is just bullying, which, as you know from school, is a cowardly thing to do. But umpires meekly put up with it – and sometimes sledging almost redeems itself by being quite witty. See page 117 for a few examples.

TICK TOCK

0.79 SECONDS

Time the ball takes to reach the batsman, if bowled at 50mph – the pace of Graeme Swann on a good day *(Calculation: 50mph = 24.44 yards per second. Time taken = 19.33/24.44 = 0.79 seconds)*

0.44 SECONDS

Time the ball takes to reach the batsman, if bowled at 90mph – the pace of Stuart Broad on a good day. *(Calculation: 90mph = 1.5 miles per min = 0.025 miles per second = 44 yards per second. Distance from bowler to batsman = 22 yds – 8ft = 58ft = 19.33 yds. Therefore time taken = 19.33/44 = 0.44 seconds)*

3 MINUTES

Time allowed for a new batsman to get into position, from the fall of the previous wicket – otherwise he can be timed out (see page 11).

4 MINUTES

Recommended length of a Test-match over. A fast bowler tends to take five minutes, a slow bowler three. Teams are supposed to bowl 90 overs in a six-hour day.

11 MINUTES

Fastest genuine fifty ever made in first-class cricket, by Big Jim Smith of Middlesex against Gloucestershire at Bristol in 1938. It is thought to have taken him only 12 balls. Although mainly a fast bowler, Smith was also "a batsman whose entry always roused a hum of excitement," according to his obituary in the 1980 *Wisden Cricketers' Almanack*. "His principal stroke (perhaps his only one!) was to advance the left foot approximately in the direction of the ball and then swing with all his might. If the ball was well up (and the foot on the right line) it went with a low trajectory an astonishing distance." A fifty was made in eight minutes by Clive Inman of Leicestershire against Nottinghamshire at Nottingham in 1965, but the bowlers were deliberately bowling badly to hasten a declaration, so *Wisden* mentions it only in a footnote and the record still belongs to Big Jim.

20 MINUTES

Time allotted for tea break in Test and most first-class cricket. Many players say it is too short – especially those who have to bowl straight afterwards with a cucumber sandwich and two Jaffa Cakes in their gullet.

28 MINUTES

The fastest Test fifty in terms of minutes, made by Jack Brown of England against Australia at Melbourne in 1894–95. "All the reports of the match agreed," noted *Wisden*, "that his innings was absolutely free from fault." And it really made a difference: Brown, a stumpy Yorkshireman with a powerful cut shot and a good sense of humour, made 140, England cantered to their target of 297, and they won the series 3-2. The match was timeless, but Brown was a young man in a hurry. Perhaps he sensed that he would not live long: he died of heart failure ten years later, aged only 35.

35 MINUTES

The fastest hundred in first-class cricket, by Percy Fender of Surrey against Northamptonshire at Northampton in 1920.

40 MINUTES

Time allotted for lunch break in Test and most first-class cricket.

1 HOUR 6 MINUTES

Time the ball is actually in play in a six-hour day, according to one study.

1 HOUR 41 MINUTES

The slowest-ever duck in Tests, by Geoff Allott of New Zealand against South Africa at Auckland in 1998–99. He faced 77 balls and couldn't prevent the follow-on but did help his team draw the match. The series, appropriately if not very excitingly, finished 0-0.

1 HOUR 53 MINUTES

The fastest double-century in first-class cricket, by Ravi Shastri of Bombay against Baroda in 1984–85. Shastri became only the second player ever to hit six sixes off an over (see page 111).

2 HOURS 45 MINUTES

Time allowed for a Twenty20 match. Each innings is 20 overs, to be bowled in 75 minutes, and there is a 15-minute break between innings.

3 HOURS 1 MINUTE

The fastest triple-century in first-class cricket, by Denis Compton for MCC against North Eastern Transvaal at Benoni, South Africa, in 1948–49. MCC (Marylebone Cricket Club) was what the England team were called in those days when they were touring abroad and playing warm-up matches between Tests.

3-4 HOURS

Typical time taken to make a Test century.

6 HOURS

Official length of a Test-match day – normally three sessions of two hours each. In practice, the fielding side usually get behind with the over rate, so the day runs to about 6½ hours.

7 HOURS 45 MINUTES

Official length of one-day international match – two innings of 50 overs, lasting 3½ hours each, and a lunch or supper break of 45 minutes.

9 HOURS 17 MINUTES

The slowest Test century of all, by Mudassar Nazar of Pakistan against England at Lahore in 1977–78. As if they hadn't suffered enough, the crowd were tear-gassed by the police following disturbances provoked by the appearance of the wife and daughter of the deposed prime minister Zulfikar Ali Bhutto.

4 DAYS

Length of a first-class match between English counties or Australian states.

5 DAYS

Length of a Test match if it goes the distance.

10 DAYS

Length of the longest match ever – the Timeless Test at Durban in 1939. South Africa made 530, England (who were 1-0 up in the series) 316, and South Africa 481. All of that took six days. England finished the sixth day on 0 for none, needing 696 to win. They nearly made it, reaching 654 for five towards the end of the tenth day (not counting two rest days and one day lost to rain). But then it rained again, and there couldn't be an 11th day as England had to catch the boat home (see page 100).

47 DAYS

Length of the 2007 World Cup. Even the man in charge, Chris Dehring, admitted that this was too long. The football World Cup takes a month.

10 YEARS

Typical length of a successful international career.

20 YEARS (AND COUNTING)

Length of international career, so far, of Sachin Tendulkar. He made his Test debut for India at 16, in November 1989, and is now 37. He is the first person to play 600 times for his country – 171 Tests, 442 ODIs and one Twenty20 match to October 13, 2010 – and the only one to score over 30,000 international runs (see page 72).

30 YEARS

Span of the longest international career – that of Wilfred Rhodes, the Yorkshire slow left-armer, who played 58 times for England from 1899 to 1929–30. He made his Test debut in 1899, aged 21, alongside W.G. Grace, who was playing his last Test at the age of 50. Grace was the oldest Test cricketer – until Rhodes played at 52.

THE LANGUAGE

Every sport has its own vocab, and cricket more than most. Here are 101 terms you need to know, not including the fielding positions (see page 66) – plus a few extras.

KEY ● mainly to do with bowling ❧ mainly to do with batting ●❧ to do with both ⑪ mainly to do with fielding

101 EVERYDAY TERMS

appeal ●⑪ ask the umpire if the batsman is out by saying "Howzat?"

arm ball ● a ball from a spin bowler that goes on with the arm rather than turning

back-of-a-length ● just short of a traditional good length

beamer ● full-toss heading for the batsman's head. Usually followed by a gesture of apology

blockhole ❧ part of the crease where the batsman taps his bat, and which the bowler aims for with a yorker

bouncer ● fast short-pitched ball aimed at batsman's head

boundary ●❧ the rim of the outfield, or a shot that reaches it ("Afridi's got 48, all of them in boundaries")

bump ball ❧ shot that looks like a catch but isn't because the ball hit the ground just after the bat

carry your bat ❧ to open the innings and still be there when all 10 of your colleagues are out

chance ⑪ possible catch

chuck ● bowl with a less than straight arm ("Bloggs definitely chucks his bouncer")

close (of play) ●❧ (aka stumps) the end of the day's play

crease ●❧ a line across the pitch. The crease usually means the batting or popping crease, 4ft from the stumps. The bowling crease means the line the stumps sit on. The return crease is the line joining the two

cross ❧ (of batsmen) to pass each other before a catch is taken, so the man who was the non-striker becomes the striker, and the new batsman starts at the bowler's end

dead bat ❧ a shot with no follow-through and usually no scoring intent

death ●❧ the closing overs of a one-day innings: usually frenetic

declare ❧ to decide you've got enough runs and would rather bowl now

the deep ⑪ part of the outfield near the boundary, usually occupied (or patrolled) by resting bowlers

dolly ⑪ easy catch

doosra ● legbreak bowled by an offspinner to fox the batsman

dot ball ●❧ a ball that is not scored off, going down as a dot in the scorebook

duck ❧ a completed innings of 0; **golden duck:** out for 0 first ball

extras ❧ runs that didn't come off the bat – either byes, leg-byes, wides or no-balls

false stroke ❧ a mis-hit, edge or otherwise unintended shot

first-class ❧ type of cricket – professional or equivalent, and not one-day

fish ❧ to play with the bat well away from the body, which tends to be perilous

five-for ● haul of five wickets by the same bowler in one innings

flight ● (of a slow bowler) the trajectory of the ball, especially if he gives it air

follow on ❧ to have your second innings straight after your first, because you've done so badly. The fielding captain can ask his opponents to follow on if they are a certain number of runs behind – 200 in a Test

full-toss ● delivery that doesn't bounce before it reaches the batsman. Traditionally considered a bad ball, but now sometimes used deliberately at the death to flummox the batsman

gardening ❧ patting the pitch down to make it flatter. Curiously, batsmen are allowed to do this

gate ❧ the gap between bat and front pad. Technically, there shouldn't be one

give the ball air ● (of a slow bowler) to bowl in a loop rather than fire it in

go back ❧ to move your back foot (the right, if you're right-handed) towards the stumps

go down the pitch ❧ to take a couple of steps out of your crease to meet the ball, usually to a slow bowler, although Kevin Pietersen does it to the quicks too

go forward ❧ to move your front foot (the left, if you're right-handed) down the pitch to meet the ball

googly ● offbreak bowled by a legspinner to fox the batsman

guard ❧ place where a batsman habitually puts his bat as the bowler runs in

half-volley ● ball that lands a yard or less in front of the batsman's front foot – usually the easiest ball to hit. Curiously, volley is not a cricket term – it belongs in tennis, football and volleyball

hat-trick ● three wickets in successive balls by the same bowler in the same match

in ❧ currently batting, or seeing the ball well ("I was just getting in, when I was out")

innings ❧ a go at batting, either for an individual or team

inswing ● movement through the air, in towards the right-hander's legs

jaffa ● perfect ball, usually pitching on off stump and leaving the batsman

leading edge ❧ shot that goes to the off side when aimed towards leg

leg (side) ●❧ the half of the ground behind the batsman as he stands at the crease

length ● how close to the batsman the ball lands

length ball ● ball on a good length, making the batsman unsure whether to go forward or back

23 TERMS THAT ARE NOT ESSENTIAL, BUT ENTERTAINING

agricultural ❧ ungainly or primitive, of a shot that probably goes to cow corner

bits-and-pieces ●❧ player who can bat a bit and bowl a bit, but is sometimes a bit useless

buffet bowling ● so poor that batsmen help themselves

chin music ● hostile, short-pitched bowling

corridor of uncertainty ● channel just outside off stump, making batsmen unsure if it's safe to leave the ball

cow corner ❧ deep mid-wicket, where agricultural shots go

dibbly-dobbly ● medium-paced bowling

Dilscoop ❧ outrageous shot played off the fast bowlers on one knee over your own head – and Sri Lanka opener Tillekeratne Dilshan during the 2009 World Twenty20

do the hard part ❧ get to 20 or so – usually mentioned if the batsman then gets out

donkey drop ● a comical delivery which goes high in the air before approaching the batsman almost vertically

ferret ❧ hopeless No 11 batsman, so called because he goes after the rabbits

filth ● terrible bowling

A CRASH COURSE

line lateral position of the ball as it reaches the batsman. A good line is usually just on or outside off stump

line-and-length sustained accuracy

long hop a short ball that sits up and begs to be hit for four

maiden an over in which no run goes against the bowler's name, ie there are no runs off the bat, no wides and no no-balls (byes and leg-byes allowed, as they are not considered his fault)

middle (verb) to hit the ball with the middle of the bat, or time it well; (noun) the crease or pitch

nip back to move into the right-handed batsman off the seam

no-ball improper delivery, usually because the bowler has overstepped the crease

non-striker batsman who is in but not facing

not out either still batting ("at lunch, Sehwag was 99 not out") or left unbeaten at the end of the innings ("Lara 400 not out")

nurdle to deflect the ball rather than whack it

off (side) the half of the ground the batsman faces when standing at the crease

off the mark no longer on 0

on a pair still on 0 in your second innings, when you made 0 in the first

one short when the batsmen have run two or more, but one of them hasn't grounded his bat properly, so the umpire deducts one from the tally

out dismissed; no longer batting; back in the hutch

outfield outer part of the ground, further from the bat than the men in catching positions

outswing movement through the air, away from the right-handed batsman

over set of six balls bowled by the same bowler from the same end. He can't bowl the next six

over rate average number of overs bowled per hour – 15 is meant to be par in Tests, but 13 is the norm

overthrows extra runs taken by the batsmen when the ball is thrown at the stumps, misses, and eludes anyone who is backing up

pad up to get your batting kit on or, once batting, to play with the pad rather than the bat

a pair two ducks in the same match by the same player – short for a pair of spectacles; **king pair:** two first-ball ducks in the same match

pitch (verb) to bounce (of a ball bowled); (noun) the 22-yard strip on which the batting and bowling takes place

play and miss to play a shot but not connect with the ball – a moral victory for the bowler

played on bowled out via the edge of the bat

reverse swing same as inswing, but with an older ball and more last-minute. No one is exactly sure why it happens, but it can be deadly

rough the part of the pitch that has been roughed up by the fast bowlers' follow-through. Usually outside the left-hander's off stump. Can provide huge turn

run-up bowler's approach to the wicket, even if he prefers to walk it, like Shane Warne

seam sideways movement off the pitch; the stitching on the ball, which enables this; type of bowler – the faster kind, even including bowlers who use swing rather than seam

short (of a length) pitching a few yards in front of the batsman, giving him time to go back and pull or cut

shoulder arms to play no stroke

sightscreen screen on the boundary, behind the bowler, that allows the batsman to pick up the ball. White if the ball is red; black if the ball is white

sitter easy catch. Strangely, the word is only used if it is dropped

6-3 or 7-2 field having six or seven fielders on the off side and only two or three on the leg

sledging chat from fielders, designed to put a batsman off or get under his skin. Unsporting, but usually allowed

slog a big hit disapproved of by the coaching book

slog-sweep lofted sweep, not in coaching book but increasingly vital ploy for batsmen facing spinners

slower ball delivery from a fast or medium-paced bowler which is deliberately bowled a lot slower to trick the batsman into playing too early and being bowled or caught. Usually achieved by switching to a spinner's grip

spell bowling stint by one bowler, consisting of anything

from one to forty or even fifty overs, but usually about six for a quick and nine or ten for a spinner

square the mown area (more often a rectangle) in the middle of the ground, containing the pitches

stance the batsman's posture as he waits for the ball – often distinctive

stock bowler one who is expected to keep runs down more than take wickets

the strike being at the end facing the next ball

strike bowler one who is expected to take wickets

sundries Australian word for extras

swing sideways movement through the air

tail-ender batsman who has been picked as a bowler, normally down at No 9, 10 or 11

time it to hit the ball sweetly

two guard between middle and leg stumps

the V area between mid-off and mid-on where a classical strokeplayer likes to hit the ball – although the idea rather takes it for granted that the bowling will be of full length

walk to give yourself out without waiting for the umpire's decision. Considered sporting by some people in the game, and mad by others

wicket a dismissal; the pitch; the stumps ("and he's at the wicket now")

wrong'un Australian name for a googly

yorker ball that lands in the blockhole, near the batsman's toes

---

Harrow cut (or Chinese cut or French cut) inside-edge which diverts the ball close to the stumps – often for runs

heavy ball a delivery that slams into the shoulder of the bat

hit-and-giggle sniffy name given to Twenty20

milk to help yourself to singles, usually off a spinner

Nelson a score of 111, or its multiples, often considered unlucky in England. Named after Horatio Nelson, because he had one eye, one arm, and one ... what was the third thing?

rabbit inept tail-ender

shirtfront a ridiculously flat pitch

stonewall to block the ball or score very slowly ("dear old Hoggard, stonewalling as usual")

streaky unconvincing or lucky ("he edges it, and that's a streaky way to get off the mark")

switch-hit a batsman swaps his hands on the handle and in effect changes from a right-hander to a left-hander, or vice versa. Mastered by Kevin Pietersen

the yips heebie-geebies that can afflict bowlers, making them unable to land the ball in the right place. Left-arm spinners are especially prone to them, although the most glaring example among recent England players was a right-arm medium-pacer, Gavin Hamilton. His fate was to go back, after a single Test, and play for his previous international team – Scotland

SHANE WARNE
FROM BEACH BUM
TO LEGEND

Once there was a little boy who grew up in a place called Ferntree Gully, a suburb of Melbourne, the most sports-mad city in Australia (and possibly the world). The boy was blond, cheerful, chubby and rather accident-prone. One day he was playing with a boomerang, didn't realise it would come back to him, and got a cut on his forehead that needed stitches. Another time, a boy at school jumped down on him and he broke both legs. His legs were put in plaster and he had to spend a year on a special low trolley, lying on his tummy and wheeling himself around with his arms. Later, he wondered if all that wheeling had built up strength in his shoulders and wrists.

The boy spent hours playing cricket in the garden with his brother Jason. Aged nine, he played for his primary school, East Sandringham Boys. He wanted to be a fast bowler like Dennis Lillee, Australia's most exciting player of the time, but he was also intrigued by how spin bowlers could make the ball turn. He was shown how to bowl a leg-break by his school coach, Ron Cantlon. A useful club legspinner himself, Cantlon had noticed that the West Indies, then the world's best team, were not great players of spin. "Keep at it," he told the boy, "because in 10 years' time they'll be scouring the country for a leggie." He had just shown Shane Warne how to do the thing that was going to make him a legend.

At secondary school, Shane preferred batting, and often went in in the top four for the 1st XI. He was also naughty enough to get several canings from the headmaster. "I guess I could have paid more attention to my studies," he said. A rough translation of this is: "I didn't do any work at all." Picked to play for Victoria Schools against New South Wales Schools, he travelled all the way to Sydney, 500 miles away, and took five wickets. Aged 19, he spent a summer in England, playing club cricket in Bristol. He drank so much beer, he put on three stone. He was a beach bum first and a cricketer second.

Back home, he won a place at the Australian Cricket Academy – but he didn't do well there and they chucked him out. He played a few games for Victoria and the Australian Test selectors, who hadn't had a major spin bowler for decades, decided to take a punt on him. They picked him in a Test against India, whose batsmen are probably the best players of spin. Warne took one wicket – for 150 runs. The next three innings he bowled in, he took none for 185, so his Test average was now 335.

The Academy invited him back. He went, and studied legspin under Terry Jenner, a fine coach and what Aussies call a larrikin – someone who doesn't always obey authority. Warne was picked for the tour of Sri Lanka and the Australian captain, Allan Border, trusted him to bowl as Australia pressed for victory on the last day. He took three for 11, and turned a corner.

In the 1992 Boxing Day Test in his home town of Melbourne, he faced the mighty West Indies, the world's No 1 team. He took seven for 52 to bowl Australia to victory. Shane Warne had arrived. He took more wickets in New Zealand and then went to England for his first taste of the Ashes. The Manchester groundsman generously prepared a turning pitch. Australia were all out for 289, a poor score. England were a comfortable 80 for one when Warne came on to bowl to Mike Gatting, a skilful player of spin. His first ball was spun so hard that it dipped and curled to leg before pitching well outside leg stump and then turning a full 18 inches past a startled Gatting and clipping the off stump. It soon became the most famous ball ever bowled in the Ashes: the wonderball.

Warne destroyed England in that series with 34 wickets. Australia won 4-1 and he was chosen as one of *Wisden*'s Five Cricketers of the Year. He was getting wickets all the time, and conceding few runs, unlike most legspinners. So he gave his captain everything: control and a cutting edge. In the next Ashes series, he did even better, and in the Boxing Day Test, 1994, he took a hat-trick against England. All three deliveries were leg-breaks, but he spun them different amounts. The only team who could cope with him were India.

He became a superstar. He was also a handy, fearless No 8 batsman, and a very good slip fielder. But the naughty boy never quite went away. He smoked throughout his career, even though he once accepted money to give up. In September 1994, at a Sri Lankan casino, he made a more serious misjudgment. He was introduced by a team-mate, Mark Waugh, to an Indian bookmaker known only as John. John said he was a person who bet on cricket. He offered Warne 5,000 US dollars (about £3,000) in return for information on pitches and weather, and Warne took the money.

When Australian officials heard about this from reporters, they fined Warne 8,000 Australian dollars (also about £3,000) and Waugh 10,000 – but kept the fines secret until a reporter got hold of the story four years later. After that, an independent report by a leading lawyer concluded that the fines were too small and the two players should have been banned. "They must have known it is wrong," the lawyer said.

It could have been worse. The very worst thing a cricketer can do, in cricket, is match-fixing – agreeing to try to lose, in order to make money – and Warne hadn't done that. But it looked as if that was what he was being set up for. He accepted that he had been "naive and stupid".

The 1998–99 season was a bad one on the field too, as Warne, returning from shoulder surgery, took only four wickets in four Tests. People wondered if he might be losing it. But then Australia bounced back from a poor start to win the 1999 World Cup, with Warne taking vital wickets, and in 2000 he received a huge honour: he was named as one of *Wisden*'s Five Cricketers of the Century. He was the only current player among them, and the only one without a knighthood: the others were Sir Don Bradman, Sir Garry Sobers, Sir Jack Hobbs and Sir Viv Richards.

In 2003, he planned to retire from one-day cricket after the World Cup. But then he was caught taking a banned drug, a diuretic. He reacted like a little kid: he blamed his mum, saying she had given him the pills to help him lose weight. He was banned for a year, and the World Anti-Doping Agency said it should have been more.

He turned this disgrace into a bonus by coming back refreshed in 2004. He soon reached 500 Test wickets, only the second man to do so after Courtney Walsh. Then, after Muttiah Muralitharan had pinched Walsh's world record, Warne nipped past him – only for Murali to reclaim the record 11 months after Warne retired from Tests. But the drugs scandal, and a few other stories alleging that he had been unfaithful to his wife, meant that he missed out on the Australian captaincy. He has often been described as "the best captain Australia never had". When he was made captain of the unfancied Indian Premier League side Rajasthan Royals in 2008, they won the competition at the first time of asking. His wife got fed up too: they divorced in 2006, although two years later they were rumoured to have got back together, and in April 2007 their three kids moved to schools in England, where Warne was captaining Hampshire.

Warne carried on eating Englishmen for breakfast and in the 2005 Ashes, at the grand old age of 35, he took 40 wickets, and made plenty of runs, yet finished on the losing side. He became the first man to claim 600 Test wickets and set a new record for most Test wickets in a calendar year (96). In the 2006–07 Ashes, he started

badly again, but in the second Test he led Australia's charge to a victory so astonishing that England never recovered from it. They lost every match in the series.

He announced that he would retire from Tests, and from cricket in Australia, at the end of the series. This gave him two last Tests, in Melbourne and Sydney, to say goodbye and reach 700 wickets. He finished with 708, and many fond farewells were said – not least by England players who were delighted not to have to face him again. Just about the only thing he hadn't achieved was a Test century. His top score was a tantalising 99. "The one

statistic that does annoy me," he said in 2006, "is having the most Test runs in the history of the game without a hundred. I don't like that."

Many people said he was the best bowler ever. That is hard to prove, as the game has changed so much from one era to another. He may not even have been the best bowler of his time (Murali retired from Tests in 2010 with 800 wickets), or the best in his team (Glenn McGrath, in a quieter way, was a genius too). But Warne was certainly a fantastic bowler, a fascinating character and a great entertainer. And, by making legspin fashionable again, he changed the game. Not many cricketers can claim that.

Why is international cricket like a Mars bar? Because it comes in three different sizes. Here's a quick guide to them all.

THE LONG AND THE SHORT OF IT

◀ Three of a kind
Daniel Vettori, captain of New Zealand, in a Test, a one-dayer and a Twenty20.

TEST

Full name?	▶	Test match
How long does it last?	▶	Five days, 90 overs a day
How many innings per side?	▶	Two
And matches per series?	▶	Two to five, most often three
What does it look like?	▶	Traditional – red ball, white kit, no names or numbers
Any special rules?	▶	New ball after 80 overs
Any meal breaks?	▶	Lunch and tea
What's a big score?	▶	500 (though you can still lose)
What's a good scoring rate?	▶	Four an over
Team scoring record?	▶	952 for 6 dec by Sri Lanka v India, Colombo, 1997 (see page 105)
Individual scoring record?	▶	400no by Brian Lara, West Indies v England, Antigua 2003-04 (see page 104)
Best bowling in a match?	▶	19 for 90 by Jim Laker, England v Australia, Old Trafford, 1956 (see page 104)
What's so good about it?	▶	Ebb and flow Full canvas, wide variety High drama Scope for tactics
When did it start?	▶	1877
How many matches so far?*	▶	1973
How is it for batsmen?	▶	Ultimate examination, takes great skill and patience
How is it for bowlers?	▶	Tough, as pitches tend to be flat, but there is time to relax and settle in
How is it for fielders?	▶	Tough for catchers, but places to hide for the donkeys
What's not so good?	▶	Dull if too slow or high-scoring
Who's best at it now?	▶	India – but they should play more Tests
Where are England?	▶	Fourth going into the 2010–11 Ashes
Who's the best team ever?	▶	West Indies in the 1980s (the scariest, thanks to fearsome pace attack) or Australia under Steve Waugh in 2000–03 (the fastest-scoring)
Overall verdict?	▶	The highest form of the game. Not called Tests for nothing. But there need to be more five-Test series for maximum drama

*all figures to October 14, 2010

ODI

Full name? ▶	One-day international
How long does it last? ▶	One day – 50 overs a side
How many innings per side? ▶	One
And matches per series? ▶	Usually three, five or seven
What does it look like? ▶	Football with long trousers – names, numbers, white ball
Any special rules? ▶	Fielding circles, powerplays, umpires strict on wides, rain delays in 2nd inns mean target revised using Duckworth/Lewis system (don't ask)
Any meal breaks? ▶	Lunch or tea
What's a big score? ▶	300
And a good scoring rate? ▶	Six an over
Team scoring record? ▶	443 for 9 by Sri Lanka v Holland, Amstelveen, 2006
Individual scoring record? ▶	200no by Sachin Tendulkar, India v South Africa, Gwalior, 2009–10
Best bowling in a match? ▶	8 for 19 by Chaminda Vaas, Sri Lanka v Zimbabwe, Colombo, 2001–02
What's so good about it? ▶	Exciting if close Draws big crowds Often a feast of runs Fairly fast-moving Sometimes floodlit
When did it start? ▶	1970–71
How many matches so far?* ▶	3056
How is it for batsmen? ▶	Easy – loaded in their favour, but expectations are high and run-chases hard on the nerves
How is it for bowlers? ▶	High pressure – short spells, no leeway
How is it for fielders? ▶	Tougher – quick singles taken all the time, nowhere to hide
What's not so good? ▶	Dull if one-sided or too low-scoring
Who's best at it now? ▶	Australia, by so far that it's embarrassing
Where are England? ▶	Fifth – but not far behind India, Sri Lanka and South Africa
Who's the best team ever? ▶	The Australian teams that won three World Cups in 1999, 2003 and 2007: powerful top order, varied and accurate attack, great ground-fielding
Overall verdict? ▶	Has given fine entertainment, but now a bit tired. Too many games, not enough possibilities. Powerplays have helped, more tweaks needed

T20

Full name? ▶	Twenty20 international
How long does it last? ▶	Three hours – 20 overs a side
How many innings per side? ▶	One
And matches per series? ▶	Usually one, sometimes two
What does it look like? ▶	ODIs, but colours may vary
Any special rules? ▶	Same as ODIs but players in dug-out, not pavilion
Any meal breaks? ▶	No – 15 minutes between innings
What's a big score? ▶	200
And a good scoring rate? ▶	Ten an over
Team scoring record? ▶	260-6 by Sri Lanka v Kenya, Johannesburg, 2007–08
Individual scoring record? ▶	117 by Chris Gayle, West Indies v South Africa, Johannesburg, 2007–08
Best bowling in a match? ▶	5 for 6 by Umar Gul, Pakistan v New Zealand, The Oval, 2009
What's so good about it? ▶	Fits in with school and work Draws big crowds, new fans Often a feast of runs Very fast-moving All over by suppertime
When did it start? ▶	2005
How many matches so far?* ▶	191
How is it for batsmen? ▶	They have a ball, as long as they get on with it
How is it for bowlers? ▶	Medium pressure – only four overs each, and expectations very low
How is it for fielders? ▶	Toughest of all – plenty of singles get turned into twos
What's not so good? ▶	Dull if one-sided or too low-scoring
Who's best at it now? ▶	England, who lifted the World Cup in the Caribbean in 2010
Where are England? ▶	There isn't a table yet, but they would be high up if there was one
Who's the best team ever? ▶	Hard to say – stints on the throne tend to be short-lived. But Pakistan have the best win/loss ratio among the major teams
Overall verdict? ▶	Sparkling entertainment and a great introduction to the game – but there is danger of overkill. Does cricket really need a Twenty20 World Cup every two years?

T20 WORLD XI

Twenty20 gets called "hit-and-giggle" cricket by the traditionalists, which means they think it's all about throwing the bat and having a laugh. But even the grumpiest grandpa would enjoy seeing our World XI in action, with its big hitters and clever bowlers. If you don't agree with the choice, send an email to lawrencebooth@hotmail.com to let us know just where we went wrong…

KEY

sr = strike-rate; ave = average (batting average if it follows runs, bowling average if it follows wickets); wkts = wickets; r/o = runs per over; 6s = sixes

1 DAVID WARNER
Australia, born 1986

Small and deadly left-handed opener – but yet to play a Test

Teams New South Wales Blues, Durham Dynamos, Delhi Daredevils, Middlesex Panthers

T20s 20, runs 644, strike-rate 151, average 29, 6s 31

Finest hour 89 off 43 balls on T20 debut v South Africa at Melbourne, January 2009

2 CHRIS GAYLE
West Indies, born 1979

Nonchalant destroyer of new ball, handy offspinner

Teams PCA Masters XI, Jamaica, Stanford Superstars, Kolkata Knight Riders, Western Australia Warriors

T20s 20, runs 617, sr 144, ave 32, 6s 34; wickets 12, runs per over 7.29, ave 21

Finest hour First T20 international 100, v South Africa at Jo'burg, 2007

3 KEVIN PIETERSEN
England, born 1980

Clean-striking master of the switch-hit

Teams Nottinghamshire Outlaws, Hampshire Hawks, Royal Challengers Bangalore

T20s 28, runs 911, sr 141, ave 37, 6s 24; wkts 1, r/o 12, ave 36

Finest hour Player of the tournament at the 2010 World Twenty20

4 YUVRAJ SINGH
India, born 1981

Brutal left-hander with a swagger to match

Teams Yorkshire Phoenix, Kings XI Punjab

T20s 22, runs 555, sr 153, ave 32, 6s 38; wkts 7, r/o 8.70, ave 24

Finest hour Hitting Stuart Broad of England for six sixes in an over, Durban 2007 (see page 111)

5 MIKE HUSSEY
Australia, born 1975

Expert finisher and alert fielder

Teams Northamptonshire Steelbacks, Gloucestershire Gladiators, Chennai Super Kings

T20s 27, runs 457, sr 150, ave 35, 6s 17

Finest hour Mowing Pakistan's offspinner Saeed Ajmal for 22 in four balls to reach World T20 final in 2010

6 SHAHID AFRIDI
Pakistan, born 1980

Hits sixes for fun and bowls surprisingly miserly legbreaks

Teams Kent Spitfires, Karachi Dolphins, Deccan Chargers, South Australian Redbacks

T20s 39, runs 630, sr 143, ave 18, 6s 22; wkts 48, r/o 6.17, ave 19

Finest hour Man of the match in the 2009 World Twenty20 final

7 BRENDON McCULLUM
New Zealand, born 1981, wk

T20 his natural home, combative keeper

Teams Canterbury Wizards, Glamorgan Dragons, Otago Volts, Kolkata Knight Riders, Sussex Sharks

T20s 40, runs 1100, sr 128, ave 33, 6s 39

Finest hour 158 on the opening night of the Indian Premier League in 2008

8 DANIEL VETTORI
New Zealand, born 1979, capt

Best economy-rate in the world among regular bowlers

Teams Northern District Knights, Delhi Daredevils

T20s 28, runs 187, sr 109, ave 13, 6s 2; wkts 35, r/o 5.36, ave 17

Finest hour Scrooge-like figures of 4-1-6-3 v Bangladesh at Hamilton, February 2010

9 DARREN SAMMY
West Indies, born 1983

Nagging medium-pacer, handy lower-order hitter

Teams St Lucia, Stanford Superstars, Windward Islands

T20s 19, runs 140, sr 121, ave 15, 6s 7; wkts 24, r/o 6.24, ave 14

Finest hour 4-0-14-1 and two run-outs v England in Trinidad, March 2009

HOW TO PICK A TWENTY20 TEAM

Don't look at the average first. In Twenty20, where time is of the essence, the first stat to look for is the batsman's strike-rate (the runs he scores per 100 balls) or the bowler's economy-rate (the runs he concedes per over). A great strike-rate is anything above 140; a great economy-rate is anything under 6.5. Averages still tell you something: a batting average of 30+ says the player is good at staying in and can anchor the innings; a bowling average below 15 shows a wicket-taker. And wickets still win matches. But so do sixes…

OFF YOU GO!

10 UMAR GUL
Pakistan, born 1984

Master bowler of yorkers and reverse swing

Teams Peshawar Panthers, Kolkata Knight Riders, Western Australia Warriors

T20s 32, runs 56, sr 112, ave 8, 6s 4; wkts 47, r/o 6.19, ave 14

Finest hour 5 for 6 to blow away New Zealand in the 2009 World T20 semi-final at The Oval

11 AJANTHA MENDIS
Sri Lanka, born 1985

Mystery spinner whose party trick is the carrom ball

Teams Sri Lanka Army Sports Club, Wayamba, Kolkata Knight Riders

T20s 19, runs 7, sr 50, ave 3.50, 6s 0; wkts 33, r/o 5.68, ave 12

Finest hour Combined figures of 5 for 18 in 7 overs v New Zealand and West Indies, 2009 World Twenty20

All figures are for Twenty20 internationals only, to October 14, 2010

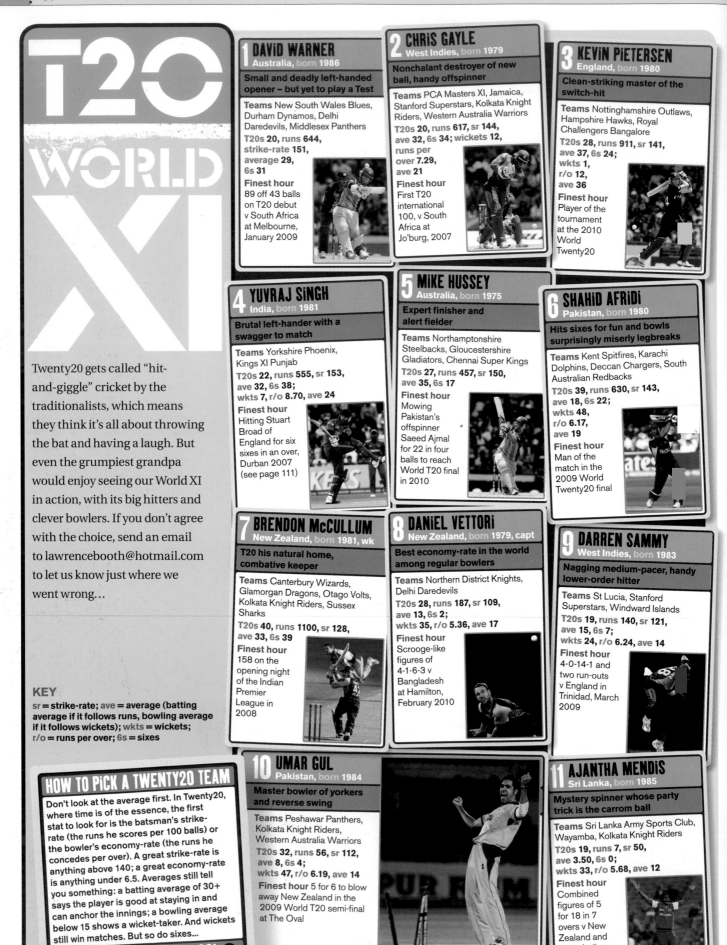

T20 SNAKES & LADDERS

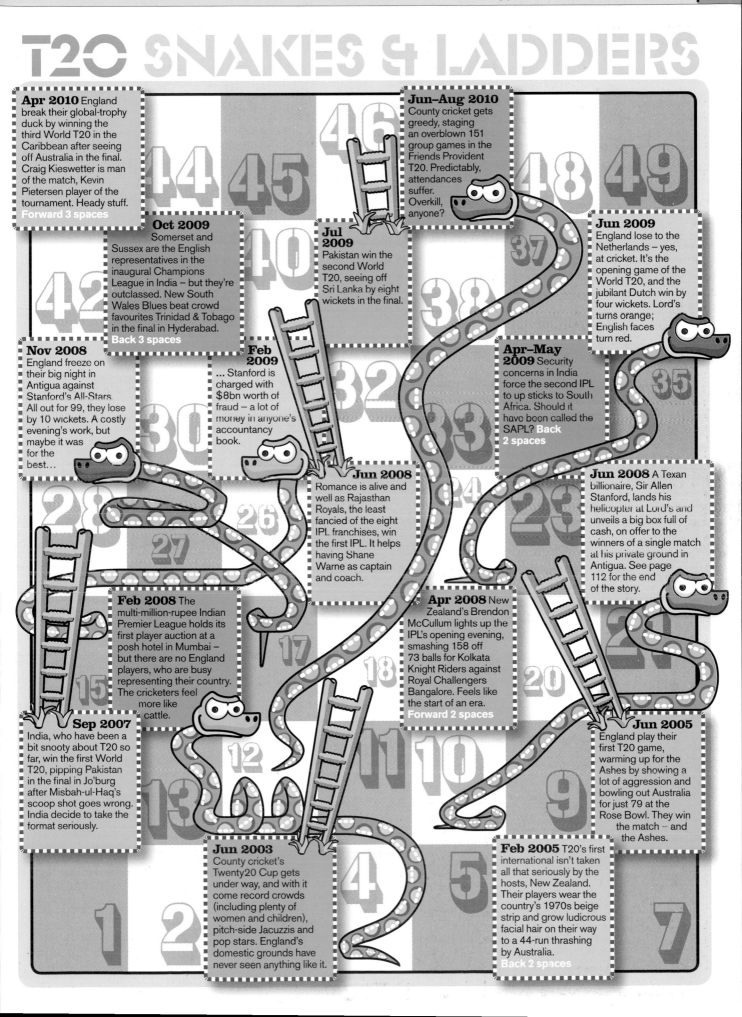

Apr 2010 England break their global-trophy duck by winning the third World T20 in the Caribbean after seeing off Australia in the final. Craig Kieswetter is man of the match, Kevin Pietersen player of the tournament. Heady stuff.
Forward 3 spaces

Oct 2009 Somerset and Sussex are the English representatives in the inaugural Champions League in India – but they're outclassed. New South Wales Blues beat crowd favourites Trinidad & Tobago in the final in Hyderabad.
Back 3 spaces

Nov 2008 England freeze on their big night in Antigua against Stanford's All-Stars. All out for 99, they lose by 10 wickets. A costly evening's work, but maybe it was for the best…

Feb 2009 …Stanford is charged with $8bn worth of fraud – a lot of money in anyone's accountancy book.

Feb 2008 The multi-million-rupee Indian Premier League holds its first player auction at a posh hotel in Mumbai – but there are no England players, who are busy representing their country. The cricketers feel more like cattle.

Sep 2007 India, who have been a bit snooty about T20 so far, win the first World T20, pipping Pakistan in the final in Jo'burg after Misbah-ul-Haq's scoop shot goes wrong. India decide to take the format seriously.

Jun 2003 County cricket's Twenty20 Cup gets under way, and with it come record crowds (including plenty of women and children), pitch-side Jacuzzis and pop stars. England's domestic grounds have never seen anything like it.

Jun–Aug 2010 County cricket gets greedy, staging an overblown 151 group games in the Friends Provident T20. Predictably, attendances suffer. Overkill, anyone?

Jul 2009 Pakistan win the second World T20, seeing off Sri Lanka by eight wickets in the final.

Jun 2008 Romance is alive and well as Rajasthan Royals, the least fancied of the eight IPL franchises, win the first IPL. It helps having Shane Warne as captain and coach.

Apr 2008 New Zealand's Brendon McCullum lights up the IPL's opening evening, smashing 158 off 73 balls for Kolkata Knight Riders against Royal Challengers Bangalore. Feels like the start of an era.
Forward 2 spaces

Jun 2009 England lose to the Netherlands – yes, at cricket. It's the opening game of the World T20, and the jubilant Dutch win by four wickets. Lord's turns orange; English faces turn red.

Apr–May 2009 Security concerns in India force the second IPL to up sticks to South Africa. Should it have been called the SAPL? **Back 2 spaces**

Jun 2008 A Texan billionaire, Sir Allen Stanford, lands his helicopter at Lord's and unveils a big box full of cash, on offer to the winners of a single match at his private ground in Antigua. See page 112 for the end of the story.

Jun 2005 England play their first T20 game, warming up for the Ashes by showing a lot of aggression and bowling out Australia for just 79 at the Rose Bowl. They win the match – and the Ashes.

Feb 2005 T20's first international isn't taken all that seriously by the hosts, New Zealand. Their players wear the country's 1970s beige strip and grow ludicrous facial hair on their way to a 44-run thrashing by Australia.
Back 2 spaces

COUNTY CRICKET

Why is county cricket like a maze?
Because it's very confusing … but also fun.
Here is the lowdown on every trophy and team.

KEY ⬤ = Test venue; **(Eng, 3)** = has played 3 Tests for England; **Ch'ship** = Championship; **Form** shows how the teams have done up to and including 2010

THE THREE COMPETITIONS

	LV COUNTY CHAMPIONSHIP	CLYDESDALE BANK 40	FRIENDS PROVIDENT T20
started life as	County Championship, 1890 (only 8 teams)	John Player League, 1969	Twenty20 Cup, 2003
type of cricket	first-class, four-day	one-day, 40 overs	one-day, 20 overs
structure	two divisions of nine, all play all twice	three groups of seven, all play all once, semi-finals (three group winners plus next-best team) and final	two groups of nine, all play all twice, then quarter-finals, semi-finals, final
how is that decided?	on merit – two up, two down	at random – but one of the three minnows (see below) per group	geographically – North and South
extra teams?	no	Netherlands, Scotland and Unicorns – the best of the Minor Counties	no
time of year	whole season – April to September	sprinkled throughout the summer, final in September	midsummer – June to July, final in August
days of the week	all over the shop – as angry fans keep saying	mainly Sundays	any day will do, Fridays and Sundays most popular
floodlights	rarely	sometimes	increasingly, especially on weekday evenings
TV	Sky do the odd game	Sky do plenty	Sky do plenty
prestige	high	low	high
crowds	low with the odd high	medium	not quite as record-breaking as five years ago
prize money	£500,000 (Div 1 winners), £115,000 (Div 2)	£125,000 (Div 1), £55,000 (Div 2)	£80,000
feels	like a museum	like a picnic	like a party

did you know ? cricket now has a money-spinning Champions League? Counties can qualify by reaching the final of their own Twenty20 tournament – even though this proved impossible in 2010 because the CL, held in South Africa, clashed with the end of the County Championship. Somerset (Sabres) and Sussex (Sharks) did play in the 2009 edition in India, though, which had a prize pool of £6.5m. Unfortunately, they won only one out of seven games between them.

SOMERSET

home County Ground, Taunton – bags of runs, and now the headquarters of England Women

captain Marcus Trescothick (Eng, 76 Tests), stiff-legged blaster

stars Craig Kieswetter (Eng 12 ODIs), clean-hitting, World T20 hero; James Hildreth, silky strokemaker

form bridesmaids – second in all three competitions in 2010

heyday 1970s – great one-day side

legends Ian Botham, Viv Richards and Joel Garner, 1970s superstars

strange but true missed out on their first Ch'ship title in 2010 by the narrowest margin: same points as Notts, but one fewer win

GLOUCESTERSHIRE

home Nevil Road, Bristol – slow, seaming

captain Alex Gidman, dependable middle-order batsman

stars Jon Lewis (Eng, 1), classical nagging seamer; James Franklin (NZ, 26), upright bowling allrounder

form poor in Ch'ship – never won it, now seem to be marooned in Div 2

heyday 1999–2004, seven one-day trophies

legends W.G. Grace, captain 1870–98 – the first celebrity cricketer; Wally Hammond, master batsman of 1930s

strange but true champion county three times in the 1870s, before the Ch'ship officially started

GLAMORGAN ⬤

home Sophia Gardens, Cardiff (or the Swalec Stadium, if you prefer) – low and slow

captain Alviro Petersen (SA, 5) replaced Jamie Dalrymple (Eng, 27 ODIs) in time for 2011

stars Mark Cosgrove (Aus, 3 ODIs), tubby biffer; James Harris, up-and-coming seamer

form poor since Ch'ship win in 1997, won 40-over league in 2002 and 2004

heyday 1948 and 1969 – champions

legend Wilf Wooller, 1948 captain and great believer in fielding

strange but true the Welsh county hosted England's first "home" Test outside England: in the 2009 Ashes

FIRST-CLASS COUNTIES IN THE SOUTH

SURREY

home The Oval, London – historic, big, flat, takes spin

captain Rory Hamilton-Brown, young thruster – risky choice

stars Mark Ramprakash (Eng, 52), run machine (see page 48); **Steve Davies** (Eng, 6 ODIs), improving keeper with a flashing blade

form poor – coaches call it a "transition period"

heyday 1952–58, seven Ch'ships; 1999–2002, three Ch'ships

legend Sir Alec Bedser, immaculate seamer; **Peter May**, elegant batsman; **Sir Jack Hobbs**, master opener

strange but true Oval was used to house German POWs in World War II

MIDDLESEX

home Lord's, London – majestic setting, flat pitch (apart from the slope)

captain Neil Dexter, promising South African-born allrounder

stars Eoin Morgan (Eng, 6), gloriously talented; **Steven Finn** (Eng, 8), giant seamer; **Andrew Strauss** (Eng, 77) lesser-spotted England captain

form poor – Div 2 since 2007, but won Twenty20 Cup in 2008

heyday 1976–93 – seven Ch'ships

legend Denis Compton, debonair batsman, 1940s

strange but true they started wearing pink one-day shirts in 2007 to support a breast-cancer charity

ESSEX

home County Ground, Chelmsford – flat, with short straight boundaries

captain James Foster (Eng, 7) one of the world's best keepers, increasingly valuable with the bat

stars Alastair Cook (Eng, 60), cool-headed opener; **Ravi Bopara** (Eng, 10), gifted middle-order batsman

form yo-yo – up and down in the Ch'ship

heyday 1983–92, five Ch'ships

legend Graham Gooch, majestic opener; **Keith Fletcher**, shrewd skipper

strange but true after 83 years with no trophies, they won 12 in 14 years

HAMPSHIRE

home Rose Bowl, Southampton – handsome, getting better for batting

captain split between **Dimitri Mascarenhas** (Eng, 20 ODIs), and **Dominic Cork** (Eng, 37)

stars Michael Lumb (Eng, 7 T20s) World Twenty20 opener in 2010

form hot in one-dayers: won 50-over trophy in 2009, added T20 Cup in 2010

heyday 1961 and 1973 – champions

legends Barry Richards, South African opener; **Shane Warne**, irrepressible Australian leggie

strange but true they built the ground without providing enough roads, so the traffic is terrible

SUSSEX

home County Ground, Hove – sea breezes, swing – but pretty flat

captain Mike Yardy (Eng, 19 ODIs), nuggety left-hander, flightless spin

stars Murray Goodwin (Zim, 19), veteran run-gatherer; **Monty Panesar** (Eng, 39), cult-hero slow left-armer

form waning – relegated in 2009 after three Ch'ships in five years

heyday A couple of years ago

legends KS Ranjitsinhji, Indian prince and England batsman; **Tony Greig**, controversial England captain

strange but true in 1611, two men from Sidlesham in Sussex missed church to play cricket. They were fined a shilling (5p) each

KENT

home St Lawrence Ground, Canterbury – attractive, flat

captain Rob Key (Eng, 15), hard-hitting batsman, poker player and promising TV pundit

stars Martin van Jaarsveld (SA, 9), correct batsman and ace slip fielder

form so-so: finally relegated in 2008, the last county to taste life in Div 2

heyday 1973–78, eight trophies

legends Frank Woolley, lordly left-hander; **Tich Freeman**, tiny legspinner; **Colin Cowdrey**, regal cover-driver; **Alan Knott**, master keeper

strange but true for decades, a lime tree stood inside the boundary; only four men ever hit the ball over it for six

GLAMORGAN
GLOUCESTERSHIRE
ESSEX
MIDDLESEX
SOMERSET
SURREY
KENT
HAMPSHIRE
SUSSEX

FIRST-CLASS COUNTIES IN THE NORTH

LANCASHIRE

home Old Trafford, Manchester – excellent pace, bounce and turn

captain Glen Chapple (Eng, 1 ODI), tireless, canny seamer

stars Jimmy Anderson (Eng, 52), swing-bowling attack leader; **Shiv Chanderpaul** (WI, 126) crab-like Guyanese run-hoarder

form nearly men – 2nd five times since 1998

heyday 1970s and late 90s – two great one-day teams

legends Brian Statham, pinpoint seam bowler; **Clive Lloyd**, WI capt; **Wasim Akram**, sultan of swing

strange but true they blame their near misses on the Manchester rain

YORKSHIRE

home Headingley, Leeds – green seamer on dank days, can turn flat

captain Andrew Gale, increasingly imposing top-order batsman

stars Ajmal Shahzad (Eng, 1), bubbly seamer, adept at reverse-swing; **Adil Rashid** (Eng, 5 ODIs), feisty legspinning allrounder

form getting better – third in 2010

heyday 1893–1968 – champions 29 times in 76 years

legends dozens: **Lord Hawke, Wilfred Rhodes, Sir Len Hutton, Fred Trueman, Geoff Boycott** …

strange but true they're always arguing with each other

DURHAM

home Riverside, Chester-le-Street – seamer-friendly

captain Phil Mustard (Eng, 10 ODIs), rustic left-hander, safe keeper

stars Steve Harmison (Eng, 63), nasty fastie; **Michael Di Venuto** (Aus, 9 ODIs), remorseless left-handed opener

form anti-climactic – fell away in 2010 after…

heyday …**two successive Ch'ship titles** – not bad for a team that entered first-class cricket in 1992

legend Ian Botham – helped start them off

strange but true nearby Lumley Castle is said to be haunted by the ghost of Lady Lily Lumley

DERBYSHIRE

home County Ground, Derby – low and slow

captain In 2010 it was **Chris Rogers** (Aus, 1), left-handed opener with a taste for big hundreds – then he joined Middlesex

stars resolutely starless

form poor – usually low in Div 2

heyday 1936 – their only Ch'ship

legends Dean Jones, dynamic captain and one-day batsman of the 1990s; **Devon Malcolm**, short-sighted but fiendishly quick

strange but true they turned their square 90 degrees onto a north–south axis in 2010 because the setting sun kept stopping play

NOTTINGHAMSHIRE

home Trent Bridge, Nottingham – much-loved, especially by swing bowlers

captain Chris Read (Eng, 15), quiet Devonian, skilful gloveman

stars Stuart Broad (Eng, 32), England's golden boy; **Graeme Swann** (Eng, 24), world's best spinner

form top – pipped Somerset to title in 2010 five years after previous triumph

heyday 1980s – won Ch'ship under Clive Rice and…

legend …**Sir Richard Hadlee**, master seamer

strange but true ball swings more since they built a new stand in 1998

LEICESTERSHIRE

home Grace Road, Leicester – low, slow and usually empty

captain Matthew Hoggard (Eng, 67), gnarled swing bowler, wacky bloke

stars James Taylor, pint-sized middle-order batsman

form perennial also-rans, but won Twenty20 Cup in 2004 and 2006

heyday 1996–98 – champions twice

legends Ray Illingworth, canny captain who led them to first Ch'ship; **David Gower**, dreamy left-hander

strange but true Taylor looks like he should be a national hunt jockey – like his dad, Steve

WORCESTERSHIRE

home New Road, Worcester – green and pleasant (especially for seamers), next to cathedral

captain Daryl Mitchell, local lad, solid opening batsman

stars Vikram Solanki (Eng, 51 ODIs), wristy middle-order stylist; **Shakib Al Hasan** (Bang, 21), watchable spinning allrounder

form indecisive: promoted or relegated five seasons in a row 2006–10

heyday 1988–89, consecutive Ch'ships

legends Graeme Hick, unquenchable front-footer; **Ian Botham**, who joined for those victorious Ch'ships

strange but true New Road is often flooded in the winter by the River Severn

WARWICKSHIRE

home Edgbaston, Birmingham – good sporting surface

captain In 2010 it was **Ian Westwood**, then he stepped down

stars Ian Bell (Eng, 57), elegant on-driver; **Jonathan Trott** (Eng, 13), no-frills grinder

form respectable – but no major trophies since 2004 Ch'ship

heyday 1993–95 – six trophies including the triple in 1994

legends Brian Lara, record-breaking star of '94; **Dennis Amiss**, 1970s opener who made 35,000 runs

strange but true England often play better at Edgbaston, perhaps because the crowd make a lot of noise

NORTHAMPTONSHIRE

home Wantage Road, Northampton – flat and slow

captain Andrew Hall (SA, 21), aggressive batsman, skilled death bowler

stars David Sales beefy hitter

form threadbare – never champions

heyday 1899–1904 – four Minor Counties Ch'ships

legends Colin Milburn, rotund 1960s big-hitter; **David Steele**, 1970s blocker who looked like a bank clerk; **Allan Lamb**, 1980s batsman who took six Test hundreds off West Indies

strange but true they have the smallest main ground of any county – capacity just 4000

THE LIE OF THE LAND

England and Wales have dozens of counties, but only these 18 can play first-class cricket. The rest can enter the Minor Counties Championship.

The 18 counties together form the England and Wales Cricket Board (ECB), which runs the game for them. Most of the ECB's income comes from television deals and ticket sales for the England team. The profits are divided up to give each county a hand-out of over £1m a year, and the ones that stage Tests get more than the rest. Counties also raise money from ticket sales and sponsorship, staging events like rock concerts, and subscriptions from members. The county with the most members is usually Lancashire.

Many people believe there is still too much cricket played, even after the ECB reduced the number of competitions from four to three in 2010 by axing the 50-over tournament. That meant a reprieve for the 40-over format, which was strange given its lack of a counterpart in the international game. But then English domestic cricket has often moved in mysterious ways…

DURHAM

YORKSHIRE

LANCASHIRE

DERBYSHIRE

NOTTINGHAMSHIRE

LEICESTERSHIRE

WORCESTER-SHIRE

WARWICKSHIRE

NORTHAMPTONSHIRE

▼ **Bottoms up** Chris Read, Nottinghamshire's captain, lifts the LV= County Championship trophy at Old Trafford in September 2010 after a nerve-racking final day.

WOMEN

IN CRICKET

For centuries, bowling was underarm. The first man to bowl round-arm at Lord's was John Willes of Kent in 1807. The umpire called no-ball and Willes is reported to have got on his horse and ridden away "in high dudgeon". Round-arm bowling was banned for 21 years, until finally MCC, the game's then rulers, saw that it was here to stay. Overarm bowling followed in 1864. You may be wondering why I'm telling you this on a page about women. The reason is that John Willes is thought to have got the idea from his sister, Christina. The story goes that he would get her to bowl at him in the barn, which may have been the world's first indoor net. She tried to bowl underarm but couldn't because her voluminous skirts got in the way. So she bowled round-arm, and changed the course of sporting history. (Willes also trained his dog to field. It was said that Willes, his sister and his dog "could beat any team in England".)

Women have been playing cricket for centuries. The first recorded county match between two female sides was Surrey v Hampshire in 1811. Women's Test cricket began in 1934. The first cricket World Cup was contested by women in 1973, two years before the men. There are women cricket writers, photographers, physios, scorers, press officers, committee members and administrators. Behind almost every promising young cricketer there is a long-suffering mum, equipped with a car, a washing machine, formidable powers of organisation and a shoulder to cry on after a golden duck. Yet some men still behave as if cricket was an all-male game. It's not just sexist – it's stupid.

In 1985, Lancashire CCC had a vote to decide whether to allow women into the pavilion at Old Trafford. "Let them in," said one member, "and the next thing you know, the place will be full of children." The sexists won that battle, but lost the war. Lancashire has had women members for years and the place is not full of children. In any case, why would it be a bad thing if it was?

Lord's was not much better. It did host a women's one-day international in 1976, and arranged for the dressing-room attendant to be replaced for the day by his wife. But the members, who enjoy the best views in the house at the best ground in the world, repeatedly refused to allow women to join the club. The only woman who could sit and watch a Test match from the pavilion was **the Queen**.

In 1989, the club secretary said there was "not a hope in hell" of the members voting to admit women. In 1998, they came up against an MCC president, Colin Ingleby-Mackenzie, who was determined to push the change through. He was a charming figure who had captained Hampshire and led his team to the County Championship after telling them, with a straight face, that they had to be in bed before breakfast.

He held a members' vote on the issue in February 1998. They voted in favour by 56 per cent to 44, but the rules required a two-thirds majority, so even though most members were now in favour of the change, it still didn't happen. He kept fighting, and some of his opponents helped him out by saying ridiculous things. One man declared that women shouldn't become members because they wouldn't be able to afford the subscription, then around £300. Another said he liked to get to the Lord's Test early to bag a seat with his *Daily Telegraph*, and how would he be able to go on

5 GREAT CRICKET WOMEN

Martha Grace

Mother, and coach, of three Test cricketers. In 1859 she wrote to George Parr, who ran the England XI: "I … ask you to consider the inclusion of my son, E.M. Grace – a splendid hitter and most excellent catch – in your England XI. I am sure he would play very well and do the team much credit. It may interest you to learn that I have a younger son, now 12 years of age, who will in time be a much better player than his brother because his back stroke is sounder, and he always plays with a straight bat. His name is W.G. Grace."

Myrtle Maclagan

In any cricket, a bowler who can take wickets while keeping the runs down is a captain's dream. If they can also make runs, they are priceless. Myrtle Maclagan did all this for England against Australia in the first women's Test series ever played, in 1934–35. Opening the bowling in the first Test at Brisbane, she took 7 for 10 in 17 overs of offbreaks as Australia capitulated to 47 all out. Then she opened the batting and showed how it was done by making 72 out of England's 154. England cruised to victory, and in the second Test, at Sydney, she followed a tidy four-for with 119, the first women's Test century, to wrap up the series. Later, she served as a soldier. "At various times in her life," *Wisden* reported, "she won prizes for squash, tennis, badminton and knitting."

Rachael Heyhoe-Flint

Most male batsmen are either attacking or defensive. Rachael Heyhoe-Flint was both. She hit the first six by a woman in a Test, for England v Australia in 1963, in the 25th women's Test, and 14 years later she made 179 in nearly nine hours to save an Ashes Test and series. She captained England against Australia in the **first women's match at Lord's** in 1976. "I cried all the way to the wicket," she said. "We had arrived." She finally joined the MCC committee in 2004, became a Lady in 2010, and is still the biggest name in women's cricket – though not the longest. That honour has passed to the England allrounder Ebony-Jewel Cora-Lee Camellia Rosamond Rainford-Brent.

Belinda Clark

She didn't just captain the Australian team – she was chief executive of Women's Cricket Australia. A hugely consistent opener, she had been an international for eight years before she was dismissed in single figures. Her 229 against Denmark at Mumbai in 1997–98 was the first double-hundred in a one-day international by a man or woman. She was *Wisden Australia* Cricketer of the Year in 1998. She retired in 2005 with averages of over 45 in both Tests and ODIs.

Clare Connor

Clare Connor has been the Rachael Heyhoe-Flint of the 21st century, a pioneer who has got results and changed attitudes. An allrounder and slow left-armer, she captained England to the 2005 Ashes, their first series win over Australia for 42 years. But years before that, she had made waves by playing for Brighton College 1st XI, with 10 men. Years later, she commentated on men's cricket on Channel 4 and became the first woman to play in the public-school old-boys' tournament, the Cricketer Cup. She returned to Brighton as an English teacher, and although she retired as a player in 2006 – when she was awarded an OBE – she became head of girls' cricket. One of her pupils, the slow left-armer Holly Colvin, has played for England since 2005. At Brighton they even have a Clare Connor Scholarship. In 2010, she joined the Sport England board.

---

doing that when he had been brought up to give up his seat to a woman?

Ingleby-Mackenzie announced another vote for September, only seven months after the previous one. He sent the members a glossy brochure arguing the case and pointing out that they might suffer from "future legislation" if they continued to block women – a subtle reference to the fact that there was a Labour government for the first time in 18 years. On September 28, the members voted – 9394 in favour of women, 4072 against. The percentage was 69.8 and that was enough. "Life as we know it," said one disgruntled member, "is over."

A few honorary women members joined, and later, some playing members. Life went on. The Lord's pavilion is still overwhelmingly male, but at least it's possible for any cricket lover to apply for membership, regardless of their colour, creed or gender.

Women's cricket is now thriving. Junior forms of the game like Kwik cricket and inter cricket give more girls a chance to wield a bat. There are still not many women's Tests – England have played only 86 in 73 years – but they get more publicity than they ever have. Like the men, they won the Ashes in 2005. And, like the men, they headed to Australia in 2010–11 to defend them.

20 QUESTIONS FOR ENGLAND CAPTAIN CHARLOTTE EDWARDS

Why did fortunes improve for the England women's team?

The first batch of central contracts came through in 2008, which meant we could finally commit to training without worrying about our jobs outside cricket. We also got Mark Lane and Keith Birkenshaw in as coaches around that time. But we'd also had the same team together from around 2004. There were probably a few players on the outskirts of the team who felt hard done by. But we weren't just picking on ability: it was about fitting into the team dynamic. We needed selfless players.

How has the game changed during the time you've been involved?

I first played for England in 1996, and one of the first changes we made was that we no longer had to play in skirts! That first Test, against New Zealand at Guildford, was in a skirt but everything after that was in trousers. People said we looked nice, but we were there to play cricket! If we played in skirts we'd have no skin left on our knees now. Now our fielding is at a new level. When I started I also had to pay for my own jumper and blazer. There was no sponsor – we just wore some random T-shirts someone had given to us for free.

When did you feel perceptions about women's cricket really started to change?

In 2005, when we won the Ashes and joined the men's team in Trafalgar Square. That made people sit up and think: "OK, the women actually play at a decent level." They started to get behind us.

You lost in West Indies and India in 2010 – is the rest of the world closing the gap?

We rested a lot of players for those series. When we peaked in 2009 – winning the 50-over and Twenty20 World Cups and the Ashes – we wanted to give players time to recover. Defeat was hard to take, but there were benefits because we're now picking from a bigger squad and have unearthed some potential stars.

You prepared that summer against boys schools' first XIs. What was that like?

It was brilliant. We're so used to playing other women, so it really took some of the girls outside their comfort zone. Some of the boys were more like men, and it was a good battle but if I recall I think we won all our games and we outfielded everyone. The boys were definitely pumped – for many of them it was their big game of the season and they definitely didn't want to lose to us or get out to a girl.

CLAIRE TAYLOR
on England's golden 18 months: February 2008 to July 2009

Feb 15–18, 2008 **Test**	Feb 25, 2008 **ODI**	Feb 28, 2008 **ODI**	Aug 6, 2008 **ODI**	Aug 14–Sep 7, 2008 **ODIs**	Feb–Mar, 2009 **50-over World Cup in Australia**	Mar 17, 2009 **World Cup**
Beat Australia by six wickets at Bowral to retain the Ashes (Taylor 79 and 64no) To perform so well in a single match at the home of Don Bradman was very special. Isa Guha bowled really well to take nine wickets, and I was delighted to put on 159 with Charlotte Edwards – we'd been through a lot against Australia.	**Beat New Zealand by nine wickets at Lincoln (Taylor 111no)** We'd lost the first game of the series, because we didn't adjust to conditions after being in Australia, where the pitches were slower. We didn't have the best record against New Zealand, so this was a massive result and I enjoyed batting with Caroline Atkins.	**Beat New Zealand by six wickets at Lincoln (Taylor 70)** This set us up for our 3-1 series win, which got the monkey off our backs: we'd never done well in Australia or New Zealand. Sarah Taylor batted superbly to make 86 and we put on 145. To build up our confidence ahead of the World Cup in Australia the following year was vital.	**Beat South Africa by 121 runs at Canterbury (Taylor 83 off 70 balls)** I was starting to feel in really good form, tactically and mentally, and I had a good idea of what was expected of me. I aimed to be the anchor at No 3 – to assess a situation and bat to it. It was important someone took responsibility for an innings.	**Won five straight games v South Africa and India (Taylor scored 162 runs without being dismissed)** We kept batting second and it kept on working out for us. We certainly didn't want to be caught on a damp track at Arundel or somewhere, and I loved playing that anchor role and finishing us off – almost two roles in one!	We arrived about 10 days before the start of the tournament because we really wanted to hit the ground running. People said we were favourites, but we knew we'd face a battle against a) Australia and b) the Australians. We were also out-of-season. But we adapted quickly.	**Beat West Indies by 146 runs at Sydney's Drummoyne Oval (Taylor 65)** My best innings of the tournament, because the pitch was slower than the others we played on and we knew it was important to maintain the tempo in case run-rate came into play in the Super Sixes.

Do you get the recognition you deserve?
It's so much better now. We're always going to get compared to the men, but there's not a lot we can do about that.

How would you sell women's cricket to the sceptics?
I'd just encourage them to come and watch it for themselves – most people who do can't believe how good it is. The fielding is top-class, and the bowling is faster than it looks on TV. Hopefully with time there will be more sixes too.

The Ashes or the World Cup?
The 50-over World Cup will always be the pinnacle for us. It's a shame we don't play as many Tests as the men.

Why is that?
Other countries just aren't as keen on it as England and Australia. Teams like India and New Zealand can only take so much time off work. I wouldn't be surprised if Twenty20 becomes the way forward.

You've won everything – so what still motivates you?
I want to stay at the top for as long as possible and retain the World Cup in 2013 in India. But it's not just about trophies: it's the chance to play with great people all over the world.

So what's your favourite place to tour?
Australia is always the best, but there's something about India. I may spend a lot of time there pulling my hair out, but the culture and the way cricket reigns supreme make it different.

What do you do on tour away from the cricket?
These days you're likely to be in the gym or recovering in the pool. If there's a shopping centre nearby the girls will be down there looking for a new outfit.

Which men's player do you enjoy watching the most?
Swanny. I've known him for years and I'm so pleased he's come through. He's a nice lad and whenever he gets the ball in his hand he's a threat.

What's your personal career highlight?
It has to be winning the World Cup in 2009 in Sydney, followed closely by the Twenty20 win at Lord's later that year.

And your biggest disappointment?
Getting knocked out of the World Twenty20 tournament in May 2010. We lost to Australia and West Indies by such slender margins: we tied with Australia, but it went to a boundary countback, and we lost to West Indies by two runs. After the hype of 2009, it was so disappointing.

What sort of contact do you have with the men's team?
It's mainly limited to dinners and official functions, but they're very supportive of us. Whenever you get the chance to chat to Andrew Strauss and Andy Flower, you want to pick their brains.

What's your favourite shot?
The pull. When a fast bowler's trying to bounce you, there's nothing better than whacking her for four.

What one thing would you change about the women's game?
I'd introduce more Powerplays into the 50-over game. You want the field to come up to encourage batters to hit over the top and make the middle overs less predictable.

Name an England star of the future.
Lydia Greenway [left-hander, aged 25]. In the last year she's really started to show some potential.

What's your one hope for the women's game over the next decade?
Getting as many people in to watch as possible. Bums on seats are the key.

Mar 22, 2009 **World Cup final**	**June 2009** **World Twenty20 in England**	**June 19, 2009** **World Twenty20 semi-final**	**June 21, 2009** **World Twenty20 final**	**July 10–13, 2009** **Test**	**And one more thing...**
Beat New Zealand by four wickets at the North Sydney Oval (Taylor 21)	**Taylor scored 199 runs in the tournament off 147 balls for once out**	**Beat Australia by eight wickets at The Oval (Taylor 76no off 53 balls)**	**Beat New Zealand by six wickets at Lord's (Taylor 39no off 32 balls)**	**Drew with Australia at Worcester to retain the Ashes**	Being named one of *Wisden*'s Five Cricketers of the Year in 2009 was an immense honour for me and not one I was expecting. I had team goals, of course, and individual targets, but I was gobsmacked when the editor, Scyld Berry, mentioned it to me. It was great, both for my profile and that of the women's game – although I have to admit this was the first copy of *Wisden* I'd ever actually owned.
It was so nerve-racking watching the last few overs. When we won, there was this sense of shock. The celebrations were good, but I wanted to remember the evening, so I started buying ginger beer and pretending it was cider!	We wanted to be the most skilful side in all three disciplines. We dominated the teams in our group (India, Sri Lanka and Pakistan) and kept getting better. The games against boys' teams before it started were key.	It's not often you play an innings that ticks all the boxes, but this was one that did: the way I played, the pressure of the situation and the quality of the opposition. I was ultra-determined and to overcome their total of 163 felt like a huge hurdle.	It was amazing to play at Lord's and do it in front of our home crowd. And the bowlers came back superbly after the battering against Australia. It was just a joy playing for a team where everyone did their jobs.	I'll remember this one for Beth Morgan's stonewalling to help us get the draw we needed: 58 in 262 balls in the first innings, 9no in the second off 92. Rain helped us a bit on the last day, but the reality was they needed to win to regain the Ashes and they weren't able to manage it.	

STUART BROAD
FIERY BLOND WITH CRICKET IN HIS DNA

Stuart Broad wasn't the only cricket-mad boy who grew up playing the game in the back garden with his dad. But he was one of the lucky few whose dad had played for England. Chris Broad opened the batting in 25 Tests in the 1980s and starred in an Ashes-winning team, making hundreds in three successive Tests in Australia in 1986–87. A generation later, Stuart did something similar with the ball, sweeping through the Aussie batting at The Oval in 2009 to set up a series victory.

Stuart is 6ft 6in tall these days, but when he was half that height he would go to Trent Bridge to watch Chris play for Nottinghamshire, sometimes even following him out to the middle when it was his dad's turn to bat. Later, Stuart's mum, Carole, would drive him to games and provide catching practice, while his sister, Gemma, was keen enough to end up as a stats analyst for the England men's team. When Stuart said, "I guess I was born to be a cricketer," it was not so much a boast as an understatement. Cricket is part of his DNA.

It's quite common for cricketers' sons to become cricketers themselves, but rare for both generations to be top players. Stuart began life as an opening batsman, like Chris – and a short one at that. But at the age of 16 he grew a whole foot in a year. Soon after, in an age-group game for Leicestershire against Derbyshire in which he had already scored 197, his captain threw him the ball on a flat wicket – more out of hope than expectation. Broad took four quick wickets. As he said later: "They were like, 'Oh, you can bowl then!'"

Until that moment, he had toyed with a career in hockey, which he played well enough to have trials with England age-group sides. But that four-wicket haul settled the matter, and in the winter of 2004–05 he headed for Australia, where he learned how to charge in fast and – as the Aussies say – cop an earful during a six-month spell with the Hoppers Crossing club in Melbourne. The boy had become a man – although he hung on to his boyish good looks.

Stuart went to a private school, Oakham in Rutland, where he learned his cricket under two former England players, Frank Hayes and David Steele. The school pitches were good enough for county matches to be held there, and in 2005, when he was 18, Leicestershire picked him to play there. The following year, he topped Leicestershire's championship bowling averages with 44 wickets at 31 apiece and helped them win the Twenty20 Cup, and caught the eye of the England selectors. Broad made his international debut in a Twenty20 game against Pakistan that September, removing two high-class batsmen in Shoaib Malik and Younis Khan, and played for England's 50-over side soon after. His rise was what pundits like to call "meteoric" – and there was more to come, including a World Cup appearance at the age of 20.

Not everything went smoothly, mind you. During a World Twenty20 game against India on a muggy September evening in Durban, South Africa, in 2007, Broad was hit for six sixes in one over by Yuvraj Singh. This battering might have destroyed his confidence, but Broad had inherited some robust genes from Chris and Carole. He decided his mistake had been to keep bowling on a traditional good length: a time-honoured tactic in first-class cricket, but too predictable against the world's best one-day batsmen.

Instead, he worked on his variations – so successfully that England's Test captain at the time, Michael Vaughan, called him "the most intelligent bowler I have worked with". He handed Broad a Test debut in December 2007 at the heart-breakingly flat Sinhalese Sports Club in Colombo. Sri Lanka racked up 548 for 9 declared (Broad 1 for 95 from 36 overs). But at least his Test career was up and running.

He advanced steadily after that, becoming one of the leading one-day bowlers in the world, and getting enough bounce and movement in Tests to become established as England's fourth seamer. But he mostly took two-fors and three-fors and it was not until the third day of the 2009 Oval Test that he became a star – and found himself labelled "the new Flintoff". The comparisons were misleading: Broad is a more thoughtful bowler than Flintoff was, and potentially a classier batsman, even if he doesn't destroy attacks the way Flintoff occasionally did.

At The Oval, with the series poised at 1-1, Australia had moved ominously to 73 for none in reply to England's 332. The captain, Andrew Strauss, gave Broad a simple order: "just try to get some wickets".

Luck of the English: Broad bowls Ricky Ponting during his great spell at The Oval in 2009.

He rose to the challenge, trapping Shane Watson lbw in his first over. He took out Ricky Ponting, Michael Clarke, Mike Hussey and Brad Haddin, all for single figures, and bowled 12 overs off the reel to take 5 for 37. The Ashes were all but won. It was the stuff of dreams.

This time, his good length worked a treat, making full use of a wicket that had been under-prepared and spiced up by rain. Like most memorable spells, this one contained an ounce of luck. As Broad let go of the ball that bowled Ponting (above) off the inside edge, he thought to himself: "Oh no, I've dragged it down." Sometimes the worst balls produce the best results.

Everything changed after that. Broad returned to the England dressing-room to find 75 texts waiting on his mobile phone, and soon appeared on the BBC1 talk show *Friday Night with Jonathan Ross* – almost unheard of for a sportsman, let alone a cricketer. Unlike previous England players who had tasted Ashes success, however, Broad kept his feet on the ground – even if, like his dad, he did have the occasional temper tantrum.

As his bowling improved, his batting suffered, although he barely got a go in South Africa in 2009–10. But one day at Lord's in 2010, everything fell into place. With England reduced to 102 for 7 by Pakistan, Broad joined forces with Jonathan Trott and added a world-record 332 for the eighth wicket (see page 7). Broad's share was an elegant, grown-up 169 – two more than Flintoff's Test best.

Broad dedicated his innings to his stepmother, Miche, who had died a few weeks earlier from motor neurone disease. He looks forward to life as a genuine Test allrounder. Watch this space!

THE QUALITIES

BATSMEN

BOWLERS

	BATSMEN	BOWLERS
PATIENCE	**loads** a big score will take three hours or more, and Test batsmen have to be able to bat all day	**lots** even the best will bowl 50 balls for each wicket
FOCUS	**loads** one mistake and you could be out; must switch on and off	**lots** every ball must be on the spot, but they do get long breathers
A GOOD EYE	**very** must judge length and line of the ball in fractions of a second	**not very** some have been hopeless batsmen and fielders
GUTS	**lots** the ball is hard and it may be coming at your head at 90mph	**some** got to keep being yourself when all is going wrong
REFLEXES	**fast** you have half a second to make a decision and carry it out	**none** unless the ball is hit straight back at you
BRAINS	**some** judgement, ability to read the conditions and know when to attack or defend	**some** same as for batsmen, plus a good memory – knowing how this batsman tends to get out
ATHLETICISM	**some** can get away with little, but it helps, especially for running between the wickets	**a lot** unless bowling spin, in which case you can be portly or even elderly, and wreak havoc as long as your name is Shane
STOICISM	**loads** could get several low scores in a row	**loads** could get smacked around, and sure to get injured at some point
DEDICATION	**plenty** most spend long hours in nets	**loads** as for batsmen, but it's harder work and bowlers get more injuries

CRICKETERS NEED

FIELDERS

some could be out there all day

loads if fielding close, less if in deep

very good if close in, less so in the deep

lots if close in, especially when the bowling is slow – the ball comes at you from point-blank range

fast if fielding close or saving one, average in the deep

hardly any just need to decide which end to throw the ball to, and how hard

a little if catching, a lot if saving one, some in the deep

some could drop easy catch

plenty the best fielders practise like demons

CAPTAINS

less always busy, but sometimes have to wait for a breakthrough

loads must notice everything

no more than other fielders

lots may have to make tricky decisions, tell mates they are dropped

none unless fielding close, but may need to react fast to changing situations

loads although it may be cricket intelligence rather than academic

none as shown by the former Pakistan captain Inzamam-ul-Haq

loads could do everything right and still lose

loads must have big appetite for every facet of the game

PATIENCE

FOCUS

A GOOD EYE

GUTS

REFLEXES

BRAINS

ATHLETICISM

STOICISM

DEDICATION

CRICKETERS' BODY SHAPES

THE BEANPOLE

height	6ft 4 to 6ft 8
weight	12–13 stone
build	slim
job	fast bowler
current example	Steven Finn (England)
past master	Curtly Ambrose (West Indies)

The beanpole looks as if he is built for basketball rather than cricket, but he is a key member of most teams. He takes the new ball or comes on first change, gliding to the wicket with a run-up which is rhythmic and deceptively mild, and getting the ball up into the batsman's ribs. His height means that the ball is 8 or 9ft above the ground when it leaves his hand; on some grounds, it is above the line of the sightscreen, which makes the batsman's task harder and gives the beanpole a touch of menace. He fields in the deep and bats at No 10 or 11, where he is either endearingly hopeless or a handy slogger. He gets called "lanky" by the press, and "streak of piss" by the coach (excuse his language). He becomes captain only if his team are a bit stuck and he has been around a long time, like Bob Willis of England in the 1980s and Courtney Walsh of West Indies in the 1990s.

THE HULK

height	6ft 2 to 6ft 5
weight	14–17 stone
build	hefty
job	fast bowler, batsman, or both
current example	Shane Watson (Australia)
past master	Andrew Flintoff (England)

The hulk has always found cricket easy because he was so much bigger than the other boys. When he's not struggling with injury, his bowling has more than pace: it has weight, so that he delivers what the pros call "a heavy ball" – a delivery that seems to lose little of its pace when it pitches, so it slams into the top of the bat. As a batsman he can be unstoppably destructive, using his reach and muscle to strike the ball crisply off the front foot, but when things go wrong, they go very wrong. His movements become wooden and he mis-hits the ball into the hands of mid-off or mid-on. He fields well for a big man, often standing in the slips and grabbing most of what comes his way, using what the papers call his big bucket hands. He may become captain by sheer force of personality ("larger than life," allegedly), but is no great tactician as he has never had to think much about his own game.

6 FT

5 FT

4 FT

3 FT

2 FT

1 FT

MR AVERAGE

height	5ft 9 to 6ft 2
weight	11–13 stone
build	medium
job	batsman or slow bowler
current example	Andrew Strauss (England)
past master	Mike Atherton (England)

If you saw him in the street, you wouldn't guess he was a sportsman. Standing in a huddle with his team-mates, he may look a bit dull – he's Mr Middling, six inches taller than some of his mates and six inches smaller than others. But he is needed too. He either opens the batting or comes in at number five, as a canny accumulator and one-day finisher. He tends to have a normal personality: easy-going, level-headed, could make a great captain. If he bowls, he is probably a spinner, like Monty Panesar (6ft 1) or Shane Warne (variously described as 5ft 11 and 6ft). Extra height, producing extra bounce, helps spinners just as much as fast bowlers, but it's not essential: Murali is only 5ft 7. If the everyman is a batsman, he fields at slip or short leg. If he's a spinner, he is probably tucked away at square leg or mid-on, although a few spinners down the years, like Warne and Phil Edmonds, have been top-class catchers.

THE TITCH

height	5ft 3 to 5ft 7
weight	10–12 stone
build	wiry
job	batsman or wicketkeeper
current example	Sachin Tendulkar (India)
past master	Brian Lara (West Indies)

There's a saying, "small is beautiful". And it is often true of batsmen. If you're one of the shorter ones in your class, don't worry – you can still be a giant of the game. You probably won't be a fast bowler, because you won't get enough bounce, but you can be a top batsman or keeper. Short players tend to be deft and well-organised, and they have the low centre of gravity which helps with most ball games because it gives good balance. They are nearly always back-footers, adept at the cut and the pull. Don Bradman, the greatest batsman of them all, was only 5ft 7. They usually field close in and may well become captain. They may not be so good at that: superstars like Tendulkar and Lara seldom make great leaders. But some little guys are a big hit as captain, like Mahela Jayawardene of Sri Lanka.

THE ROLY-POLY

height	5ft 8 to 6ft
weight	12–16 stone
build	comfortable
job	batsman or slow bowler
current example	Jesse Ryder (New Zealand)
past master	Mike Gatting (England)

One of the best things about cricket is that you don't have to be slim to play it. Or even athletic. There's a long tradition of cricketers with an ample frame. They are nearly always batsmen, although the first famous example, W.G. Grace, managed to combine a formidable waist measurement with a long career as an allrounder. These days, bowling is out, but the well-padded sportsman can still be a top-order batsman. Remember how important it is to get your weight into the shot? If he strikes the ball well enough, and stands at slip, he won't have to run much; if he is from the subcontinent, and has a lordly air about him, he can walk most of his runs, like the former Pakistan captain Inzamam-ul-Haq – proof that the roly-poly can end up in charge, and may have great success. Arjuna Ranatunga lifted the World Cup for Sri Lanka in 1996, combining the guile of a fox with the girth of a horse. And England's last portly captain, Mike Gatting, led them to an Ashes win in 1986–87. Gatting also had the distinction of facing the ball of the century from Shane Warne in 1993. It swung into him, pitched outside leg stump, turned viciously the other way, and clipped the top of off. Martin Johnson wrote in the *Independent*: "How anyone can spin the ball the width of Gatting boggles the mind."

A DAY IN THE LIFE OF

MARK RAMPRAKASH

Mark Ramprakash is one of the all-time great county cricketers. After captaining Middlesex and playing 52 Tests for England with only two centuries and too many failures, he has devoted himself to piling up runs for Surrey. In his first 91 matches for them, he made 39 hundreds, equalling the legendary Peter May (who took 208 matches). He has since taken his tally to an eye-watering 60, in the process becoming possibly the last player to make 100 first-class hundreds. He also won *Strictly Come Dancing*, a challenge he described as more nerve-racking than Test cricket. Aged nearly 40 he was touted for a Test recall ahead of the Ashes decider at his home ground in 2009, only for the selectors to plump for Jonathan Trott instead. But Ramps remains a phenomenon. Here he talks us through a typical day in his life.

6.45AM TO 8.30
getting up and out

For a home game, I set the alarm for about a quarter to seven. Quick shower, make my way down to the station by car – I did have a good intention to ride my bicycle down there, it's six or seven minutes by bike, but early season it was often wet so I ended up taking the car. I go to the Metropolitan Line station near where I live in north-west London. If it's a weekday, I always take the train. The journey takes around an hour. I read the paper or read a book, currently a Robert Ludlum thriller. I get to The Oval at half eight and go to the caff round the corner for baked beans on toast and scrambled egg.

9.00 TO 10.20
warming up

I get to the ground at nine. Quick change and then out to the nets with the bowling coach, Geoff Arnold, or another player, to do some throwdowns. It's not a full net, it's someone throwing balls off about 16 yards, seam up, different lengths, mixing it up. I like to get my batting out the way early. Sometimes I have a net, particularly early season. Surrey usually warm up as a team about 9.45 – a team stretch, led by one of our physios, then a five-minute game of football to get loose. I play now and again for the Arsenal charity side. Then some fielding, some catching. I like to go up to the dressing-room pretty early, about 10.20.

10.20
autograph time

When I come off the pitch, I'll often sign a few autographs. It really depends where you're playing. What we're finding at the outgrounds more and more is that people are in your face at every opportunity. I've noticed a big change in the last couple of years. Last week at Worcester, I arrived at the ground at five to nine, parked at the far end, a couple of guys came racing over to get autographs then, and it will happen constantly through the day, and I left quite late and three or four of them were still waiting at 7 o'clock at night. That's not just me, all the players are finding this – people bring books, pictures, four or five things each often – I don't quite know what they're doing with them. *Going on eBay, maybe?* Yes, possibly. *Do you still sign?* I certainly try and do all the kids that I can. It depends a little bit on what time of day you catch me. If I'm in the car park at the end, I'm a bit reluctant, my working day is done, I'm not so inclined to sign them as I've started at nine in the morning. Unfortunately the players are getting a little bit more careful about it – we'll do them at 10.20, we'll do them at lunchtime, but not at the end of the day.

▲ **Here we go again** En route to 188 v Hampshire at the Rose Bowl in 2007.
◄ **Still got it** Ramprakash has never lost his enthusiasm in the field.

10.30
tea and thinking

I'll have a cup of tea and a few biscuits and get the mind right. The captain does the toss at half ten and we'll find out whether we're batting or bowling. I usually have a little think before about the bowlers. Obviously most of them you know, but if there's someone new I'll try and find out whether anyone knows about him and his style of bowling, if we've got anything on the computer, try and take in any information.

11.00
start of play

If we're batting, I pad up straightaway – as a No 3, I have to be ready from ball one. Whilst I'm waiting to bat I will often keep an eye on the cricket, but also perhaps be sitting around reading some of the other papers or watching the TV: I want to get the balance right between being ready to go in and not losing energy. If there's an early wicket, I don't mind that – get in early, 'cause the opposition are attacking, there are gaps, as a No 3 you can't mind getting in early. Having said that, if the openers hang around, then great, because they see off the new ball and when you go in, the ball may be doing less. There are probably only four or five top-class spinners playing county cricket at the moment, so if you can see off that burst when the ball is new, and if the pitch is good and you're concentrating well, you want to go on to a big score. *Are you playing differently the last couple of years? Different mindset, or playing different strokes?* A little bit of both, I think. On the mental side, I saw John Crawley [an England contemporary] play yesterday and I heard Shaun Udal [Hampshire and England spinner] say that he may be 36 or whatever but he doesn't stop learning about the game. That's true. The last three or four years, my balance has been a lot better at the wicket, you're constantly tinkering with bits and pieces, constantly exploring the best way to do it for you.

I've never been a slip fielder. For Middlesex I was always at square cover. Now I've managed to find my way into the gully. I've always liked square of the wicket and at gully you do have to be quite sharp, quite on the ball. I like to make sure I've had a few flat catches, make sure the hands are ready. As the day wears on, I'll be anywhere around the outfield. I find with the long days in the field, I'm having to stretch constantly, you're out there for three sessions of two hours, it's easy to get stiff. You may have not much to do for half an hour, then suddenly you have to chase a ball. *Is your fielding as good as ever?* No. I've lost some pace, and diving is quite hard work, the grounds are hard, the back gets a little stiff, getting down is a little harder.

1.15PM
lunch

Lunch is generally very good, we get a choice of perhaps fish, pasta or a lamb shank, something like that. The food at The Oval is excellent and we get treated very well. If I'm batting, I don't tend to eat as much – a bit of fruit or ice cream. If we're fielding, I pile it on.

after batting

If I've made runs, I'm happy to sit down, have a rest and recover, and I'll be in a good mood. If I've had a long day, I have the dreaded ice bath. It's very refreshing for the legs, I'm a convert to it. If I've missed a straight one, as can happen, I will perhaps have a gym session, working on either core stability or a bit of strength work or aerobic work. It's important to take any opportunity you can to

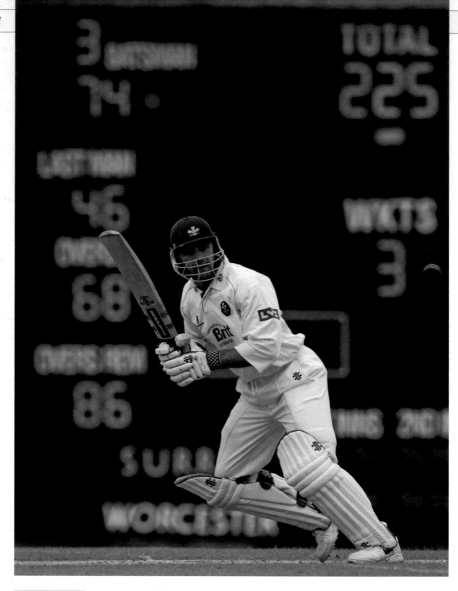

▲ **On the ball** Ramprakash clips to leg during his 142 v Worcestershire in 2007.

keep ticking over. As you get older you've got to work hard at trying to stay in shape. You work very hard in the winter to get in shape and then in the summer you're trying to maintain it. I'm lucky with my weight, I'm probably slightly lighter than I was at 18 – not for lack of trying, I've got a very sweet tooth. I don't drink alcohol, so that may help. When I did *Strictly Come Dancing*, I wasn't in the gym for about 14 weeks so I was losing strength. It's a different type of fitness. Dancing is mainly balance.

4.10
tea

The sandwiches are quite good but I often have to bring in my own tea. I often go along to the caff and get a couple of chocolate chip cookies. I've really made an effort to cut down on cups of tea, it's not very good for you, it can dehydrate you, so I just

have two or three in a day. As I've got older, I've paid much more attention to my nutrition and fluid intake. I try and drink the required amount of water, and if we've had a particularly tough day there is a powdered mix of stuff to rehydrate us. They say we should drink between 1.5 and 2 litres of water. If you can get close to that, you're doing pretty well. *Does that mean you have to think about when you can get to the loo?* (laughs) In the morning is when I try and drink as much as I can, 500 mls of water. While I'm waiting to bat, I often have to go, because I'm trying to get hydrated for the day. Only last week I was actually in the gentlemen's room when a wicket went down. It didn't make me late but it was close. I don't know how other sports people handle it, footballers and that, they seem to be drinking all the time, but I suppose they've only got to spend 90 minutes out there.

6.30
close of play

I don't really do warm-downs, it's a long enough day as it is. We come off at 6.30 or sometimes later, slow change, possibly an ice bath, then a shower, looking to leave around 7ish. Usually get a lift with Nayan Doshi [Surrey spinner] to Finchley or one of the Metropolitan stations so that saves me a bit of walking, and hopefully I'm back to the station near my house at 8.15, home by 8.30. It's a long day but it was my choice to go to Surrey and not to move house. My journey is not dissimilar to a lot of players'. Sometimes it's a relief when we're playing away because you stay [in a hotel] a lot closer to the ground. We don't tend to go for drinks, because everyone's got journeys. When I started, at Lord's, we'd go to the Tavern, but that really doesn't happen now unless you have a very good friend that you've been touring with over the years. At Worcester Ian Salisbury [Surrey and England spinner] and I went out for dinner with Graeme Hick [England contemporary] and his wife. Players are more inclined to get back to their families, I've got two young girls and I want to see them, I value my time at home.

8.30
home again

The girls are in bed, but they come running down, so I have a chat with them for five to ten minutes. My wife will have already eaten. I'll have my dinner and we'll watch something like an episode of CSI. Then to bed about 10.15 and the whole thing starts again. *If anyone reading this wants to be a cricketer, would you recommend it?* Oh yeah, without a doubt. I can't express how lucky I've been to be a professional cricketer. I've travelled all over the world, Australia, the Caribbean, Asia, and in the English summer, I'm not stuck in an office. Of course, it is a job, and you have to work very hard at it, because it's a competitive life and the results are there for all to see. But it is a great life. I'm 41 now and making the most of the time I've got left.

Mark Ramprakash hundreds, 2006–2010

Most cricketers fade away once they pass their 35th birthday, but Ramprakash has just got better. In his last five seasons for Surrey, Ramprakash – who turned 41 in September 2010 – has scored an astonishing 34 hundreds in the county championship. He even found the time to win the BBC's *Strictly Come Dancing* tournament, collecting a perfect 40/40 from the judges for his salsa. Once a perfectionist, always a perfectionist. Here are those hundreds in full:

2006

Score	Opponent, Ground
113	v Leicestershire, Grace Road
292	v Gloucestershire, The Oval
118	v Worcestershire, The Oval
156	v Glamorgan, Swansea
155	v Northamptonshire, Northampton
167	v Somerset, Guildford
301no	v Northamptonshire, The Oval
196	v Worcestershire, New Road

2007

Score	Opponent, Ground
115	v Yorkshire, The Oval
107no	v Hampshire, The Oval
120no	v Warwickshire, The Oval
266no	v Sussex, Hove
108	v Kent, Whitgift School
142	v Worcestershire, Guildford
188	v Hampshire, Rose Bowl
175	v Warwickshire, Edgbaston
196 and 130no	v Lancashire, The Oval

2008

Score	Opponent, Ground
118	v Lancashire, The Oval
123	v Sussex, Hove
112no	v Yorkshire, Headingley*
200no	v Somerset, Taunton
178	v Sussex, The Oval
127	v Kent, Canterbury

Ramprakash's 100th first-class 100. Next in the list of current players comes Sachin Tendulkar on 76, followed by Ricky Ponting on 73. So Ramprakash has left some pretty good players in his wake.

2009

Score	Opponent, Ground
133	v Middlesex, The Oval
138	v Glamorgan, Cardiff
136	v Middlesex, Lord's
274	v Leicestershire, The Oval
134no	v Derbyshire, Whitgift School

2010

Score	Opponent, Ground
102	v Derbyshire, The Oval
223 and 103no	v Middlesex, The Oval
248	v Northamptonshire, The Oval
179no	v Leicestershire, Grace Road

YEAR	MAT	RUNS	HS	AVE	100/50
2006	15	2278	301*	103.54	8/9
2007	15	2026	266*	101.30	10/4
2008	14	1235	200*	61.75	6/1
2009	11	1350	274	90.00	5/4
2010	16	1595	248	61.34	5/5

Scores (first-class only) from Cricinfo.com

DON BRADMAN
THE BEST BATSMAN EVER

Click! Clack! Click! Clang! The noise rang down the street, all day long. It was made by a small boy, a golf ball, a cricket stump, a water tank and a brick stand. The tank stood on the stand, behind the boy's home. Hour after hour, under a harsh sun, the boy would hit the ball with the stump against the stand, which was curved, so the ball would bounce back at odd angles. Hitting it with the stump took patience, concentration and an amazing eye.

Without knowing it, the boy was giving himself a great training for Test cricket. After that stump, a bat always felt like a luxury. Donald Bradman was the fifth and youngest child, so he always had company and competition, but he liked solitude too. Destiny was designing the perfect character for a team game with a strong individual element.

The Bradmans lived in Bowral, outside Sydney. In 1920, aged 12, Don made his first hundred for Bowral school. His uncle played for the town team and Don became their scorer. Once, they let him bat, at No 10, and he made 37 not out. He was given his first bat, a battered old thing, as a thank-you. It was too big, so his father cut 3 inches off the bottom. His dad also took him to Sydney to see a Test match – Australia v England. Australia were 4-0 up and wanted a whitewash. They got it. "I shall never be happy," Don announced, "until I play on this ground." His father smiled "with affectionate tolerance".

By 14, Don had left school and gone to work for an estate agent. Pressed for time, he spent one summer playing tennis, not cricket. When he picked up his bat again, he made 234 for Bowral against Wingello. In a district final against Moss Vale, a match spread over five Saturdays, Bradman made 300.

He joined a Sydney team, St George, and made a hundred on debut, but went back to Bowral to make 320 not out in another final against poor Moss Vale. On debut for his state, New South Wales, he made 118. He moved to Sydney, faced England for the first time in a tour match, and made 87 and 132 not out. At 5ft 7, he wasn't big, but he was quick, nimble, crafty, attacking … and insatiable.

Picked for Australia aged 20, he surely couldn't fail. But he did. He made 18 and 1 as England inflicted a humiliating 675-run defeat. He was dropped; Australia lost again. He was recalled; Australia lost yet again, but he starred with 79 and 112 – the youngest man to make a Test hundred. He added another as Australia won a consolation victory. A year later, against Queensland, he made 452 not out, a world first-class record. He mostly evaded the field, but once, batting against Victoria, he announced "a round-up" and hit the ball to each fielder in turn, going anti-clockwise from slip to fine leg.

Touring England in 1930, the prodigy became a legend. In the Tests, he made 8, 131, 254, 1, 334, 14 and 232, and Australia won back the Ashes. The 334 at Headingley, then a Test record, is still famous because he made 309 in a day, but Bradman himself preferred the 254 at Lord's as "practically … every ball went where it was intended to go." A businessman sent him £1000, worth £30,000 today; his team-mates noted that he still didn't buy them a drink. The Australian public didn't mind. To them, he was a hero and a symbol of national strength.

In 1932 Bradman married Jessie Menzies in what he called the best partnership of his life. Under pressure to make huge scores, he usually succeeded, although his health suffered. The English, desperate to stop him, hatched a dastardly plan: to bowl at the batsman's body with a slip cordon on the leg rather than the off. It was labelled Bodyline. Bradman missed the first Test because of a row over his newspaper column, then returned to a standing ovation – and was out first ball. But he made a hundred in the second innings and Australia were level at 1-1. He kept making runs, but his series average of 56 was the worst of his Test career. England won the series and lost the goodwill of the cricket world. Bodyline was outlawed.

The Bradmans moved to Adelaide and Don became a stockbroker. Even a genius couldn't be a full-time cricketer in those days. Back in England in 1934, he made 244 and 304 to win back the Ashes, but then fell ill. After having his appendix out, he got peritonitis, a dangerous disease of the gut. Jessie set off for England not knowing if he would be alive when she got there. King George – of Australia as well as Britain – asked to be kept informed. Bradman pulled through.

He became Australia's captain. They went 2-0 down in the 1936–37 Ashes, and he shocked his fans by making consecutive ducks. But then he piled up 270, 212 and 169 to engineer a fairy-tale 3-2 win. In 1939, he took up squash to keep fit – and won the South

Don Bradman is applauded out to bat during the fourth Test against England, at Headingley, Leeds, in 1938.

Australia Open Squash Championship. His glittering career was rudely interrupted by the Second World War: he tried to serve as an airman, then a soldier, but was thwarted by a bad back. The army even said he had poor eyesight. Just think how well he might have batted if he'd been able to see properly.

In 1948, aged 40, Bradman led the Australians on one last Ashes tour. They were so good, they were labelled The Invincibles. "Next to Mr Winston Churchill," said *Wisden*, "he was the most celebrated man in England."

In his final innings, at The Oval, he needed just four runs to keep his Test career average above 100. The crowd gave him a thunderous ovation and the England team gave him three cheers. A modest legspinner, Eric Hollies, bowled a googly, and Bradman, who (some said) had a tear in his eye, missed it. He was out for 0; his average was 99.94. No other man has managed more than 60 over a complete career. He wasn't just the best batsman ever: he was the best by miles.

Find out more at www.bradman.org

BATTING
ATTACK AND
DEFENCE

The art of batting comes down to two
things. Do make runs; don't get out.
So a batsman must be able to attack
and to defend.

Attack

When lions are stalking a herd of
antelope, they bide their time until one
of the weaker ones gets separated from
the rest. Many batsmen take a similar
approach. They wait for the bad ball,
then pounce.

The weakness may be the ball's length
– either too short or too full. The batsman
shifts his weight accordingly, rocking
back or stepping forwards. Or it may be
the line – either wide of off stump, or
heading for the batsman's pads. That
allows him to swing the bat. Result:
the short ball, or long hop, gets cut past
cover, pulled through midwicket, or
hooked to deep square leg. The
full ball, or half-volley, gets
driven through the covers,
down the ground ("in the V"),
or flicked through square leg.

The best batsmen can attack
good balls too, if their eye is in and
the pitch is trustworthy. They treat
a good-length ball like a half-volley,
hitting through the line as the pros say.
That really freaks the bowler out. If
the good balls are going for four, what
should he do? Bowl a bad one?

Defence

These days most batsmen are strokeplayers who prefer to attack, which makes cricket more fun to watch. But every batsman has to do some defending, and even a great attacking innings will contain dozens of defensive shots.

Traditionally, most teams have had at least one blocker, someone who doesn't fret if the runs come slowly. Often he's an opener, because the fast bowlers are most dangerous early on – fresh, hungry and armed with a shiny, hard ball.

The last blocker to open for a major Test team was **Mark Richardson** of New Zealand, who retired in 2004. He plodded along with a strike rate (runs per 100 balls) of 37. It worked for him: his batting average was 44.

He was a slow runner too, so he started a tradition whereby, at the end of a Test series, he would challenge his least athletic opponent to a charity race. Richardson would squeeze himself into a bodysuit which was tight, beige and hideous. That's the thing about slow scorers: they're not bothered about looking good.

The last England star in the same mould was **Mike Atherton**, who played 108 Tests, retiring in 2001, and also had a strike rate of 37. At Johannesburg in 1995–96, England had to bat for 10 hours to save a Test – so that's what Atherton did. He survived for 643 minutes, faced 492 balls and made 185 not out. He wore the same kit throughout, thinking it might be bad luck to change. "I must have smelt like a polecat," he wrote in his autobiography, "but superstition was stronger than the smell or the discomfort."

Between attack and defence

Between attack and defence lies nudging and nurdling. A batsman may have a short backlift and no follow-through, but he is picking out the gaps, so the runs tick over. Remember, four runs an over is a good scoring rate. A strokeplayer like Kevin Pietersen will get them with one handsome shot. A nudger like **Paul Collingwood** might get them with a scampered two and a single and another single if his partner gives him back the strike. The end result is just the same – except that Collingwood is a lot sweatier.

Beyond attack and defence

Attack and defence are not quite the opposites they seem. There are times when attack brings hardly any runs – say if the ball is moving around a lot and you can't middle it. And sometimes defence brings quite a few – say if there is no third man, and you have a solid defensive technique, keeping the ball down even when you edge it. Or when a player of great strength, like Shane Watson, blocks the ball and it goes for four.

Attack can be an effective form of defence. Imagine you're facing a spinner who has three men round you, waiting for the bat-pad catch, like dogs hoping for a piece of cheese from the table. If you **hit a few fours**, those men will go back into run-saving positions. And then you'll be able to edge the ball into your pad and get away with it.

◄ **Attack**
India's Gautam Gambhir takes evasive action to avoid being hit by Michael Clarke of Australia.

BATTING
THE 4 CHOICES

A batsman is forever choosing between pairs of opposites.

PLAY OR LEAVE

Illustrations by Major J.A. Board, from the *MCC Cricket Coaching Book*, 1952

Sometimes, especially early on, the batsman won't play a stroke at all. It's usually because the ball is wide of off stump, and he would have to reach for it, which might mean edging a catch to the wicketkeeper or slips.

Leaving isn't as passive as it sounds. It tells the bowler he is wasting energy bowling wide, which makes him bowl straighter. Then the batsman can tuck the ball off his legs, a shot most top players find easy. But the key to leaving it is choosing the right ball. If the ball moves in and clips the off stump, it looks horrible.

BACKWARD OR FORWARD

When we first play cricket, we think batting is all about hitting, so we swing the bat. And we often miss the ball, because we haven't moved our feet. A good shot needs your weight in it as well as your hands, and it's your feet that carry your weight. You need to decide: am I playing back or forward? You may take a small step, like the Indian opener Virender Sehwag, or a giant one, like **Kevin Pietersen**. The choice hinges on the length of the ball. If it is short, you need to be on the back foot; if it is pitched up, the front. Come to think of it, Pietersen hardly ever goes back. Maybe he should try it.

STRAIGHT BAT OR HORIZONTAL

Defensive shots are usually played with a straight bat. That's because the ball is usually straight – ie probably hitting the stumps. By playing with an upright bat, you have the best chance of making contact. You can afford to misjudge the length a bit: it will just mean that the ball arrives higher or lower on the bat, which may jar (because it will hit solid wood, not the springs) but won't get you out. Most batsmen would rather be in pain than back in the pavilion.

A horizontal bat is mostly for short deliveries. If they're wide as well, you cut them. If they're aimed at your body, you pull them. If they're at your head, you hook them. If they're over your head, you leave them and hope the umpire signals wide.

The other horizontal-bat shot is the sweep, normally played to a spinner. You stretch forward to meet the ball on the half-volley or close to it, and sweep it towards square leg or finer. You have to get your head low. And you can even infuriate the bowler by flipping the blade in the other direction and playing a reverse-sweep, like **Eoin Morgan** of England.

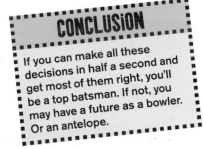

4

OFFSiDE OR ONSiDE

Little kids having their first go at cricket often try to hit everything to leg, because that's a natural swing. Pushing out, away from your body, comes less naturally, but the top players have to master it. Most players end up stronger on one side or the other, just as some prefer the back foot or the front.

Of course the direction of the shot depends on where the bowler bowls. Anyone facing South Africa when Jacques Kallis is bowling needs to be strong on the off side, as Kallis loves to bowl eight inches outside off stump. Facing Graeme Swann, a right-handed batsman needs to be strong through the leg side, as he turns his stock ball from off to leg. Only two shots, the pull and the sweep, normally involve going from off to leg, although the best players of the on-drive, like Sachin Tendulkar of India, can do it from off stump. Only the reverse sweep goes from leg to off, and not many players – Morgan apart – try it.

One of the most classical shots, the straight drive, is played straight down the ground. As well as delighting elderly coaches, it is a winner in one-day cricket, because there is never a fielder directly behind the bowler. Don't go too straight, though: you'll hit the other set of stumps, and if the bowler has got a fingertip to the ball, your partner could be run out.

CONCLUSiON

If you can make all these decisions in half a second and get most of them right, you'll be a top batsman. If not, you may have a future as a bowler. Or an antelope.

FAST BOWLING

It is one of the most stirring sights in sport: a fast bowler racing in off a long run-up and hurling the ball at 90mph towards the batsman's feet, chest or head. It gets the heart pumping even if you're just watching from the safety of the sofa. But there is a lot more to fast bowling than brute force. It's an art that consists of five separate strengths…

90 mph Pace

Most top batsmen are comfortable facing bowling at 80–85mph. If a bowler can get past 90, that comfort evaporates, and the batsman can be hurried or unnerved, which is a polite word for terrified. Duncan Fletcher, the England coach from 1999 to 2007, was always looking for that extra few mph, and was prepared to select a bowler like Sajid Mahmood, who offered pace without much control. The ploy backfired: Mahmood became the most expensive one-day bowler England had ever had. But pace has its place – it's great for blasting out tailenders.

The fastest bowlers in the world today are **Shaun Tait** of Australia, who clocked 100mph during a one-day international at Lord's in 2010, but puts so much strain on his body that, at the age of just 27, he decided to concentrate on limited-overs cricket only. And there's **Shoaib Akhtar** of Pakistan, who is always getting into trouble – whether for alleged ball-tampering, alleged drug-taking, or for not playing through the pain – but can still crank it up at the age of 35 and, at Cape Town in the 2003 World Cup, with a strong wind behind him, bowled the first 100mph ball ever recorded, to Nick Knight of England. I was there, *writes Tim de Lisle*, and although it did seem lightning-fast, it wasn't very eventful. Knight played it easily enough, nudging it to square leg. The trouble was that it didn't have any …

Movement

A ball that goes straight, however fast, is a ball a good batsman can usually handle. If it moves sideways, it's another story. Fast bowlers move the ball in one of three ways: seam, swing or reverse swing.

Seam means keeping the seam upright and landing the ball on the seam, which makes it deviate a little or a lot depending on the pitch (see page 16). If it seams away, the batsman may edge the ball for a catch behind the wicket. If it seams in, he may be bowled or lbw. The new ball moves most because the seam sticks out less once the ball gets bashed around. The leading seamers in the world today are Mohammad Asif of Pakistan – when he's not getting into trouble with the authorities – and probably Stuart Broad of England, tall men with upright actions, who get lift (see top right) as well as movement.

Swing achieves the same effect through the air. Late swing is especially dangerous. Orthodox swing happens with the new ball, which is shiny on both sides, or with a ball which is shiny on one side: the ball swings away from the shiny side. And it is helped by cloud cover. A leading swing bowler is Jimmy Anderson of England, who naturally moves the ball away from the right-hander and into the left-hander, but has developed a wicked delivery that swings across the bows of the left-hander and opens up the possibility of a catch in the slips. Reverse swing happens with the old ball, when it has been roughed up by an abrasive surface. The swing comes later in the ball's trajectory and it is usually inswing, homing in on the batsman's feet. Lasith Malinga

of Sri Lanka (Malinga the Slinger) produced a fabulous spell of reverse swing against South Africa in the 2007 World Cup, taking four wickets in successive balls with what appeared to be laser-guided missiles. Unfortunately South Africa spoiled the story by clinging on to win by one wicket. Somehow, despite bowling round-arm, **Malinga** has developed plenty of …

Control

Even pace and movement are not much use without control. Control means making the ball pitch where you want. It comes with experience, and often increases as pace fades. Some bowlers use control to land the ball in the same place again and again. Andrew Flintoff used to be like that before his body packed in. When Hawk-Eye showed his pitch map, all the blobs were in a cluster, in what Geoff Boycott famously called the corridor of uncertainty: around off stump, on a good length, or in Flintoff's case, a touch shorter – back of a length, as the players call it.

Other bowlers use control to create variations. In one-day cricket, a bowler can't just keep putting the ball in the same place. If he has movement and control, a bowler may not need pace. **Glenn McGrath** of Australia became almost medium-paced in his mid-thirties, but kept on taking wickets. He ended up with 563 of them in Tests, more than any other seamer, and was also the leading wicket-taker in the 2007 World Cup. It helped that he had …

Lift

If the ball stays low, the batsman can get his head over it and control it. If it bounces, it is much harder to keep down. Lift comes from two things: a bouncy pitch, and a tall bowler. If you ever bump into a cricket team at an airport – quite likely, as they do a ridiculous amount of flying – you'll notice that a third of them are giants. Mainly fast bowlers.

Tall bowlers are lethal on uneven pitches, when some balls scuttle through at ankle height, because the difference between that and their normal delivery is that much greater, so it's as if the batsman is playing on a trampoline one moment and an ice-rink the next. Steven Finn of England gets a lot of lift, like Steve Harmison, who is quick but has a drifty action: the ball slows down after bouncing. His mate Flintoff didn't have this flaw: he bowled a so-called heavy ball, which seemed to retain its pace all the way to the top of the bat. And Flintoff had an extra helping of …

Heart

Fast bowling may be glamorous, but it's also hard work. In each spell, the bowler has to run 25 yards or so, 30 to 50 times, and walk back the same distance. It takes perseverance and determination. A bowler with a big heart will keep steaming in even late in the day when he has taken none for plenty. **Merv Hughes** of Australia (1985–94) was a prime example. In fact, he seemed to consist entirely of a big heart and a moustache to match. But he took 212 Test wickets and some of them were superstars.

FLiNG iT LiKE FLiNTOFF
Five fast-bowling tips from the man himself

1 **Develop a comfortable, rhythmic run-up** but not necessarily longer – it won't make you any quicker

2 **Accelerate through your run-up** so you explode into the crease

3 **Keep your wrist steady behind the ball** a hard trick to learn, but it gets easier with practice

4 **Bowl at 90% pace most of the time** save the extra 10% for the big effort balls – yorkers and bouncers

5 **Develop variations** to become a bowler your captain can call upon in any conditions

Adapted from the website of Andrew Flintoff's agents, ISM. For full text, see www.cricketism.com.

SLOW BOWLING

It's not fast, but it is clever. And it can tie even the best batsmen in knots.

About 25 years ago, spin bowling was heading for the rubbish dump. The cricket world was ruled by West Indies, who often didn't even pick a spinner – they just had four top-class fast bowlers pounding in all day at the hapless batsman. But spin never died out on the Indian subcontinent, and soon a legspinner, Abdul Qadir, was winning matches for Pakistan. Australia went through years of very ordinary spinners, but then along came Shane Warne, who for a while would become the biggest wicket-taker of all. He made spin bowling fashionable again, and was soon joined on his pedestal by Sri Lanka's **Muttiah Muralitharan**, the world's weirdest bowler, with his double joints, his huge turn and his bulging eyes, forever expressing astonishment at how many wickets he was taking. Thanks to these two, a healthy balance developed between slow bowling and fast, between guile and force. In fact, if anything – even after the retirement from Test cricket of both Warne and Muralitharan – we could do with some more fast bowlers.

Spin bowling is one of the best things about cricket. It looks gentle and friendly and hittable, yet it can be devastating. It comes from either the wrist or the fingers. Usually, it is hard for wrist-spinners to control the ball, so they go for a lot of runs, but Warne changed that. Finger-spinners have more control, but less turn, although **Graeme Swann** of England, with his big-turning offbreaks, may have changed that.

Both types of spinner need more than spin. They need flight, also known as loop or dip – something to sow doubt in the batsman's mind about whether to play forward or back. The young Warne even brought swing into it – his leg-breaks would swerve into the batsman before spinning the other way, which was a fabulous trick. Spinners also need a variation ball (see table opposite), sometimes called a mystery ball. And they may even vary their stock ball, changing their pace and making

▲ **The eyes have it** Muralitharan in action in his final Test.

it turn more or less. When Warne took a hat-trick against England at Melbourne in 1994–95, all three balls were leg-breaks, but they all had different amounts of spin on them.

To bat against spin, you need to be able to read it, ie spot which way the ball is spinning. Some batsmen can do that from the hand, by noticing a change of action. Others do it off the pitch, which means they usually have to play back, to give themselves time to adjust.

As bats gets heavier and boundaries shorter, spin bowling keeps being written off. But it always bounces back. And a great spinner can keep going for longer, both on the day and through a career. The biggest Test wicket-taker of all time is Murali, followed by Warne and Anil Kumble, who bowled brisk legbreaks and googlies for India. Between them they took 2127 Test wickets. It's hard to see another trio ever coming close.

◀ **Hat-trick**
Melbourne, 1994–95: Shane Warne gets his third wicket in three balls, Devon Malcolm caught by David Boon. The other two wickets were Phil DeFreitas lbw, and Darren Gough caught by Ian Healy. England were all out for 92.

TYPE OF SPIN	BOWLED WITH	COMES FROM	TURNS FROM	VARIATION/S	COMMON?
Legspin	right arm	wrist	leg to off	googly – off to leg flipper – shoots straight on	not very
Offspin	right arm	fingers	off to leg	(traditional) arm ball – gentle outswinger (modern) doosra – leg to off	very
Slow left-arm	left arm	fingers	leg to off	arm ball – gentle inswinger	quite
Chinaman	left arm	wrist	off to leg	wrong 'un – leg to off	not at all

TYPE OF SPIN	INCISIVE?	EXPENSIVE?	BEST EXPONENT TODAY	BEST EVER
Legspin	can be very	can be very	Danish Kaneria (Pak) – 261 wkts* at 34, although he was dropped by Pakistan during their tour of England in 2010.	Shane Warne (Aus) – 708 wkts at 25, and a phenomenal ability to rise to the occasion. Not so hot against India though.
Offspin	moderately	not very	Graeme Swann (Eng) – 113 wkts at 26, he has revived the art of orthodox offspin, especially against left-handers, who can no longer simply pad the ball away: Hawk-Eye has shown that far more deliveries go on to hit the stumps than anyone realised.	Muttiah Muralitharan (SL) – 800 wkts at 22, he could turn it on anything. Of the old school, Jim Laker (Eng) – 193 at 21, one-tenth of them in one Test (see page 104).
Slow left-arm	moderately	not very	Daniel Vettori (NZ) – 325 wkts at 33, with a priceless ability to make use of his variations when the conditions don't suit him.	Bishan Bedi (Ind) – 266 at 28, he earned top marks for style and a few for sportsmanship: he used to applaud batsmen who hit him for six.
Chinaman	occasionally	can be very	Simon Katich (Aus) – 21 wkts at 30, a more-than-handy occasional bowler, but if an opening batsman like Katich is the best it doesn't say much for the rest.	Probably Johnny Wardle (Eng; 102 at 20), who used to switch from normal slow left-arm when the mood took him. He was also rather a good cartoonist.

*all figures are for Tests

ALLROUNDERS

Cricket is designed so that everybody gets a breather – except the umpires, and one type of player. The allrounder. He is the only person expected to be a frontline batsman and a frontline bowler.

He needs bags of energy and two completely different sets of skills. He may even show two different sides of his personality. Sir Richard Hadlee, New Zealand's greatest player, batted like a millionaire and bowled like a bank manager.

Captains and selectors love allrounders for the same reason that your mum or dad likes special offers at the supermarket: they're getting two for the price of one. When Andrew Flintoff played, England had five bowlers at their disposal, which meant it didn't matter too much if one of them was having an off day.

You don't have to have one. In fact, two of the best teams of all time didn't bother with allrounders. The West Indians of the 1980s just picked six batsmen, a wicketkeeper, and four fast bowlers.

And, for more than a decade, the Australian team up to 2006–07 played six batsmen, a wicketkeeper, three fast bowlers and Shane Warne. But both those teams did have sort-of allrounders, because their wicketkeepers, Jeffrey Dujon and Adam Gilchrist, were also frontline batsmen.

Different teams have different habits when it comes to allrounders. Pakistan produce lots of them, India very few. South Africa and New Zealand produce more than Australia, who despite that have great hopes for their hard-hitting young legspinner Steve Smith. West Indies haven't had many allrounders over the years, but they did have Garry Sobers, probably the greatest of them all.

KEY
✎ batting style
⚫ bowling style
⚠ point of interest

1 GARRY SOBERS
WI 1954–74, 93 Tests
✎ left-hander, great power
⚫ left-arm, both fast and slow
⚠ born with a sixth finger on each hand, swiftly removed
8032 runs at `57.78`
235 wickets at `34.03`
difference `+ 23.75`

2 JACQUES KALLIS
SA 1995–, 140 Tests
✎ rock-solid No 4
⚫ beefy fourth seamer
⚠ greedy against minnows – average v Bang and Zim is 124
11,126 runs at `55.07`
266 wickets at `31.59`
difference `+ 23.48`

3 IMRAN KHAN
Pak 1971–92, 88 Tests
✎ correct No 8 who rose to 5
⚫ top-class inswing
⚠ a great captain as well, now a politician
3807 runs at `37.69`
362 wickets at `22.81`
difference `+ 14.88`

4 AUBREY FAULKNER
SA 1906–24, 25 Tests
✎ gritty, unorthodox battler
⚫ leggie with a quicker ball
⚠ became a famous coach but ended up killing himself
1754 runs at `40.79`
82 wickets at `26.58`
difference `+ 14.21`

5 KEITH MILLER
Aus 1946–56, 55 Tests
✎ classical No 5
⚫ genuine quick
⚠ ex fighter pilot: "Pressure," he said, "is a Messerschmitt up the arse"
2958 runs at `36.97`
170 wickets at `22.97`
difference `+ 14.00`

6 SHAUN POLLOCK
SA 1995–2008, 108 Tests
✎ elegant No 8 or 9
⚫ immaculate swing
⚠ 26 Tests as captain, when his averages were 41 and 21
3781 runs at `32.31`
421 wickets at `23.11`
difference `+ 9.20`

The traditional test of a true allrounder is this: is his batting average higher than his bowling average? Flintoff retired from Tests with a batting average just under 32 and a bowling average just under 33, but that was slightly deceptive because he got off to a poor start. Between the middle of December 2003 and the end of the 2005 Ashes he averaged 45 with the bat and 24 with the ball – top stuff.

The one problem with this yardstick is that it favours batsmen who don't bowl much. It's not hard to have a bowling average of 35 if you only bowl a bit. Here are the top allrounders in Test history, using the averages yardstick, but with one qualification. I've left out those who have played fewer than 25 Tests, as stamina is a big part of being an allrounder – although this is harsh on Willie Bates, the England offspinner of the 1880s,

whose career was cut short after 15 Tests because he was hit in the eye by a ball. And although it was tempting to exclude players who have taken two wickets per Test or fewer, that would have meant leaving out Jacques Kallis, who deserves a place for sheer longevity alone.

There should really be extra marks for being a successful captain, which would bring Imran Khan and Monty Noble up the list, and to some extent Shaun Pollock and Tony Greig. An allrounder-captain is three players in one, which is an amazing, gravity-defying achievement. There should also be an extra credit for being a genuine fast bowler, like Imran, Miller, Gregory and Flintoff. Anyone who can do that and make a hundred as well is a genius. So the greatest allrounder of all time is Sobers … but Imran is right up there too.

THE MOST AMAZING ALL-ROUND TEST MATCH
Ian Botham
England v India, Bombay, 1979-80

⚠ First he took **6 for 58** as India scored 242.

⚠ Then he went in with England wobbling at 57 for 4 and made **114** to see them to 296.

⚠ Then he took **7 for 48** and India were all out for 149.

⚠ Then he put his feet up as England's openers knocked off the 96 they needed.

⚠ **A hundred and a five-for** in the same Test has been done 26 times.

⚠ Botham has done it more than anyone else – **five times**.

---

7 TREVOR GODDARD
SA 1955–70, 41 Tests

✎ correct, left-handed opener
⬤ accurate left-arm swing
⚠ "a walking coaching manual," Cricinfo says, later an evangelist preacher

2516 runs at `34.46`
123 wickets at `26.22`
difference `+ 8.24`

8 TONY GREIG
Eng 1972–77, 58 Tests

✎ No 6, aggressive front-footer
⬤ third seamer and offspinner
⚠ grew up in SA, captained England and recruited for Kerry Packer

3599 runs at `40.43`
141 wickets at `32.20`
difference `+ 8.23`

9 JACK GREGORY
Aus 1920–28, 24 Tests

✎ left-handed blaster, didn't use gloves
⬤ hostile quick
⚠ giant who played "like a nuclear explosion," as Neville Cardus wrote

1146 runs at `36.96`
85 wickets at `31.15`
difference `+ 5.81`

10 MONTY NOBLE
Aus 1898–1909, 42 Tests

✎ adaptable No 1, 2, 3, 4, 5…
⬤ medium-pacer and offspinner
⚠ also a shrewd captain, his nickname was Mary Ann

1997 runs at `30.25`
121 wickets at `25.00`
difference `+ 5.25`

11 IAN BOTHAM
Eng 1977–92, 102 Tests

✎ hard-hitting No 6
⬤ king of the swingers
⚠ superstar, charity walker, now a commentator

5200 runs at `33.54`
383 wkts at `28.40`
difference `+ 5.14`

12 RICHARD HADLEE
NZ 1973–90, 86 Tests

✎ left-hander, useful slogger
⬤ immaculate seamer
⚠ so good that he was knighted before he retired

3124 runs at `27.16`
431 wickets at `22.29`
difference `+ 4.87`

Bubbling under
Chris Cairns (NZ 1989–2004) + 4.13
Kapil Dev (Ind 1978–94) + 1.41
Trevor Bailey (Eng 1949–59) + 0.53

WICKETKEEPING

◀ **Best in the world**
– but not in the Test
side. Chris Read of
Nottinghamshire
stumps his Durham
counterpart Phil
Mustard in a
Championship match
at Trent Bridge, 2010

In most groups of people, there's somebody who is busier than everyone else. They are always in the thick of things, making things happen, knowing what's going on, chatting, bustling, oozing energy. In a cricket team, it's nearly always the wicketkeeper.

The keeper is different. He is the only fielder wearing gloves and pads. He is the busiest person on the field, touching the ball about four times an over. He has the best view of anyone apart from the umpire. He is seldom the captain – he's just too busy – but he is the hub of the team.

Three jobs in one

The keeper needs three distinct sets of skills. When the fast bowlers are on, he is a goalie, throwing himself sideways – except that he is not supposed to tip the ball round the post, and he should probably refrain from punching it. When the spinners come on, he has to be an artist, standing up to the stumps, reading the spin, whipping the bails off if

the batsman wanders out of his crease. And all day long, he has to be a cheerleader, bossing the fielders, praising the bowlers ("Like it, Swanny!"), and holding the whole show together. Matt Prior, who took over as England keeper in May 2007, talks about trying to create "bubble and intensity". Paul Nixon, who kept for England in the 2007 World Cup, said he tried "to drip-feed negativity into the batsman's ear".

He also has to bat, so that's a fourth job. For decades, keepers

were allowed to average about 27 in the lower order. Then along came Adam Gilchrist of Australia, who averaged 50 and destroyed attacks. So now most teams want a batsman-keeper rather than the other way round. The best keeper in the world is probably Chris Read, of Nottinghamshire and England, who has immaculate soft hands. But whenever he got into the England team, he got dropped again, because he didn't make many runs.

THE WACKY WiCKY

Many wicketkeepers become quite eccentric. Jack Russell, the Gloucestershire and England keeper in the 1990s, wore the same hat through his whole career from 1981 to 2004. It needed repairing at regular intervals and the only person allowed to do the mending was Russell's wife, Alison. Russell was also very particular about what he would eat for lunch: two Weetabix, soaked in milk for exactly 12 minutes, and a mashed banana.

He drank about 20 cups of tea a day, all made with the same teabag, which he would hang on a nail in the dressing-room, ready for the next cup. But he was a fantastic keeper, who could stand up to fast-medium bowlers and take stumpings down the leg side, and he was a big reason why Gloucestershire were the best county one-day team of the early 2000s. He is now a successful painter, specialising in cricket scenes.

FIELDING

Fielding is almost the opposite of wicketkeeping. A fielder may have very little to do, and he could be miles from the centre of the action. But when the ball comes to him, he has to be wide awake and ready to catch it, stop it, chase it, dive for it and fire it into the stumps. Fielding is a measure of a team's spirit, because 90 per cent of it doesn't show up on the scorecard. It is really four different arts:

Slip catching

The good news for slip fielders is that they get to stand around all day and there's always someone to talk to. The bad news is that the ball comes at them like a bullet, without warning, and out of a bobbly background made up of distant spectators in their summer clothes. Oh, and if they drop it, everyone blames them for all the runs that the batsman concerned goes on to make.

A good slip fielder is a great thing. The best ones go either at first slip, deeper than the keeper, or at second, level with the keeper. First slips tend to be calm, no-fuss types, and can even be portly, like Shane Warne and his predecessor Mark Taylor. Second slips are usually more athletic and extrovert, like Ian Botham and Andrew Flintoff. Third slips can be either type – quietly efficient like Andrew Strauss, or brilliantly gymnastic like Paul Collingwood. The best slip of recent years is reckoned to be Mark Waugh of Australia, who was wonderfully consistent and apparently effortless. He held the world Test record of 181 catches until Rahul Dravid of India went past him in 2009.

Outfielding

The best outfielders normally go at cover or midwicket in Tests, and at backward point in one-day games, although modern captains will move them to counter the strengths of a particular batsman. They're a magnificent sight, prowling the covers with an animal presence, so that the batsman feels hunted and trapped. Andrew Symonds of Australia is a great prowler, and his hairstyle alone makes it hard to get the ball past him. His captain, Ricky Ponting, is almost as good. But the best outfielder of recent times was **Jonty Rhodes** of South Africa, the man who made backward point such an important position. As the cricket writer Neil Manthorp said, Rhodes could leap like a salmon, throw down the stumps when off balance, and prevent quick singles by reputation alone. He went on to become South Africa's fielding coach.

Bat-pad catching

When a ball from a spinner takes the edge of the bat, it often hits the pad as well, and pops up towards the man at silly point or short leg. These positions are in front of the bat, so they demand courage – and helmets, and shinpads – as well as lightning-fast reflexes. David Boon, who played for Australia in the 1990s, was a great bat-pad catcher, even though he looked like he had just wandered in from a pub in the outback.

Boundary fielding

Traditionally, fielding in the deep was a job for fast bowlers looking for a rest. They would amble round the boundary to collect the ball, keep their whites clean, and often bowl the ball back in to protect their shoulders. Not any more. Thanks to one-day cricket, even fast bowlers will slide, dive and ping the ball in to the stumps, flat and hard. And some teams use the relay throw, when the fielder in the deep throws the ball to a team-mate half-way to the stumps to send on. This, studies have shown, is quicker than one long, high throw – as long as the man in the middle gathers the ball cleanly.

HOW TO SET A FIELD

The ground is big and flat and the ball zips across it as if on a giant pool table. So where does the captain put his fielders? Here are four examples, showing how to attack and defend with both fast and slow bowlers.

▲ **Field marshal**
Andrew Strauss moves his fielders at Lord's.

BOWLING: FAST

Fine leg

SLIPS

2nd 1st
3rd
4th
Keeper

Gully
Leg gully

Cover point
Short leg

Mid-off
From 4th slip if another wicket doesn't fall

Mid-on from leg gully if another wicket doesn't fall

SCORE 20-2

The fielding side have started well and want more. They are happy to leave gaps to invite the drive, which could produce an edge to the slip cordon. This field is for a right-arm seamer bowling to a right-hand batsman. The ball is hard and shiny, and the pitch is offering some sideways movement: if it wasn't, one or two slips would move to catching positions in front of the bat, such as short extra and short mid-on. The pitch is also bouncy, so short leg is in, under the helmet, ready to pounce when the batsman fends off a rib-tickler. If the second wicket doesn't come, leg gully – the most unusual position here – will go out to mid-on, and soon afterwards 4th slip will drop to mid-off.

SCORE 200-3

The batting side have recovered well through a big partnership. The ball has gone soft, the pitch seems to have flattened out and the fielding captain has switched to the defensive, hoping to bore the batsmen out. He has just the one slip and a gully, and five of his nine fielders are in a ring, saving the single, to build the pressure. The only easy singles available are to third man and fine leg, who are protecting the boundaries against deflections – often the shots that go fastest off the bat, because the ball retains much of its pace.

Third man
Fine leg

1st slip
Keeper

Gully

Square leg

Cover point

Extra cover

Mid-on

Mid-off

Field diagram (top)

Slip
Keeper
Short fine leg
Backward point
Deep square
Backward short leg
Midwicket
Sweeper
Mid-on
Mid-off
Long-on
from mid-on

250-5

The batting side are on top but not by much, with the tail only a wicket away. The spinner is on and he has what's known as an in-out field. There's a bit of turn, so he has a slip and one man at bat-pad, ready to snaffle an edge. But he is aware that the batsman wants to milk him, so he also has a ring of five and protection in the deep on both sides of the wicket. This field is for an offspinner like Graeme Swann, turning the ball into the right-hander. The bat-pad man is at backward short leg, and the ring is 2-3 (two on the off, three on the leg), with one man out for the sweep and another for the square drive or cut. If the bowler was a slow left-armer like Monty Panesar, turning the ball away from the right-hander, the man under the helmet would jump across to silly point, and the ring would be 3-2. If a wicket doesn't fall for a while, mid-on might drop back to long-on to deter the lofted on-drive.

BOWLING: SLOW

70-3

It's the fourth innings now and the pitch is breaking up. Swann is the main attacking weapon, and he already has a wicket or two. He crowds the batsman with four men round the bat, but he still wants some protection so as not to give away easy runs. He has one man out for the sweep, which leaves four fielders for the ring. These are divided 2-2, so that the leg side, towards which his turn goes, is reasonably well patrolled. So the field ends up as 4-5, and Swann mustn't give the right-hander too much width outside off stump to free his arms. The batsman knows if he can thread it through that ring of four, he will probably reach the boundary. But he has to be careful about aiming through the leg side: if he plays too early, he could get a leading edge. A left-arm spinner would move backward short leg over to gully, and short midwicket to extra cover. All these plans can be tailored to individual batsmen. It makes you wonder, as the 1970s England spinner Derek Underwood once said, "Why do so many players want to be captain?"

Field diagram (bottom)

Slip
Keeper
Backward short leg
Deep backward square
Cover point
Silly point
Short leg
Midwicket
Mid-on
Mid-off

▶ **Claustrophobic**
Swann, on a hat-trick, at Cape Town in January 2010 bowls to South Africa's Mark Boucher as England's small army of close fielders wait. Boucher survived.

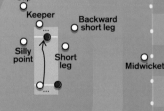

SACHIN TENDULKAR
CRICKET'S BIGGEST STAR

The boy was 12, and this was his daily timetable: 7–9am, cricket; 9.30am–4.30pm, more cricket; 5.30–7pm, even more cricket. He played in the park near his home in Mumbai, India. When he batted, the coach would put a one-rupee coin on top of the stumps. Any bowler who dislodged the coin could keep it. Otherwise, the boy would keep it. He still has 13 of the coins.

Some great sportsmen are naturally gifted. Others are hard workers who make the best of their talents. Sachin Tendulkar is both. He has also needed a third quality: the ability to keep your head while all around are worshipping you. There are a billion people in India and their biggest hero is this small, quiet, modest man. India teems with life and noise, but it's said that when Tendulkar bats, India goes quiet. They call him Sachin, like a member of the family.

He scored his first century when he was 13. At 14, he batted in a schools semi-final with his friend Vinod Kambli. They came together at 84 for 2 and were still together at 748 for 2. Tendulkar made 326 not out and it wasn't even the top score, as Kambli got 349 not out. Tendulkar's average for the tournament was over 1000.

At 16, he played for India against Pakistan. He was too young to sign his own contract, so his father, a professor, signed it for him. He made only 15 in his first Test, but managed 59 in his second. He faced three great fast bowlers – Wasim Akram, Waqar Younis and Imran Khan – and was surprised to find Akram sledging him. "Why do you do that," he apparently asked, "when your bowling is so good?" Where many players would have gone down to Akram's level, Tendulkar rose above it, and paid him a compliment.

In his first two one-day internationals, he made 0. But his progress was unstoppable. In his second Test series, in New Zealand, he reached 88; then, in England, still only 17, he made his first Test hundred. Touring Australia, where Indian batsmen often struggle with the bounce, he made two more hundreds. His Test average was already 41.

How did he do it? By having what coaches call the three Ts: talent, technique and temperament. By applying himself, studying the conditions, seeing what was needed. By being strong – he is only 5ft 5, but chunky – and yet being able to caress the ball, the way some powerful men, like Andrew Flintoff, cannot.

In one-day cricket, he reached the top less directly. He kept getting fifties but went 78 matches without a single hundred. He was promoted to open the innings and finally, in Sri Lanka, against Australia, a hundred came along. Even then, he followed up with three ducks in a row. But the hundreds began to come at a steady rate, and now he has 46, far more than the next man (Ricky Ponting with 29). That's Tendulkar: unbelievably steady.

For years there was a debate over whether he was the best player in the world. His contemporaries included two other all-time greats, Shane Warne and Brian Lara. Each has been the greatest in a different way. Warne had the most impact on the game; Lara was an exceptional entertainer, match-winner and record-breaker. Tendulkar has been the most gracious of the three, and it has been grace under phenomenal pressure: the burden of carrying a billion hopes. He has also shone in hand-to-hand combat, playing Warne quite comfortably. Tendulkar has 11 hundreds against Australia, seven while Warne was still playing; Warne only one five-for against India – and Tendulkar wasn't playing on that occasion.

He has been compared to Bradman by many, including Bradman, who told his wife, Jessie, his style reminded him of himself. But he has also known failure. In the Test Ratings, he has never reached 900, a level Ponting, Mohammad Yousuf, Kevin Pietersen, Shivnarine Chanderpaul and Mike Hussey have all achieved. As captain of India, in 25 Tests spread over two stints, he started well, only to end up with four wins, nine defeats and too many draws.

But he has also been part of a new era of Indian cricket, tougher and more attacking than before. He has been central to several triumphs – beating Australia at home four times and drawing away, winning in Pakistan. He has gone way past Sunil Gavaskar's world record for the most Test centuries, and is the only man to make 30,000 international runs. Aged 37, he recently scored a Test double-century against Australia. That came not long after he became the first man to score 200 in a one-day international. "Sachin is a genius," Lara once said. "I'm a mere mortal."

Off the field, he is a family man who likes driving and praying. He is so famous that both these activities have to be done in the middle of the night. He stays up

*Then and now: a fresh-
faced 17-year-old Tendulkar
is applauded off by England
(above) after scoring his
maiden Test century, at
Old Trafford. Twenty years
later (and with rather more
stubble) he enjoys a lap of
honour (left) after helping
India beat Australia at
Bangalore in October 2010.
His first-innings 214 was
his 49th Test century, which
took him past 14,000 runs
and lifted him to the top of
the ICC rankings for the first
time since 2002.*

late to drive fast cars in the deserted streets of Mumbai and to go to the Hindu temple. Along with the fame, and the fans, has come fortune. Tendulkar is probably the highest-earning cricketer of all time. His current deal with his agents is reported to guarantee him 60 crore a year, around £7m. He has been paid to promote cars, tyres, credit cards, televisions, shoes, biscuits, banks, cameras, Pepsi and Adidas.

So Tendulkar is one of the great success stories. But you may be wondering what happened to his friend Kambli. He played for India with Sachin, although it took him three years longer to get there. He was an instant hit,

making 224 and 227 in consecutive matches. After seven Tests, he had an average of 113, but then the gods stopped smiling on him. The runs tailed off, he had trouble playing bouncers, and he became obsessed with his bat handle, which at one point had nine grips. When he was dropped, India had many other young batsmen, and he couldn't get back. His Test career was over at 23.

Tendulkar, meanwhile, just kept on going. Once, I watched India play Australia in Mumbai *writes Tim de Lisle*. Many of the crowd cheered when Rahul Dravid was out, even though it was a blow to India's hopes. They cheered because it meant they would see Tendulkar.

PLANET CRICKET

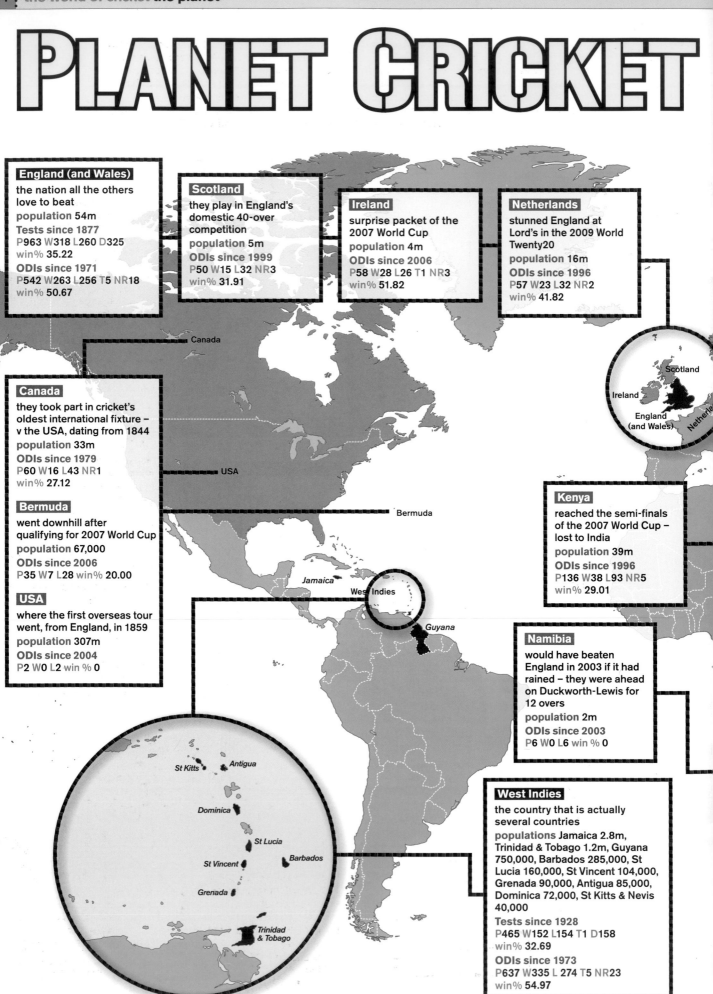

England (and Wales)
the nation all the others love to beat

population 54m

Tests since 1877
P963 W318 L260 D325
win% 35.22

ODIs since 1971
P542 W263 L256 T5 NR18
win% 50.67

Scotland
they play in England's domestic 40-over competition

population 5m

ODIs since 1999
P50 W15 L32 NR3
win% 31.91

Ireland
surprise packet of the 2007 World Cup

population 4m

ODIs since 2006
P58 W28 L26 T1 NR3
win% 51.82

Netherlands
stunned England at Lord's in the 2009 World Twenty20

population 16m

ODIs since 1996
P57 W23 L32 NR2
win% 41.82

Canada

USA

Bermuda

Jamaica

West Indies

Guyana

Scotland

Ireland

England (and Wales)

Netherla

Canada
they took part in cricket's oldest international fixture – v the USA, dating from 1844

population 33m

ODIs since 1979
P60 W16 L43 NR1
win% 27.12

Bermuda
went downhill after qualifying for 2007 World Cup

population 67,000

ODIs since 2006
P35 W7 L28 win% 20.00

USA
where the first overseas tour went, from England, in 1859

population 307m

ODIs since 2004
P2 W0 L2 win % 0

Kenya
reached the semi-finals of the 2007 World Cup – lost to India

population 39m

ODIs since 1996
P136 W38 L93 NR5
win% 29.01

Namibia
would have beaten England in 2003 if it had rained – they were ahead on Duckworth-Lewis for 12 overs

population 2m

ODIs since 2003
P6 W0 L6 win % 0

St Kitts

Antigua

Dominica

St Lucia

St Vincent

Barbados

Grenada

Trinidad & Tobago

West Indies
the country that is actually several countries

populations Jamaica 2.8m, Trinidad & Tobago 1.2m, Guyana 750,000, Barbados 285,000, St Lucia 160,000, St Vincent 104,000, Grenada 90,000, Antigua 85,000, Dominica 72,000, St Kitts & Nevis 40,000

Tests since 1928
P465 W152 L154 T1 D158
win% 32.69

ODIs since 1973
P637 W335 L 274 T5 NR23
win% 54.97

Overview: only **10 teams** have played Test cricket (although Zimbabwe are currently sitting it out because they got so bad). Nine of them are countries, and the 10th is West Indies, a group of countries. All 10 are picked out in red here. You'll notice that they're very spread out, ranging from New Zealand (11–13 hours ahead of London time) to West Indies (5 hours behind). And they're all on the edge of their continents. Why should cricket have landed up in such a scattered bunch of places? Because they were all part of the British Empire.

The countries picked out in **pink** are cricket's second division. They don't play Test cricket, but they do play one-day internationals. All of them have tasted victory, except Hong Kong, Namibia … and the USA.

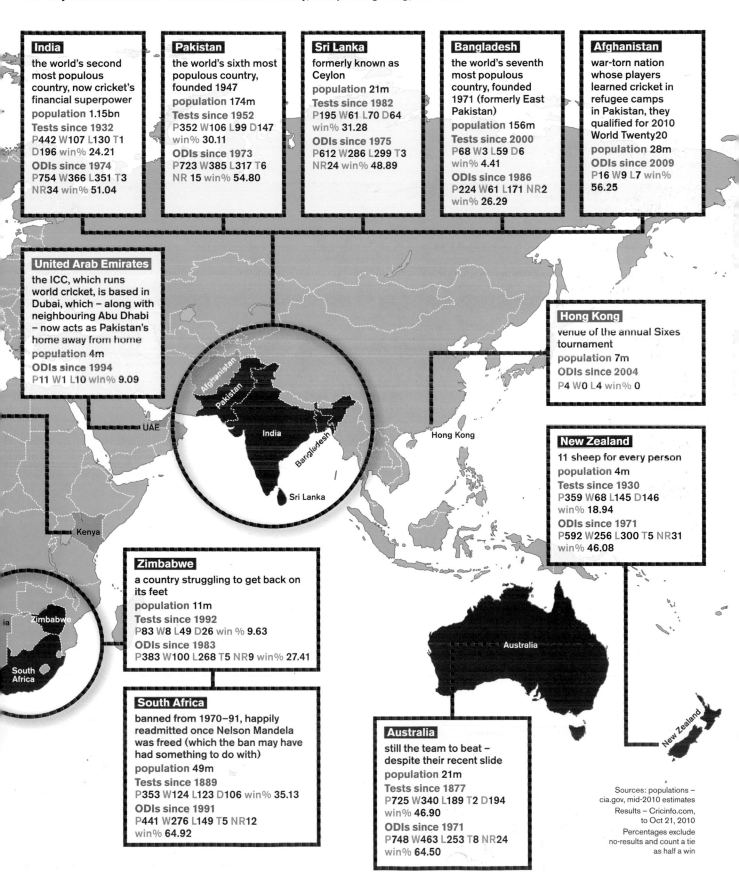

India
the world's second most populous country, now cricket's financial superpower
population 1.15bn
Tests since 1932
P442 W107 L130 T1 D196 win% 24.21
ODIs since 1974
P754 W366 L351 T3 NR34 win% 51.04

Pakistan
the world's sixth most populous country, founded 1947
population 174m
Tests since 1952
P352 W106 L99 D147 win% 30.11
ODIs since 1973
P723 W385 L317 T6 NR 15 win% 54.80

Sri Lanka
formerly known as Ceylon
population 21m
Tests since 1982
P195 W61 L70 D64 win% 31.28
ODIs since 1975
P612 W286 L299 T3 NR24 win% 48.89

Bangladesh
the world's seventh most populous country, founded 1971 (formerly East Pakistan)
population 156m
Tests since 2000
P68 W3 L59 D6 win% 4.41
ODIs since 1986
P224 W61 L171 NR2 win% 26.29

Afghanistan
war-torn nation whose players learned cricket in refugee camps in Pakistan, they qualified for 2010 World Twenty20
population 28m
ODIs since 2009
P16 W9 L7 win% 56.25

United Arab Emirates
the ICC, which runs world cricket, is based in Dubai, which – along with neighbouring Abu Dhabi – now acts as Pakistan's home away from home
population 4m
ODIs since 1994
P11 W1 L10 win% 9.09

Hong Kong
venue of the annual Sixes tournament
population 7m
ODIs since 2004
P4 W0 L4 win% 0

New Zealand
11 sheep for every person
population 4m
Tests since 1930
P359 W68 L145 D146 win% 18.94
ODIs since 1971
P592 W256 L300 T5 NR31 win% 46.08

Zimbabwe
a country struggling to get back on its feet
population 11m
Tests since 1992
P83 W8 L49 D26 win % 9.63
ODIs since 1983
P383 W100 L268 T5 NR9 win% 27.41

South Africa
banned from 1970–91, happily readmitted once Nelson Mandela was freed (which the ban may have had something to do with)
population 49m
Tests since 1889
P353 W124 L123 D106 win% 35.13
ODIs since 1991
P441 W276 L149 T5 NR12 win% 64.92

Australia
still the team to beat – despite their recent slide
population 21m
Tests since 1877
P725 W340 L189 T2 D194 win% 46.90
ODIs since 1971
P748 W463 L253 T8 NR24 win% 64.50

Sources: populations – cia.gov, mid-2010 estimates
Results – Cricinfo.com, to Oct 21, 2010
Percentages exclude no-results and count a tie as half a win

Afghanistan
Pakistan
India
Bangladesh
Sri Lanka
UAE
Kenya
Hong Kong
Zimbabwe
South Africa
Australia
New Zealand

INDIA

Test ranking 1 One-day ranking 3

Captain Mahendra Singh Dhoni age 29, 18 Tests (won 12), charismatic leader, batting powerhouse, unfussy keeper.

Coach **Gary Kirsten** (SA) was perfect for the job when he took over in 2008: unassuming and astute, he let India's big egos have their way.

Stars **Sachin Tendulkar**, master batsman and icon (see page 72). **Virender Sehwag**, opener who combines explosiveness with stamina. **V.V.S. Laxman**, elegant middle-order aesthete and occasional match-turner. **Zaheer Khan**, skilled and combative left-arm swing bowler.

Traits Increasingly efficient under Kirsten, and far less prone to collapse. Sometimes accused by an intense media of placing business interests ahead of runs and wickets. Their board belatedly saw the need to play more Tests once the team reached the No 1 ranking.

Finest hour **Beating Australia 2-1** in 2000–01, when Laxman batted like a god to grab victory from the jaws of near-certain defeat (see page 101). **Winning the first World Twenty20** in 2007 in South Africa.

Test form Most recent series first Outstanding at home, if still playing too many two-Test series. Australia (home) **won 2-0**. Sri Lanka (away) **drew 1-1**. South Africa (h) **drew 1-1**. Bangladesh (a) **won 2-0**. SL (h) **won 2-0**. New Zealand (a) **won 1-0**. England (h) **won 1-0**. Aus (h) **won 2-0**.

One-day form Most recent series first Mixed. **Lost in final of Triangular Series** in SL. **Won four-team Asia Cup** in SL. **Last out of three** in Zimbabwe Triangular. SA (h) **won 2-1**. **Lost in final of Tri-Nation tournament** in Bang. SL (h) **won 3-1**. Aus (h) **lost 2-4**.

T20 record Pretty good – world champions in 2007. **P27 W14 L11 T1 NR1**

Good at Batting on slow pitches (especially against spin), bowling with the old ball, looking imperious in front of adoring fans, signing sponsorship deals.

Not so good at Fielding. Going to the gym. Batting on fast, bouncy tracks.

▶ No 1 M.S. Dhoni with the ICC Test Championship mace.

ICC TEST RANKINGS since they were introduced in 2003

	Jun Oct Jan Apr Jul Oct Jan Apr Jul Oct Jan Apr Jul Oct Jan Apr Jul Oct Jan Apr Jul Oct Jan Apr Jul Oct
	2003 2004 2005 2006 2007 2008 2009 2010
1 Australia	
2 South Africa	
3 New Zealand	
4 England	
5 Sri Lanka	
6 India	
7 Pakistan	
8 West Indies	
9 Zimbabwe	
10 Bangladesh	*Zimbabwe lost their Test status in Jan 2006, see page 81*

5 REASONS WHY INDIA OVERTOOK THE REST

1 They are formidable at home
The last time they lost a Test series in India was in 2004–05 against a great Australian side. Before that, it was 1999–2000, when Hansie Cronje led South Africa to victory before he was unmasked as a match-fixer. And before *that*, you have to go back to 1986–87 and defeat to their bitter rivals Pakistan. That's some record.

2 They are getting better away
It used to be the case that Indian cricketers seemed to suffer from homesickness even more severely than Steve Harmison. But since 2003–04 they have won Test series in Pakistan, West Indies, England and New Zealand. And they even held the Australians to a draw in their own back yard.

3 Australia fell away
Just as India began to put together a consistent run of results, the Aussies faded badly. The Border-Gavaskar Trophy – the piece of silverware named after Australia's most battle-hardened captain and India's sturdiest opener – is becoming an Indian possession: they have won five of the last eight Tests between the sides, and lost none.

4 Their fast bowlers are no longer a running joke
India used to rely on their many spinners and the charismatic allrounder Kapil Dev, who was quick only by Indian standards. But they take fast bowling seriously now – there is a pace academy in Chennai – and they no longer rely on turning pitches. Zaheer Khan, Ishant Sharma, R.P. Singh, Irfan Pathan and Ashish Nehra have all become matchwinners.

5 Sachin Tendulkar has enjoyed an Indian summer
He was pretty good anyway, but between November 2008 and October 2010, Tendulkar scored 10 Test hundreds and averaged 80. Quite something for a man who's been playing Test cricket since the 1980s

▶ **Still got it**
Tendulkar during his 214 at Bangalore against Australia in October 2010.

SOUTH AFRICA

Test ranking 2 One-day ranking 2

Captain **Graeme Smith**, age 29, 78 Tests as capt (won 37). Almost a national institution now after taking the job on as an unknown 22-year-old.

Coach **Corrie van Zyl** (SA), age 49, was due to step down after the 2011 World Cup after just over a year in office. Replaced the highly popular and affable Mickey Arthur, who did the job for almost five years until early 2010.

Stars **Jacques Kallis**, expert grinder and useful – if reluctant – swing bowler. **A.B. de Villiers**, match-changer at No 5 or 6 and brilliant at backward point. **Dale Steyn**, lightning-quick bowler with a nasty streak. **Morne Morkel**, friendly giant, gets awkward bounce.

Traits Committed, serious and always tough to beat, but lost momentum after winning in England in 2008 for the first time in 40 years, then winning in Australia for the first time ever. Still haunted by the "chokers" tag applied to them by Steve Waugh, Australia's captain 1999–2004.

Finest hour **That triumph in Australia**, when they chased 414 to win at Perth, then claimed the series at Melbourne after J.P. Duminy and Steyn added 180 for the ninth wicket.

Test form Pretty good. West Indies (a) **won 2-0**. India (a) **drew 1-1**. Eng (h) **drew 1-1**. Aus (h) **lost 1-2**. Aus (a) **won 2-1**. Bang (h) **won 2-0**. Eng (a) **won 2-1**.

One-day form Up and down. WI (a) **won 5-0**. Ind (a) **lost 1-2**. Eng (h) **lost 1-2**. Zim (h) **won 2-0**. **Failed to qualify** from group stage of Champions Trophy in SA. Aus (a) **won 3-2**. Aus (h) **won 4-1**.

T20 record Very good. **P35 W23 L12**

Good at Fielding. Beating weak opposition. Seam bowling.

Not so good at Playing spin bowling. Keeping their heads under pressure. Big tournaments.

▲ **Almost an institution** Graeme Smith left and Dale Steyn after beating India at Nagpur in February 2010.

SRI LANKA

Test ranking 3 One-day ranking 4

Captain **Kumar Sangakkara**, age 33, 11 Tests (won 5), a qualified lawyer who loves Oscar Wilde and bats like a dream.

Coach **Trevor Bayliss** (Aus), less high-profile and influential than Tom Moody, the compatriot he replaced in June 2007. Planned to step down after 2011 World Cup.

Stars **Mahela Jayawardene**, middle-order rock, makes big runs in second gear. **Lasith Malinga**, slingy fast bowler with a blond afro who shouldn't be as accurate as he is. **Ajantha Mendis**, ex-soldier, now mystery spinner who turns it both ways and flicks his "carrom" ball with his middle finger.

Traits Elegant, unorthodox batting. Loads of spin bowling (even since Murali retired), and some swing: Malinga is first real paceman. Spectators find them charming, opponents don't always agree.

Finest hour **Winning 1996 World Cup** and reinventing one-day cricket, with Sanath Jayasuriya showing it was possible to do your big hitting at the start of the innings, not just the end.

Test form Good at home. Ind (h) **drew 1-1**. Ind (a) **lost 0-2**. NZ (h) **won 2-0**. Pakistan (h) **won 2-0**. Pak (a) **drew 0-0** – series abandoned during second Test in Lahore following terrorist attacks on buses carrying SL team and match officials.

One-day form Good at winning anonymous tournaments. **Won triangular series** (v NZ and Ind). **Lost in final of Asia Cup** to Ind. **Won triangular series** in Zim (v Zim and Ind). **Won tri-nation tournament** in Bang (v Bang and Ind).

T20 record Better than average. **P33 W19 L14**

Good at Batting at the Sinhalese Sports Club in Colombo. Spin bowling. Being every neutral's favourite team.

Not so good at Coping with non-Asian conditions. They did draw in England in 2006, but tend to flounder in Aus and SA.

▲ **That's huge** Kumar Sangakkara left and Mahela Jayawardene during their third-wicket stand of 624 against South Africa in 2006.

▲ **Champions at last** Paul Collingwood **right** and team-mates with the World Twenty20 trophy in Barbados in May 2010.

ENGLAND

Test ranking 4 One-day ranking 5

Captain **Andrew Strauss**, 33, 27 Tests (won 13), cautious but tough, leads from the front and regained the one-day captaincy in 2009. Twenty20 capt: **Paul Collingwood**, 34, sometimes reluctant but not when leading England to World Twenty20 glory in 2010.

Coach **Andy Flower**, understated but hard as nails. Averaged 51 in Tests for Zimbabwe, kept wicket, captained the side, topped the world batting rankings and famously stood up to Robert Mugabe, his country's president, by joining Henry Olonga in wearing a black armband at the 2003 World Cup. Highly respected and unafraid to be ruthless in selection. Has turned round the one-day side too.

Stars **Graeme Swann**, cheeky-chappie offspinner who allows England to get away with a four-man attack because he takes wickets *and* keeps it tight. **Kevin Pietersen**, Brylcreem Boy with the ability, when on form, to take a game by the scruff. **Stuart Broad**, blond heart-throb whose good days are very good indeed – see The Oval 2009 (and page 42).

Traits Resilient and united, with a useful tail. Bowling world-class in helpful conditions but struggles on flat pitches. Batting can be brittle, and only Pietersen is naturally dominant.

Finest hour The **Ashes victory in 2005**, bigger than 2009 because Australia still had several superstars. **Winning the World Twenty20** in 2010, when they became the last major team to win a global one-day trophy.

Test form Very good. Pak (h) **won 3-1**. Bang (h) **won 2-0**. Bang (a) **won 2-0**. SA (a) **drew 1-1**. Aus (h) **won 2-1**. WI (h) **won 2-0**. WI (a) **lost 0-1**.

One-day form Superb, which makes a change. Pak (h) **won 3-2**. Aus (h) **won 3-2**. Bang (h) **won 2-1**. Bang (a) **won 3-0**. SA (a) **won 2-1**. Champions Trophy (in SA) **lost in semi-final** to Aus.

T20 record Getting much better – now world champions. **P34 W17 L15 NR2**

Good at Bowling under cloudy skies. Playing Australia at home. Being given newspaper columns. Tweeting.

Not so good at Batting against left-arm seamers. Winning on the subcontinent.

▲ **The man with the Latin tattoo** Australia's Michael Clarke in action against New Zealand at Hamilton in March 2010.

AUSTRALIA

Test ranking 5 One-day ranking 1

Captain Ricky Ponting, age 35, 73 Tests in charge. Highly respected leader, with nearly 6,500 runs at 53 as captain.

Coach Tim Nielsen, down-to-earth ex-wicketkeeper for South Australia, took over from the more cerebral John Buchanan in 2007 – and lost four of first thirteen Test series. Buchanan lost two in seven years, but then he had great players.

Stars Ponting, No 3 and all-time great: still the big wicket after all these years. **Michael Clarke**, talented vice-captain with a tattoo on his left arm saying *carpe diem* (Latin for "seize the day"). He often does. **Shane Watson**, hulking allrounder who turned himself into a consistent opener and also gets wickets.

Traits Tough as old boots, even if the loss of several greats between 2007 and 2009 has removed their intimidating aura. Bowling now mortal, and spin ropey. Still deeply dedicated to the cause, as shown by their famous cap, the **Baggy Green** – more a national symbol than a piece of cloth.

Finest hour A hat-trick of World Cup wins in 1999, 2003 and 2007. And **16 Test wins in a row** – a world record – between Oct 1999 and Feb 2001 (under Steve Waugh), and again from Dec 2005 to Jan 2008 (under Ponting).

Test form Depends where they play. Ind (away) **lost 0-2**. Pak (in England) **drew 1-1**. NZ (home) **won 2-0**. Pak (h) **won 3-0**. WI (h) **won 2-0**. Eng (a) **lost 1-2**. SA (a) **won 2-1**. SA (h) **lost 1-2**.

One-day form Almost flawless. Eng (a) **lost 2-3**. NZ (a) **won 3-2**. WI (h) **won 4-0**. Pak (h) **won 5-0**. Ind (a) **won 4-2**. **Won Champions Trophy** in SA.

T20 record Should be better. **P38 W21 L15 T1 NR1**

Good at Fighting hard – they hate losing. Exploiting home conditions. Ground fielding (they use a baseball coach). Collecting World Cups. Singing in the dressing-room (but only after they've won).

Not so good at Winning close games. Playing high-class offspin. Keeping quiet. Being modest.

PAKISTAN

Test ranking 6 One-day ranking 6

Captain They seem to make it up as they go along. **Salman Butt**, age 25, was Test captain in England in 2010 before his alleged involvement in the spot-fixing scandal. **Shahid Afridi**, 30, had handed him the job after one Test v Australia at Lord's to concentrate on the one-day captaincy. And after Butt came **Misbah-ul-Haq**, 36, who hadn't played for nine months...

Coach Waqar Younis, a former great who was better at bowling inswinging yorkers than he is at pulling together the spikiest team in world cricket – but shelf-lives for Pakistan coaches are notoriously brief.

Stars Not as many as they had before Mohammad Amir and Mohammad Asif were accused of deliberately bowling no-balls at Lord's in 2010. But there's always **Afridi**, one-day blaster – only batsman ever with a Test career strike-rate above a run a ball (among those with 1,000 runs). **Umar Akmal**, on the rise with the bat.

Traits The word often used of them is mercurial – they're very up and down. Controversy follows them around like a demented fan.

Finest hour Winning 1992 World Cup in Australia from a near-hopeless position. Their captain, the great allrounder Imran Khan, said: "Fight like cornered tigers." And they did – assuming tigers can swing a cricket ball both ways.

Test form Miserable. Eng (a) **lost 1-3**. Aus (in Eng) **drew 1-1**. Aus (a) **lost 0-3**. NZ (a) **drew 1-1**. SL (a) **lost 0-2**. SL (h) **drew 0-0** – series abandoned because of Lahore terrorist attacks. Pakistan have not hosted any international cricket since. Ind (a) **0-1**.

One-day form Not much better. Eng (a) **lost 2-3**. **Failed to qualify from group stage** of Asia Cup. Aus (a) **0-5**. NZ (in UAE) **lost 1-2**. **Lost to NZ in semi-finals** of Champions Trophy in South Africa. SL (a) **lost 2-3**. Aus (in UAE) **lost 2-3**.

T20 record Second to none, **world champions in 2009**. **P40 W26 L13 T1**

Good at Fast bowling, especially reverse swing. Dashing one-day batting. Bickering. Defying expectations. Getting embroiled in scandal.

Not so good at Travelling. Coping with bouncy pitches – in Aus they have won 1, lost 14 since 1983.

NEW ZEALAND

Test ranking 8 One-day ranking 7

Captain **Daniel Vettori**, age 34, 27 Tests as capt (won 6). Bespectacled Harry Potter lookalike who bowls left-arm spin, bats solidly in the lower-middle order and generally has more on his plate than any boy wizard could cope with.

Coach **Mark Greatbatch** (NZ), age 47. Bristling former Test batsman who replaced an Englishman, Andy Moles, in early 2010. His persona is far more dour than his batting ever was.

Stars **Brendon McCullum**, hell-raising one-day opener who gave up the gloves to concentrate on his batting. **Jesse Ryder**, McCullum's boisterous one-day opening partner, sometimes in trouble with administrators for drinking too much. **Ross Taylor**, gifted middle-order attacker.

Traits Pragmatic, never-say-die attitude, which is probably necessary when their best sportsmen all want to play rugby. Lost a cutting edge when their fastest bowler, Shane Bond, retired in 2010.

Finest hour 1985–86. Inspired by the great seam bowler Richard Hadlee, they beat Australia home and away before going on to win in England for the first time.

Test form Disappointing. Aus (h) **lost 0-2**. Bang (h) **won 1-0**. Pak (h) **drew 1-1**. SL (a) **lost 0-2**. Ind (h) **lost 0-1**. WI (h) **drew 1-1**. Aus (a) **lost 0-2**.

One-day form Worryingly on the wane. Bang (a) **lost 0-4**. **Last in triangular tournament** in SL (v SL and Ind). Aus (h) **lost 2-3**. Bang (h) **won 3-0**. Pak (UAE) **won 2-1**. **Lost in final of Champions Trophy** to Aus in SA.

T20 record Middling. **P**40 **W**17 **L**20 **T**3

Good at Discipline. Batting deep. Making the most of limited talent. Rugby.

Not so good at Semi-finals – they have played five in World Cups and lost them all.

WEST INDIES

Test ranking 7 One-day ranking 8

Captain **Darren Sammy**, age 26, appointed October 2010. Committed allrounder and the first St Lucian to play for West Indies. Replaced the more flamboyant Chris Gayle after he'd had three years in the job.

Coach **Ottis Gibson** (WI), 41, genial but tough former fast bowler who spent two years as England's bowling coach before taking the West Indies role in January 2010.

Stars **Gayle**, opening batsman – bats like a pirate, looks like a rock star. **Shiv Chanderpaul**, adhesive batsman, crabby but effective. **Dwayne Bravo**, dashing No 6 bat and lively seamer.

Traits Always longing for their glorious past, but it will never return unless they sort out their structural problems and internal squabbles. At best, attractive; at worst, inept – especially overseas.

Finest hour 1976 to 1995 – kings of the world. Since then: **winning Champions Trophy** in England, 2004.

Test form Dismal. SA (h) **lost 0-2**. Aus (a) **lost 0-2**. Bang (h) **lost 0-2**. Eng (a) **lost 0-2**. Eng (h) **won 1-0**. NZ (a) **drew 0-0**. Aus (h) **lost 0-2**.

One-day form Almost as bad. SA (h) **lost 0-5**. Zim (h) **won 4-1**. Aus (a) **lost 0-4**. **Lost all three group games** at Champions Trophy in SA. Bang (h) **lost 0-3**. Ind (h) **lost 1-2**.

T20 record Mediocre. **P**28 **W**11 **L**15 **T**2

Good at Entertaining. Hitting sixes.

Not so good at Slow bowling. Travelling. Knuckling down.

▲Star appeal Shakib Al Hasan led his team to an unexpected one-day clean sweep at home to New Zealand in October 2010.

BANGLADESH

Test ranking 9 One-day ranking 9

Captain **Shakib Al Hasan**, age 23, 8 Tests as capt (won 1), talented No 5 and thoughtful left-arm spinner, played for Worcestershire in 2010.

Coach **Jamie Siddons** (Aus), age 46, no-nonsense, likeable Victorian who cares for his team but still manages to make entertainingly spiky comments at press conferences.

Stars **Tamim Iqbal** Fearless left-handed opener, blasts away regardless. **Mushfiqur Rahim**, Tom Thumb-sized wicketkeeper and gutsy batsman.

Traits Young, keen, fervently supported – but too often overwhelmed.

Finest hours **Beating Australia** in a one-day game in Cardiff in 2005; **winning 2-0 in the Caribbean**, even if it was against a West Indies 3rd XI; **beating NZ 4-0** in ODIs in 2010.

Test form Only one result to shout about. Eng (a) **lost 0-2**. Eng (h) **lost 0-2**. NZ (a) **lost 0-1**. Ind (h) **lost 0-2**. WI (a) **won 2-0**. SL (h) **lost 0-2**. SA (a) **lost 0-2**.

One-day form Ditto. NZ (h) **won 4-0**. Eng (a) **lost 1-2**. **Lost all three games at Asia Cup** in SL (v Ind, Pak & SL). Eng (h) **lost 0-3**. NZ (a) **lost 0-3**.

T20 record Barely any better. **P16 W3 L13**

Good at Spin bowling. Opening. Keeping the faith.

Not so good at Test cricket. Holding their nerve.

ZIMBABWE

Test ranking –* One-day ranking 11

Captain **Elton Chigumbura**, age 24, lively allrounder appointed in May 2010 to replace Prosper Utseya, who had done the job for four years but played only one Test. This was because Zimbabwe suspended themselves from Test cricket in January 2006 as their country, ruled by the dictator Robert Mugabe, and their cricket slid into turmoil.

Coach **Alan Butcher** (Eng), age 56, father of former England batsman Mark and ex-coach of Surrey.

Stars Well, almost. **Brendan Taylor**, powerful opening batsman. **Tatenda Taibu**, combative keeper and fine strokemaker in the middle order.

Traits For a few years after their Test exile, they were hopeless in one-day cricket – not surprisingly, as their best players were deserting them. But they are slowly rediscovering the gusto of old: keen, committed and athletic – but still prone to too many shockers.

Finest hour **Test: 1998–99, beat India** at home **and Pakistan** away. **One-day: their very first match**, in the 1983 World Cup, when Duncan Fletcher, later England's coach, stunned Australia with 69no and 4-42. **Twenty20: beat Australia** at World T20 in 2007.

Test form Nothing since Sept 2005 – and no win against any team other than Bangladesh since they beat India in June 2001.

One-day form Currently below Ireland – but slowly improving. Ire (h) **won 2-1**. **Lost to SL in final of triangular tournament** in Zim (also Ind). WI (a) **lost 1-4**. SA (a) **lost 0-2**. Bang (a) **lost 1-4**. Kenya (h) **won 4-1**.

T20 record Poor – but they did beat Australia. **P14 W3 L10 T1**

Good at Soldiering on. Very occasionally playing above themselves.

Not so good at Averting meltdown.

***But hoping to return**

▲On the move Brendan Taylor and Tatenda Taibu are Zimbabwe's best hopes for future success.

MY WORLD XI

Sooner or later – perhaps when rain stops play – you'll find yourself selecting your own World XI to take on the mythical cricketers of Mars. It's great fun and sure to cause plenty of debate among your friends. After all, there is no correct answer.

These line-ups tend to work better on paper than in reality, as Australia showed when they thrashed a World XI in late 2005. Most cricketers play with maximum pride for their country, and they like playing with their mates. But it's still an interesting exercise to try and pick the very best XI in the world.

Our choice has been made for a Test match. The best teams are balanced, and this side contains nine men with first-class hundreds, four right-handers and two left-handers in the top six, the world's fastest bowler, two left-arm seamers plus two spinners in case the pitch is taking turn. Only West Indies and Pakistan are not represented here, which is a pity: if he hadn't become mixed up in the spot-fixing controversy at Lord's in 2010, Mohammad Amir would have kept out Mitchell Johnson.

This team also contains one special ingredient guaranteed to pull a crowd: charisma. Virender Sehwag goes in with Tamim Iqbal in what could be the most exciting opening partnership in Test history. And what bowler would relish the prospect of trying to separate Sachin Tendulkar and Mahela Jayawardene, two of Test cricket's most gracefully immovable objects? After all that, the sight of A.B. de Villiers coming in at No 6 should demoralise the Martian bowlers even further.

When the little green men have a bat, Dale Steyn offers pace and hostility, Zaheer Khan guile with both the new ball and the old, and Johnson swing. And it would be a treat to watch Daniel Vettori and Graeme Swann in action together on a wearing pitch. But maybe you can do better…

VIRENDER SEHWAG
1 Bats **right**
Born **20.10.1978** Team **India**

Why **Can turn a game in a session**
Tests **81**, runs **7152**, average **53**
Deputy **Andrew Strauss** (England)
Reliable, but not as dashing

TAMIM IQBAL
2 Bats **left**
Born **20.3.1989** Team **Bangladesh**

Why **Ferocious and fearless**
Tests **19**, runs **1445**, average **40**
Deputy **Gautam Gambhir** (India) Classy, but not so hot in 2010

KUMAR SANGAKKARA (wk)*
3 Bats **left**
Born **27.10.1977** Team **Sri Lanka**

Why **Reads game astutely both sides of the stumps**
Tests **91**, runs **8016**, average **56**
Deputy **Jacques Kallis** (South Africa) Rock-like, but one-paced; *(as wk) **M.S. Dhoni** (India) Bruising hitter and leader of men

SACHIN TENDULKAR
4 Bats **right**
Born **24.4.1973** Team **India**

Why **All-time great, having late flourish**
Tests **171**, runs **14210**, average **56**
Deputy **Kevin Pietersen** (England) A genius struggling for form in 2010

MAHELA JAYAWARDENE

5 Bats **right**
Born **27.5.1977** Team **Sri Lanka**

Why A stylist – and a run-machine
Tests **113**, runs **9408**, average **54**
Deputy Thilan Samaraweera (Sri Lanka)
Outstanding technique

A.B. de VILLIERS

6 Bats **right**
Born **17.2.1984** Team **South Africa**

Why Brilliant counter-attacker and fielder
Tests **61**, runs **4232**, average **45**
Deputy V.V.S. Laxman (India) Artist, capable
of great things, but inconsistent

DANIEL VETTORI (capt)

7 Bats **left** Bowls **left-arm spin**
Born **27.1.1979** Team **New Zealand**

**Why Wily veteran, approaching
allrounder status**
Tests **100**, runs **3962**, average **30**
wickets **325**, average **33**
Deputy Shakib Al Hasan (Bangladesh)
Up-and-coming slow left-armer and batter

MITCHELL JOHNSON

8 Bats **left** Bowls **left-arm fast**
Born **2.11.1981** Team **Australia**

Why Pace, swing, lower-order slugging
Tests **38**, runs **1030**, average **22**
wickets **166**, average **29**
Deputy Morne Morkel (South Africa)
Giant quick who loves bounce

GRAEME SWANN

9 Bats **right** Bowls **right-arm offbreak**
Born **24.3.1979** Team **England**

Why Guile, spark – world's best spinner
Tests **24**, runs **653**, average **25**
wickets **113**, average **26**
Deputy Harbhajan Singh (India) Talented
but temperamental

DALE STEYN

10 Bats **right** Bowls **right-arm (very) fast**
Born **27.6.1983** Team **South Africa**

Why Quickest bowler on the planet
Tests **41**, runs **540**, average **13**
wickets **211**, average **23**
Deputy Ishant Sharma (India) Dangerous
beanpole striving for consistency

ZAHEER KHAN

11 Bats **right** Bowls **left-arm fast-medium**
Born **7.10.1978** Team **India**

Why Skilful and combative
Tests **74**, runs **986**, average **13**
wickets **254**, average **32**
Deputy Jimmy Anderson (England)
Lethal in swinging conditions

Figures from Cricinfo.com, to October 14, 2010

ENGLAND TEAM PROFILES

The names are familiar, but what sort of players are they? What are their Test stats? And the highs and lows of their careers so far? You may know all this – if you do, get a friend to read bits aloud, and guess who they are about.

Batsmen

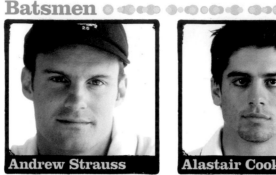

Andrew Strauss

born **1977**, county **Middlesex**. **LHB, opener and captain** **Tests 77, runs 5777, ave 43**

England's undisputed leader after forming a close bond with coach Andy Flower in the Caribbean in early 2009, and now one of the world's most respected openers. He's versatile too, and was England's leading one-day runscorer in 2009–10 after cleverly reinventing his game and scoring at a run a ball.

high **captained England to the Ashes in 2009** low **dropped for the tour of Sri Lanka in late 2007**

Alastair Cook

born **1984**, Essex. **LHB, opener** **Tests 60, runs 4364, ave 42**

Calm left-hander who already had 13 Test hundreds before he was 26 and captained England in Bangladesh in 2009–10 when Strauss wanted a break. Efficient rather than spectacular – his first 60 Tests produced only four sixes – he has learned how to score what the old pros call "ugly runs".

high **60 and 104 on Test debut, Nagpur, 2005–06** low **2010 v Pakistan, until saving his career with 110 at The Oval**

Jonathan Trott

born **1981**, Warwickshire. **RHB, No 3; RM** **Tests 13, runs 1155, ave 55 wkts 1, ave 86**

The team's best concentrator and most old-fashioned batsman, he loves to eat up time at the crease – some critics think he eats up too much time. But if you wanted to pick an England player to bat for a day to save your life, the South African-born Trott would be the man.

high **119 on Test debut to help win the Ashes** low **mental strength questioned on South Africa tour in 2009–10**

Allrounder

Stuart Broad

born **1986**, Nottinghamshire. **LHB, No 8; RFM, new or old ball** **Tests 32, runs 1096, ave 28 wkts 97, ave 34**

Tall, blond, angelic – and extremely fiery (like his dad, Chris). An aggressive fast bowler with a licence to attack, he took his batting to another level in 2010 with 169 against Pakistan at Lord's.

high **The Oval, 2009: 5-37 in 12 overs sealed the Ashes** low **Edgbaston, 2010: fined for throwing the ball at Pakistan keeper Zulqarnain Haider**

Wicketkeeper

Matt Prior

born **1982**, Sussex. **RHB, No 7** **Tests 35, runs 1896, ave 42**

England's No 1 keeper in Tests, where his counter-attacking strokeplay can change the course of an innings. Not so assured in limited-overs cricket, because he struggles to work the ball around, but his keeping has improved remarkably since his debut in 2007 – despite pressure from others.

high **126no off 128 balls on debut v West Indies** low **Only two half-centuries in 50 attempts in ODIs**

Bowlers

Graeme Swann

born **1979**, Nottinghamshire. **RHB, No 9; OB** **Tests 24, wkts 113, ave 26 runs 653, ave 25**

Where has he been all this time? Ignored for years, Swann has become England's MVP with his irrepressible offbreaks. Specialises in taking wickets in the first over of a spell and loves bowling to left-handers. Good at chipping in with the bat too, and tells the best jokes in the team.

high **Removed Mike Hussey to seal the Ashes in 2009** low **Not selected for Test cricket until late 2008**

Tim Bresnan

born **1985**, Yorkshire. **RHB, lower-order; RFM** **Tests 5, wkts 14, ave 35 runs 125, ave 41**

Solid and dependable, either as a third seamer or No 8 batsman capable of keeping a top-order colleague company. Jumps wide at the crease to angle the ball into the right-handed batsman, which makes him tricky to score off but not always a potent wicket-taker.

high **Hit 80 in the Champs Trophy semi v Aus in 2009** low **Ticked off for being rude on Twitter to a fan who teased him about his weight**

England under Andy Flower

2008–09
in West Indies
Tests (4 games) 0-1
ODIs (5) 3-2
T20 (1) 0-1
2009 at home
v West Indies
Tests (2) 2-0
ODIs (3) 2-0
2009 at home
World Twenty20
Eliminated at
Super Eight stage
2009 at home
v Australia
Tests (5) 2-1
ODIs (7) 1-6
2009–10
in South Africa for
Champions Trophy
Lost in semi-finals
to Australia
2009–10 in SA
T20 (2) 1-1
ODIs (5) 2-1
Tests (4) 1-1
2009–10 in Dubai
v Pakistan
T20 (2) 1-1
2009–10
in Bangladesh
ODIs (3) 3-0
Tests (2) 2-0
2009–10
in West Indies
World T20
Champions
2010 at home
v Bangladesh
Tests (2) 2-0
ODIs (3) 2-1
2010 at home
v Australia
ODIs (5) 3-2
2010 at home
v Pakistan
Tests (4) 3-1
T20 (2) 2-0
ODIs (5) 3-2
England also won
one-off ODIs v
Ireland (in 2009) and
Scotland (in 2010)

Kevin Pietersen

**born 1980, unattached.
RHB, No 4; OB
Tests 66, runs 5306, ave 47
wkts 4, ave 142**

Still the team's star attraction and the closest player to a celebrity in the England side, despite struggling for fitness and form for much of 2009–10. When his full repertoire is on show – with his switch-hits and flamingo whips wide of mid-on – there is no better sight.

**high man of the tournament at World Twenty20 in 2010
low dropped from the two limited-overs sides less than four months later**

Paul Collingwood

**born 1976, Durham.
RHB, No 5; RM
Tests 63, runs 4176, ave 42
wkts 15, ave 63**

A consistently under-rated Test regular and an increasingly flexible one-day batsman. Brilliant backward point or third slip, decent one-day bowler, and – after a stint in charge of the one-day side – Twenty20 captain.

**high first England captain to lift a global trophy at World Twenty20 in 2010
low Adelaide 2006-07: 22 off 119 balls as England collapsed to 129**

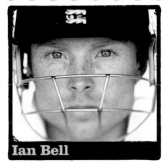

Ian Bell

**born 1982, Warwickshire.
RHB, No 3 or 6
Tests 57, runs 3863, ave 42
wkts 1, ave 76**

The team's most stylish batsman, but he only added some much-needed flint in South Africa in 2009–10. Excels at Nos 5 and 6, where he averages 56, and slowly getting better at No 3. A top-class fielder, especially at short leg.

**high Cape Town, 2009–10: batted almost throughout final day to help save Test
low Centurion, 2009–10: bowled playing no shot to SA spinner Paul Harris**

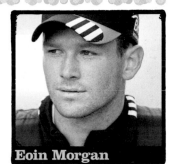

Eoin Morgan

**born 1986, Middlesex.
LHB, No 6
Tests 6, runs 256, ave 32**

Born in Dublin but pinched by England, Morgan is the shining new star of the one-day side: his reverse-sweeps are one of the joys of the modern game. An effervescent fielder, but had a mixed start with the bat in Tests, where experts fretted over his technique.

**high 103no from 85 balls to win Rose Bowl ODI v Australia, 2010
low Test duck v Pakistan at Lord's in 2010 to make it 45 runs in five innings**

Steven Finn

**born 1989, Middlesex.
RHB, No 11; RFM
Tests 8, wkts 32, ave 23
runs 13, ave 6.5**

At 6ft 8in, thought to be the tallest player ever to represent England. Disconcerting bounce is his stock-in-trade, and his action reminds observers of his mentor, the former England seamer Angus Fraser. Serious potential.

**high nine wickets v Bangladesh at Lord's in only his third Test
low Dhaka, 2009–10: bowled only 19 overs out of 219**

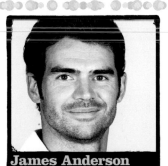

James Anderson

**born 1982, Lancashire.
LHB, No 10; RFM, new or old ball
Tests 52, wkts 188, ave 31
runs 502, ave 12**

England's attack leader in Tests and ODIs, Anderson is the world's best bowler when it's swinging. He can still be expensive when it isn't, but the good days outweigh the bad. His batting has improved too, from rabbit to nightwatchman.

**high World Cup 2003: 4 for 29 to destroy Pakistan
low replaced by Ryan Sidebottom in the 2010 World Twenty20**

Monty Panesar

**born 1982, Sussex (real name Mudhsuden).
LHB, tail-ender; SLA
Tests 39, wkts 126, ave 34
runs 187, ave 5**

Overtaken in the spin department by Swann in 2009, but Monty remains the most instantly recognisable player in the squad. A gifted, accurate spinner, with a fielding method every fan can relate to and a batting technique to match.

**high 8 for 93 v Pakistan at Old Trafford, 2006
low drifted out of contention when Swann reappeared on the scene**

Ajmal Shahzad

**born 1985, Yorkshire.
RHB, No 8 or 9; RFM, new or old ball
Tests 1, wkts 4, ave 15
runs 5, ave 5**

New to the side and refreshingly honest: part of the squad for the Lord's Test against Bangladesh in 2010, he admitted he had never been to London before. Adept at reverse-swinging the old ball, and a quirkily effective lower-order batsman.

**high spell of 4-2-10-3 on Test debut v Bangladesh
low squeezed out of the original 2010–11 Ashes squad by Bresnan**

THE GREAT GROUNDS

Six of the best places to watch cricket: all spectacular and all different.

Lord's London, England ▼

opened 1814 capacity 30,000 home of MCC and Middlesex lights yes, belatedly Tests 121 ODIs 50 T20s 8 on the side archery for 2012 Olympics

To some, it's a cathedral; to others, a stuffy old private club. But to almost everyone, it's the home of cricket, an oasis in the big city and a beautiful place in its own right. The field is a perfect green chessboard, the pavilion is a formidable Victorian edifice, and the newer stands are bold examples of modern architecture, while still being very usable. And then there are the quirks, like the eight-foot slope from one side to the other, which can befuddle both batsmen and bowlers. Take a tour on a non-match day to drink it all in, then go again when it's full. For more tips, see page 118.

MCG Melbourne, Australia ▲

opened 1854 capacity 100,000 home of Victoria lights yes
Tests 102 ODIs 131 T20s 3 on the side Aussie Rules football

For looks, you're better off at the SCG in Sydney, with its charming wrought-iron roofs. But the MCG, in the sports-mad city of Melbourne, is more of an experience. It's a colossal concrete coliseum. The Great Southern Stand alone, seating 48,000, is twice the size of most English grounds. The seats at the top are so high that they give a blimp's eye view and can cause vertigo. The pitch treats batsmen and bowlers more evenly than most grounds, while the weather is famous for its ability to lay on all four seasons in one day. The atmosphere is harsh and intimidating, with a gladiatorial edge, but it's exhilarating when your team is doing well – or so I'm told.

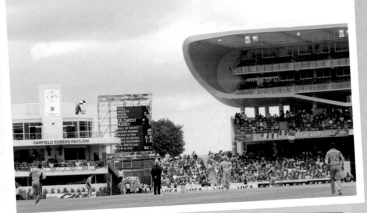

Kensington Oval
Bridgetown, Barbados, West Indies

opened 1871 capacity 28,000 home of Barbados lights yes Tests 46 ODIs 28 T20s 12

The Kensington Oval has always had a sporty surface, a glorious climate and a buzzing atmosphere, with a crowd who seem to come equipped with just the right mixture of enthusiasm, expertise and laughter. But as a set of buildings, it used to be nothing special. Now that has been put right with a handsome new ground, built for the 2007 World Cup at a cost of $45m (£23m). The design is coolly futuristic: the 3Ws stand, named after the great Barbadian batting trio of Weekes, Worrell and Walcott, is like a more laid-back version of the Lord's media centre. The ends of the ground are now named after Malcolm Marshall and Joel Garner, who took the new ball here for Barbados only 25 years ago. For the World Cup final, the ground looked a picture. It was just a shame that the weather was wet, the umpires had a nightmare and the last few overs were played out in virtual darkness. At least now they've got some lights.

Eden Gardens Kolkata, India

opened 1864 capacity 90,000 home of Bengal lights yes Tests 36 ODIs 22 T20s 0

The name suggests an innocent paradise, but the reality is a little different. Kolkata (formerly Calcutta) is a teeming city and its cricket ground – huge, plain and rudimentary – is all about the 90,000 people who stream into it. No cricket crowd is noisier or more passionate than this one. Sometimes the fervour bubbles over and there are riots; other times it inspires the Indian team to astonishing feats. In March 2001, India followed on there against Australia, 274 runs behind – and won. See page 101.

Newlands Cape Town, South Africa ▶

opened 1888 capacity 25,000 home of Western Province lights yes Tests 45 ODIs 34 T20s 9 on the side rugby, round the corner

Cricket leaves plenty of time to enjoy your surroundings, and there are none better than these. Cape Town is a spectacular city, dominated by the surreal beauty of Table Mountain – which looms over one side of the ground. It's hard to believe that something so steep could be such a close neighbour of something so flat. The mountain distracts you from the other surroundings, which include a brewery and a railway line. The pitch can be slow and the weather windy (which enabled the first official 100mph delivery to be bowled here – see page 58), but the atmosphere is lively, draws are rare, the ball turns, and the ground is a good size, big enough to have a sense of theatre, small enough to be intimate.

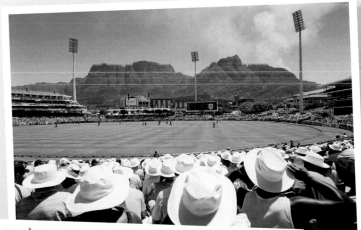

Pukekura Park
New Plymouth, New Zealand ▶

opened 1892 capacity a few thousand home of Central Districts lights no Tests 0 ODIs 1 on the side rock concerts

Its name is not encouraging, and it has hosted only one senior international, but this is a gem. No need to build a stand, as nature has provided one, in the form of a steep hill – all man had to do was carve some terraces into it for the spectators to sit on. If the cricket is a bit sleepy, which is not unknown in these parts, you can explore the park, which includes two lakes, a zoo, a waterfall, a racecourse and a 2,000-year-old tree. You may have seen the cricket field already: it appeared in the Tom Cruise film *The Last Samurai*, playing the role of a 19th-century army parade ground.

FLINTOFF'S
ASHES

It had been 16 years since England last held the Ashes, more than 18 since they had actively won them, and 24 since Ian Botham single-handedly crushed Australia in one of the most stirring summers of the lot. So you can understand why, in 2005, a nation suddenly fell in love with cricket all over again. England beat Australia 2-1 in possibly the greatest series ever played – and the star of the show was a hulking, blond, northern lad called Andrew Flintoff. If 1981 will forever be known as Botham's Ashes, then 2005 felt like the property of the man repeatedly anointed as his successor.

Flintoff was 27 when the Australians arrived for what they fondly imagined would be another Ashes triumph. Fondly, and not unreasonably: after regaining the urn in 1989, they had not let go, winning eight series in a row, most of them by embarrassing margins. But Flintoff, by now seven years into an international career bedevilled by weight issues, injury and inconsistency, was finally starting to click. Just as Mike Brearley had carefully nurtured Botham, so Michael Vaughan brought the best out of Flintoff, who readied himself for Australia by chalking up the best figures of his life. In 18 Tests from March 2004 to the start of the Ashes, he scored 1,030 runs at 46 and took 109 wickets at 23. They were the stats of a world-class allrounder – and yet a large question-mark remained. Flintoff had never played a single Test against the old enemy.

After the first Test at Lord's, which Australia won by 239 runs (despite being bowled out for 190 on a raucous opening day), the question-mark had doubled in size. Flintoff scored 0 and 3, took four expensive wickets, and looked, said Wisden, "overwhelmed by the occasion". But that defeat taught him a valuable lesson: to excel at any sport, let alone one as mentally demanding as Test cricket, you have to be yourself. Living and dying by the sword, Flintoff concluded, was far more rewarding than poking around for scraps.

A ten-day gap before the second Test at Edgbaston was just the breather he needed. The main shopping centre in Birmingham is called the Bullring, and Flintoff emerged as if he had spent the interim pawing at the turf. He blasted five sixes in a 62-ball 68 on the first day after Ricky Ponting had generously invited England to bat, then took three wickets to help his side to a lead of 99. Four more sixes followed during his second-innings 73 to make it nine in the match – an Ashes record – and Flintoff's last-wicket stand of 51 with Simon Jones meant Australia were chasing a tricky 282 rather than a manageable 231. At 47 without loss, they were looking good. But Flintoff's first over changed everything. He bowled Justin Langer off his body with his second ball, then gave Ponting a fearsome working-over before Australia's captain edged the seventh (Flintoff had bowled a no-ball – and for once he was glad he had).

He picked up two more wickets as England apparently took control, but Australia – champions that they were – fought back. Shane Warne and Brett Lee put on 45 for the ninth wicket before Flintoff persuaded Warne to tread on his stumps – only for Lee and Michael Kasprowicz to knuckle down with 62 still needed. As the tension reached unbearable proportions, not even Flintoff could part them, and it needed Kasprowicz to touch a leg-side lifter from Steve Harmison (even if his glove was off the bat at the time) with three runs needed to save England's bacon – and the series. As the batsmen slumped in disbelief and the rest of the England team went berserk, Flintoff approached Lee, put an arm on his right shoulder, and shook his hand. He later joked that he said: "That's 1-1, you Aussie bastard." But the moment, captured by photographer Tom Shaw, summed up Flintoff's chivalry. "MR INFREDIBLE", declared *The Sun*. No one disagreed.

In the third Test, at his home ground of Old Trafford, Flintoff scored 46 and 4, and took five wickets, but Australia – nine wickets down in the fourth innings – escaped with a draw. It was annoying for England, but Vaughan was quick to point out Australia's jubilation on the pavilion balcony. "Look at them," he told his team during their post-match outfield huddle. "They're celebrating a draw." The truth was Australia were rattled.

At Trent Bridge, Flintoff responded to his captain's taunt, claiming his second man of the match award in three games. His 102 in the first innings was pure class. Just as crucially, he added 177 in quick time for the sixth wicket with Geraint Jones. Flintoff again removed Adam Gilchrist – for once, looking like a bunny – and England enforced the follow-on. They won, just. Now they only needed to draw at The Oval to end 16 years of hurt and mockery.

Bad luck, mate: Flintoff consoles Brett Lee after England beat Australia by two runs at Edgbaston in 2005

Flintoff was not about to disappoint. He made 72 as England batted first, sharing a fifth-wicket stand of 143 with Andrew Strauss, then – with a good-natured but feverishly excited crowd praying for rain – produced a heroic spell of 14.2-3-30-4 on his way to a rare but deserved five-for. Kevin Pietersen's swashbuckling 158 on the final day did the rest – and Flintoff, England's man of the series, embarked on a famous all-night bender, culminating in an equally famous quote the next day as the team enjoyed an open-top bus ride to Trafalgar Square. "I've not been to bed yet," he said (or perhaps slurred). "The eyes behind these glasses tell a thousand stories."

He was easily forgiven the booze and the bragging,

because without Flintoff England would probably have lost. He scored 402 runs – more than any Australian – at an average of 40, and took 24 wickets – more than any Englishman – at an average of 27. He was named "coolest celebrity" of 2005 by CoolBrands, beating even David Beckham, and was lauded by Wisden, who said: "The manner in which he played and conducted himself made him a national hero."

Flintoff's next Ashes experience would be to captain England to a 5-0 defeat in Australia in 2006-07, and although he shone briefly during England's 2009 triumph against the Aussies, he would never properly recapture the heights of that summer. But, well, he would always have 2005. And so would the British public.

1 up to 1700

Kids, shepherds and funny words

Why is cricket like life itself? Because its origins are lost in the mists of time. It seems to have evolved from games played in the fields by shepherds or children, in which one player had a club or stick and tried to hit an object thrown or rolled by another. The object may have been a stone, a piece of wood, or a matted lump of wool. The time: anywhere between the 9th century and the 15th. The place: somewhere in northern Europe, most likely southern England – Kent, Surrey or Sussex.

The wicket may have originally been a wicket gate, and sheep may have been needed to make sure the grass was short, since the mower had yet to be invented. The name cricket may have come from creag (a game played by Prince Edward, son of Edward I, in Kent in 1300), or criquet (French for club), or kricke (Flemish for stick), or crycc (Old English for staff). There is a theory that it started as a children's game, spread to working men, and then to the gentry.

1598
a court case refers to a game called creckett being played at the Royal Grammar School, Guildford, around 1550

1598
cricket appears in an Italian–English dictionary as "cricket-a-wicket"

1610
first* "cricketing" match in Kent: the Weald v the Downs at Chevening

1611
two men from Sidlesham, Sussex, are caught missing church on Easter Sunday to play cricket, and are fined 1 shilling (5p) each

1622
first reference to a "cricket batt", in a court case

1624
first cricket fatality, in Sussex: one Jasper Vinall, a fielder hit by a batsman trying to avoid being caught

1640
Puritan clerics in Kent denounce cricket as "profane", especially if played on a Sunday

1652
a court case in Kent refers to "a certain unlawful game called cricket"

1658
first reference to a "cricket ball" by the lexicographer Edward Phillips

1666
a letter refers to a game on Richmond Green, south-west of London

1676
first reference to cricket being played abroad, by Britons living in Aleppo, Syria

1680
first reference to "wickets" in a cricket context, scribbled in an old bible and mentioning Marden in Sussex

1697
"a great match" is held in Sussex, between two sides of 11 men, for a prize of 50 guineas (£52.50)

[*first means first recorded]

THE 8 AGES OF CRICKET

2 18th century

Clubs, laws, toffs and London

Georgian Britain sounds like fun. It was lively, noisy and creative, producing some great poets, painters and architects, who made sure that, for the first time, beautiful houses were built for working people. Cricket was taken up by members of the aristocracy and became a spectator sport, although some players were so grand that they actually disliked being watched. The game was often played for money, and there was betting – and probably match-fixing. A match in 1751 between the Old Etonians and England was played for £1,500, with "near £20,000" wagered on the result. Cricket became entrenched in the southern counties and then moved into London. Islington and the City Road were briefly the centre of the cricket world, then Hambledon in Hampshire, before **Thomas Lord** led the way to Marylebone.

1702
match played at the Duke of Richmond's house, Goodwood in Sussex, now more famous for sports involving horses and cars

1706
the first match report – in Latin and in verse, written by William Goldwin, an old Etonian

1709
first county match: Kent v Surrey

1710
cricket pops up at Cambridge University

1718
controversial match at **White Conduit Fields**, Islington (then a village just north of London), between London Cricket Club and the Rochester Punch Club: London were winning, so Rochester walked off in a bid to save their stake money; a judge orders them to finish the next year (London win)

1727
the first Articles of Agreement – laws, in effect – for matches between the Duke of Richmond's team and a Mr Brodrick's

1730
match played in central London at the Honourable Artillery Company, City Road, which still hosts cricket today

1739
first All-England team – meaning an XI chosen from everybody not available to the other side – play Kent, who beat them by "a very few notches"

1744
first Laws of Cricket, saying the pitch has to be 22 yards, issued by the London Club

1744
first match recorded in *Scores & Biographies*, a series of books: Kent v All-England at the Artillery Ground

1751
a match is played in New York, "according to the London method"

1767ish
founding of the Hambledon Club in Hampshire, the leading club for the next 30 years

1769
first century, by John Minshull for Duke of Dorset's XI v Wrotham

1771
width of bat limited to 4¼ inches – still the rule today

1774
lbw law invented, possibly by a bowler

1775
first first-class century, by John Small, father of the straight bat, for Hambledon against Surrey

1775ish
third stump added

1776
first scorecards, at the Vine Club, Sevenoaks, Kent

1780
first ball with a seam, made by Dukes, who still make cricket balls today

1780ish
White Conduit Club founded in Islington

1787
Thomas Lord, a 31-year-old bowler, opens a ground in Dorset Square, Marylebone, for members of the White Conduit Club of Islington, who are fed up with playing on public ground because

they don't like the rowdy opinions of the spectators; Lord receives financial backing from two earls and founds the Marylebone Cricket Club (MCC)

1788
White Conduit play their last game against MCC

1788
MCC revise the Laws

1777
Noah Mann, father of swing bowling, dies aged 33 after partying hard and "falling upon the embers"

1794
first school match: Charterhouse v Westminster

3 19th century

Proper bowling, writing and touring

Georgian England gives way to Victorian England, which was more formal, less fun, but very good at getting things done. Round-arm bowling got going, and soon the batsmen decided they needed pads. Annual fixtures were set up between schools and universities. By the middle of the century, the railways had come along, so a team like the All-England XI could travel widely. The first foreign tour followed soon afterwards – with an unlikely destination. Two famous sporting brand-names cropped up: Lillywhite and Wisden. And round-arm turned to over-arm.

▼ **Making waves** England's cricketers on board the ship waiting to depart from Liverpool for the first overseas tour to America. In the team are **John Wisden** and **John Lillywhite**.

1805
first Eton–Harrow match: Lord Byron, later more famous as a poet, plays for Harrow

1806
first annual match between the Players (who get paid) and the Gentlemen (rich enough to play for fun); the Players usually win

1807
first round-arm bowling, by John Willes of Kent

1809
Lord's ground moves to its second site, at North Bank, St John's Wood

1811–14
cricket rudely interrupted by the Napoleonic War

1814
Lord's ground moves to its present site

1827
first annual match between Oxford and Cambridge universities, at Lord's

1828
round-arm allowed by MCC

1833
John Nyren, an ex-player, publishes the first famous cricket book, *The Young Cricketer's Tutor*, helped by a Shakespearian scholar called Charles Cowden Clarke – the game's first ghostwriter

1834
Alfred Mynn, "the Lion of Kent", makes his debut: a 23-stone giant who bowled fast round-arm, he was probably the first great player

1836ish
pads invented

1830s
the first bowling machine, the catapulta, is designed by Felix, artist, cricketer and schoolmaster, who uses the nickname in case parents disapprove of a teacher playing cricket

1839
first formal county club – **Sussex CCC**

1846
first match at the Oval in Kennington, south London

1846
William Clarke's All-England XI start touring the country, often playing against 20 or 22 local men

1848
Fred Lillywhite, of the sports-shop family, launches his *Guide To Cricketers*

1849
first Roses match – Yorkshire v Lancashire

1850
wicketkeepers start wearing gloves

1850
John Wisden, a leading fast bowler, opens a sports shop

1859
first overseas tour – of the US and Canada

1864
overarm bowling allowed

1864
Wisden launches his *Almanack*

4 1845 to 1914

W.G., Tests and a golden age

Cricket was now very popular. It had its first superstar, a Gloucestershire doctor called **William Gilbert Grace**. He was grasping, crafty, pleased with himself and dishonest, claiming to be an amateur (unpaid) while trousering vast fees. But he was an exceptional cricketer and crowds went to see him play. At some grounds, the ticket price doubled if he was playing, and he was said to be the second best-known Englishman "after Mr Gladstone" (the prime minister).

An England team sailed to Australia, and the first Test match took place: you can guess who won. Then the Australians toured Engand. Losing away was one thing, but losing at home … Some English cricket lovers were so horrified, they put a mock death notice in the paper, and the legend of the Ashes was born.

Cricket began to take the shape we know today, with a county championship, a handsome red-brick pavilion at Lord's, a third team playing Tests and an organisation called the ICC to supervise things. Batsmen developed stylish stroke-play and bowlers had to be clever, which led to the years leading up to the First World War being labelled the golden age. A book called *The Players* by Ric Sissons shows that for the professionals, it wasn't golden at all: some of them were so poor, they were sleeping three to a bed.

5 1918 to 1949

More countries, and Bradman

A sport with only three full members isn't much of a sport – especially if one of them is far too good for the others. In the 1920s, England and Australia saw the need to make the club a little less exclusive, so India, New Zealand and West Indies all joined in. West Indies made their mark quickly, inspired by the great George Headley; the others took 20 years or more to win a Test. But the period was dominated by one man – **Don Bradman**, the white Headley, the greatest run machine there has ever been.

1865
W.G. Grace starts playing for the Gentlemen v the Players: now the Gentlemen win more often than not

1877
first Test match – Australia v England

1882
England's first home defeat by Australia. **Death notice** for English cricket

placed in *Sporting Times*, which leads to tradition of the Ashes

1889
South Africa join Test cricket

1889
work begins on the present Lord's pavilion

1890
County Championship officially launched

1897
the googly invented by B.J.T. Bosanquet

1903
MCC starts running England's overseas tours

1907–08
Jack Hobbs, arguably England's greatest player, makes his Test debut

1909
ICC founded to oversee the international game: originally the Imperial Cricket Conference, it later changes its name to the International Cricket Council

1910
six runs awarded for a hit over

the boundary – previously, you had to hit the ball out of the ground

1914
golden age comes to abrupt end with the First World War

1921
Australia beat England 5-0 – uniquely (until 2007)

1926
India, New Zealand and West Indies become full members of ICC

1927
first radio commentary on cricket, on the BBC

1928
West Indies' first Test

1928
Don Bradman's first Test

1929–30
West Indies' first victory, over England. George Headley, "the black Bradman", makes a hundred in each innings

1930
New Zealand's first Test

1930
Jack Hobbs's last Test

1932
India's first Test

1932–33
Bodyline affair: England bowlers target Australian batsmen's bodies, with several catchers on leg side

1935
Bodyline outlawed by MCC

1938
the BBC televises Test cricket for the first time, from Lord's

1940–44
cricket largely shuts down for the war

In Affectionate Remembrance
OF
ENGLISH CRICKET,
WHICH DIED AT THE OVAL
ON
29th AUGUST, 1882,
Deeply lamented by a large circle of sorrowing friends and acquaintances.

R.I.P.

N.B.—The body will be cremated and the ashes taken to Australia.

6 1950s and 60s

Professionalism and caution

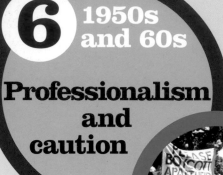

Straight after the Second World War, cricket was glamorous and colourful, as people enjoyed themselves again after the sacrifices of wartime. But after that, it became greyer and less entertaining. The game was **televised**, but it was in

black and white. Batting tended to be safety-first and although there were some famous feats, like Jim Laker's 19 wickets in a match, the atmosphere was staid. With the coming of rock 'n' roll in 1956, and then the **civil-rights** movement and the hippie movement in the Sixties, the world was changing. Cricket wasn't.

7 1970s and 80s

Pizazz, pace and Packer

Two great Australian fast bowlers, Dennis Lillee and Jeff Thomson, demolished England and West Indies – but West Indies fought back by picking four fast bowlers. Cricket began to catch up with modern life. One-day internationals arrived at last, invented almost by accident after an Australia–England Test was washed out and some light entertainment was required. They caught on instantly and a World Cup was devised. But the game was still being run high-handedly: the players were poorly paid and seldom consulted. **Kerry Packer**, an Australian media mogul, boldly offered them more money to play for him. Most of the leading Aussies and West Indians signed up, along with a few Englishmen, and the cricket world split in two. Packer pioneered coloured kit and floodlights, drew big crowds, and staged some thrilling matches. To many fans, they weren't the real thing – but nor were the so-called Tests that went ahead with less-good players. After two years, peace broke out. Packer got the TV rights to Australia's home matches, and the national boards got their stars back.

1948
first five-day Tests in England

1948
Bradman's last Test

1951–52
India's first victory, over England: Vinoo Mankad takes 12 for 108

1952
Pakistan's first Test

1952–53
Pakistan's first victory, over India: Fazal Mahmood 12 for 94

1955–56
New Zealand's first victory, over West Indies, after 25 years

1957
Test Match Special launched on BBC radio

1962
last Gentlemen v Players match

1963
the end of the amateur

1963
first major one-day competition – the Gillette Cup (60 overs a side), contested by the English counties

1968
MCC hands over the running of the game in England to the Test & County Cricket Board

1970
South Africa banned from international sport because they would only pick white players

1970–71
first one-day international

1975
first World Cup, in England, won by West Indies

1976
West Indies become dominant team, playing four fast bowlers

1977
Kerry Packer signs many of the world's leading players to join a breakaway circus, leaving several Test countries fielding second-rate teams

1978
helmets arrive in Test cricket

1979
peace treaty between Packer and Australian board

1979–80
floodlights and coloured kit come into official ODIs

1980
Australia drops the eight-ball over

1982
Sri Lanka's first Test

1983
India win World Cup – first winner other than West Indies

1987
First World Cup outside England – held in India and Pakistan, won by Australia

◀▲ **The fast and the fiery** West Indies quick bowler Michael Holding cleans up England's Allan Knott at The Oval in 1976 above. England legend Fred Trueman left signs autographs for a couple of fans.

source: Cricinfo. 2000s = all games between Jan 1, 2000 and Oct 15, 2010

8 1990 to now

Small world, big money

Pace gave way to guile as Shane Warne showed that even a slow bowler could rule the world. Australia toppled West Indies and took the game to a new level with their fast scoring – only to lose their way towards the end of the 2000s as their great names retired one by one. The cricket world was expanding. The seven Test teams briefly became ten as South Africa returned and Zimbabwe and Bangladesh joined in, then shrunk to nine when Zimbabwe suspended themselves in 2006. Twenty20 threatened to get out of control, with three World Cups in four years. The international programme ballooned, and nearly all of it was televised. Satellite TV came along to pay huge sums for the rights. India, with the most viewers, became the game's financial powerhouse, and dreamed up their own Twenty20 Premier League, awash with money and celebrities. ICC grew rapidly from four people in a corner of Lord's to something like a multinational company, based in Dubai, with a vast turnover. But when an equally big development came along on another kind of screen, the administrators barely noticed. Cricinfo, one of the first sports websites, quickly became one of the biggest and best, unearthing one million cricket lovers in the US whose existence had been a well-kept secret. When it started publishing news and comment to complement its stats and scorecards, fans had a single global noticeboard for the first time. This led to many arguments, but also to wider understanding. The cricket world had become a global village.

HOW INTERNATIONAL CRICKET HAS BALLOONED

T20s
2000s
127

ODIs
2000s
1405

TESTS

1990s
983

1980s
366

1970s
82

1990
Sky TV broadcast their first England tour, to West Indies

1991
South Africa readmitted as apartheid crumbles

1992
South Africa play in World Cup for first time, in Australia and New Zealand; cup won by Pakistan

1992
Zimbabwe's first Test

1993
Cricinfo, the first cricket website, launched by Simon King, a British scientist working temporarily in USA

1993
ICC become independent of MCC

1996
Sri Lanka win World Cup and reinvent one-day game by scoring fastest in opening overs

1997
Test & County Cricket Board replaced by England and Wales Cricket Board (ECB)

1999
ICC sell TV rights to next two World Cups and three Champions Trophies for $550m (£340m) to Rupert Murdoch's Global Cricket Corporation

1999
BBC TV loses rights to home Tests to Channel 4

2000
Cricinfo valued at $150m (£90m)

2000
Hansie Cronje, captain of South Africa, banned for life for taking bribes from bookmakers

2000
Bangladesh's first Test

2002
Cricinfo bought by *Wisden*, owned by Sir Paul Getty, for a reported £10m

2003
Twenty20 cricket launched in England: first form of professional cricket that doesn't include a meal break

2005
ICC leave Lord's for Dubai

2006
Channel 4 loses TV rights to Sky

2006
Indian board announce their sponsorship and media-rights deals now worth US$1bn (about £500m)

2006
ICC sell audio-visual rights to next two World Cups, two Twenty20 World Cups and 14 other events for a reported $1.1bn (£550m), to ESPN-Star Sports

2007
World Cup held in West Indies for first time, won by Australia for third time in a row

2007
first Twenty20 World Cup, held in South Africa, won by India

2007
ESPN buys Cricinfo; Mark Getty, Sir Paul's son, sells *The Wisden Cricketer* magazine to Sky

2008
Lalit Modi unveils the money-spinning Indian Premier League

2010
England win third World Twenty20, in the Caribbean

◄ All change
England's Kevin Pietersen batting captains Indian team Royal Challengers Bangalore in the second IPL in 2009, held in South Africa.

THE GREATEST...

... FAST BOWLER

When *Wisden* invited 100 experts to name their Five Cricketers of the Century, no fast bowler made the final five – which was curious, because most series are won by the side with the better fast bowlers. The nearest miss was Dennis Lillee of Australia, a magnificent bowler. But he struggled in the Indian subcontinent and in my book he wasn't quite as great as **Malcolm Marshall** of West Indies, a bowler for all seasons and surfaces – very fast, very hostile, very accurate and able to swing the ball both ways. His average was among the very best (20) and so was his strike rate (46). Marshall died aged only 41, but had found time to become a leading coach and to pass on his secrets to Shaun Pollock of South Africa, who finished with even more Test wickets (421) than his mentor (376).

... SLOW BOWLER

Anyone who thinks Murali's action was dodgy would say **Shane Warne**. But Murali's action either was dodgy or it wasn't, and the game has decided that it wasn't. He is not the first bowler to arouse suspicion on certain types of delivery. I'd put them equal. Warne's control was more remarkable, coming from a leg-spinner; **Murali** was more consistent on different surfaces and took more wickets. Both had their weak spots – Warne didn't do well against India, and Murali struggled in Australia.

... BATSMAN

It has to be **Bradman**. In the Five Cricketers of the Century vote, all 100 members of the panel voted for him. See page 52.

... ALLROUNDER

Not much argument about this one either. With 90 votes in Five Cricketers of the Century, it's **Garry Sobers**. See page 62 for some supporting stats.

... PERSONALITY

Shane Warne has to be in with a shout, but most experts would say **W.G. Grace**. A huge draw as a batsman, bowler, captain, showman and rogue, he was the game's first superstar.

▶ **Two sticks**
Steve left and Mark Waugh right are given cakes and walking sticks on their 36th birthday at Worcester, June 2, 2001.

... PAIR OF BROTHERS

Until 1990, it was the Chappells – Ian, a formidable captain of Australia, and Greg, a class batsman who also captained his country. But then along came **Mark Waugh**, first replacing, then joining his twin **Steve** in the Australian team. Steve, the elder by four minutes, was a gutsy percentage player, tough as old boots and eventually a great captain. Mark was a stylish touch player, a forceful one-day opener and a scintillating slip fielder. They became two of the most capped players in Test history, with Steve playing 168 times and Mark 128, and played more than 100 Tests together. Steve's Test batting average was 51 to Mark's 41, but in all first-class cricket, their figures were virtually identical – Mark 52.04, Steve 51.95.

... PLAYER FROM EACH COUNTRY

COUNTRY	PLAYER	REASON	DOUBT?	NEAREST RIVAL
Australia	Bradman	best batsman ever – in any country	no	Shane Warne, leg-spin king
Bangladesh	Habibul Bashar	only Bangladeshi to make 3,000 Test runs	some	Tamim Iqbal, pyrotechnic opener
England	W.G. Grace	allrounder + colossus – great beard too	some	Jack Hobbs, great opener
India	Sachin Tendulkar	95 international hundreds, seems ageless	some	Kapil Dev, punchy allrounder
New Zealand	Richard Hadlee	immaculate seamer, stylish batsman	no	Martin Crowe, class batsman
Pakistan	Imran Khan	ace allrounder + captain, now a politician	no	Wasim Akram, swing bowler
South Africa	Graeme Pollock	left-handed genius, elegance personified	some	Shaun Pollock, his nephew
Sri Lanka	Murali	best off-spinner ever	no	Sanath Jayasuriya, master blaster
West Indies	Viv Richards	domineering, gum-chewing batsman	some	George Headley, great opener
Zimbabwe	Andy Flower	top batsman + keeper, once ranked No 1	no	Heath Streak, swing bowler

... OPENING BATSMAN

Herbert Sutcliffe of England has the highest Test average – 60. But he didn't have to face the great West Indian fast bowlers of the 1970s. **Sunil Gavaskar** of India did, and made 12 hundreds against them, averaging 65. He is also the highest-scoring Test opener with 9607 runs.

... TAIL-ENDER

Of all the batsmen who have gone in regularly at No 9 to 11 (and made at least 500 runs), the one with easily the best average is **Shaun Pollock** of South Africa – 41.07 from 23 Tests as a tail-ender, with two hundreds. Pollock was good to watch too, with the elegant strokes of a No 6. Perhaps it was in his genes: his uncle was South African batting master Graeme Pollock.

... TEST BATTING AVERAGE (among those who have played 10 Tests)

No, it's not Bradman. It's not even a man. It's **Jo Broadbent** of Australia, who played 10 Tests in the 1990s and finished with an average of 109.25 from eight innings with four not-outs. She went on to coach Queensland Fire.

... COACH

The most successful is John Buchanan, who stepped down as Australia coach after winning another World Cup in 2007. But he had such good raw materials to work with – Warne, McGrath, Gilchrist, Ponting, Hayden, the Waughs – that it is hard to know what value he added. The late **Bob Woolmer**, whose sudden and baffling death overshadowed the 2007 World Cup, may have been the best coach of all. He was an exceptional person, always bubbling with enthusiasm, knowledge and imagination. He steered South Africa almost to the top of the tree and Warwickshire to a string of trophies, and he helped everyone from Ian Bell to Pakistan and Scotland. Some of his former charges have already become effective coaches themselves, including Allan Donald (England's consultant bowling coach in summer 2007) and Jonty Rhodes (South Africa's fielding coach at the World Cup).

... ONE-DAY NURDLER

The art of working the ball around for ones and twos is thought to have been first perfected by **Javed Miandad** of Pakistan. He was short, moustachioed, combative and forever annoyed about something, usually the fact that he had been replaced as captain because Imran Khan had decided to return to the team. But for nurdling the ball around, he was your man.

... RUN-UP

You may know **Michael Holding** as a commentator with a great voice, once memorably compared to burnt molasses. But he used to be a fast bowler, one of the great West Indian attack of the 1980s, and his run-up was worth watching on its own – long, silky, rhythmic and almost silent.

... WICKETKEEPER

Alan Knott of England just pips his 1970s contemporaries, Rod Marsh of Australia and Bob Taylor, also of England. Knott was eccentric, bendy and always had a handkerchief or two about his person, but nobody kept more neatly or nimbly, and he also made five Test centuries.

... WICKETKEEPER–BATSMAN

Adam Gilchrist of Australia, the greatest No 7 batsman in Test history, just pips Andy Flower of Zimbabwe, a brilliant player of spin who is now coach of England.

... FIELDER

In the modern age, which has been the era of athletic fielding, it's **Jonty Rhodes** of South Africa. See page 67.

3 GREAT RIVALRIES

THE ASHES

When Britain goes to war, Australia usually joins in – on the same side. But you wouldn't know it from the way they treat each other on the cricket field. This is the greatest rivalry in international cricket, because:

It's the oldest. It began in 1877, in the very first Test match, and has been going ever since, when not rudely interrupted by some other old foes – the Germans.

It's the one that is played most. England and Australia have met in 326 Test matches – including the five played in 2010–11 – twice as many as any other pair of teams. Next comes England and West Indies on 145. Most Test series are now only three matches long, but the Ashes is nearly always five or six.

It has the best name, trophy and story. As a name, the Ashes is short, vivid and memorable. As a trophy, it's lovable – tiny, plain, no airs or graces or bling. As a story, well, read on …

In 1882, England lost at home to Australia for the first time. It was quite an achievement after bowling the Aussies out for 63. Needing just 85 to win, England were suffocated by F.R. Spofforth, known as The Demon, who bagged 14

---

10 EPIC ASHES BATTLES

1920-21 Aussie whitewash
Australia win all five Tests. Their captain, Warwick Armstrong, is nicknamed the Big Ship. England's captain, J.W.H.T. Douglas, is nicknamed Johnny Won't Hit Today.

1930 Bradman's summer
A young Australian batsman, barely 22, makes 974 runs, still a world record for any Test series. Australia win 2-1. See page 52.

1932-33 Bodyline
The England captain, Douglas Jardine – actually a Scotsman – comes up with a dastardly plan to thwart Bradman: bowling at the batsman's body, with a ring of short legs to catch the ball as he fends it off. It works, but at a heavy cost. Most cricket-lovers disapprove and Australia almost breaks off diplomatic relations with Britain. See page 52.

1948 The Invincibles
England are at home, and have a powerful side, and Bradman is now 40. Somehow, Australia win 4-0. They are nicknamed The Invincibles. See page 52.

1953 Hutton's triumph
A dour series begins with four draws but sputters into life at The Oval as first Bedser and Trueman, then Laker and Lock bowl the Aussies out. England regain the Ashes after 19 years.

1970-71 Illingworth's triumph
After a tedious decade, the Ashes flicker into life again. England are captained by the canny Ray Illingworth, who deploys John Snow, a moodily brilliant fast bowler, to rip through the Aussies. England win 2-0.

1974-75 Lillee and Thomson
Australia now have a great pair of fast bowlers – one classical, the other a slinger. They terrorise an elderly England line-up and Australia win 4-1.

1981 Botham's Ashes
Australia get on top and England's captain resigns after only two Tests. Then he bounces back and plays like a superhero as England win 3-1. See page 112.

2005 Flintoff's finest hour
Australia arrive in England as firm favourites after dominating the Ashes for 16 years. At first

wickets in the match. In his last 11 overs, he took a staggering 4 for 2, as Australia squeezed home by seven runs. One spectator was reported to have dropped dead and another bit chunks out of his umbrella handle. A mock death-notice appeared in the *Sporting Times* (see page 93). The writer was a journalist, Reginald Brooks. The papers took up the phrase and England's next tour of Australia, in 1882–83, was described as a "quest to regain the ashes of English cricket." The quest was successful. The term then rather vanished until, in 1904, Plum Warner of England wrote a book called *How We Recovered the Ashes. Wisden*'s first mention of the Ashes followed in 1905.

In 1882–83, an urn had been presented to the England captain, Ivo Bligh. What it contained, nobody has ever established – maybe a bail, maybe a veil. When Bligh died in 1927, his widow gave it to MCC. It has been the official Ashes urn ever since. It is not technically a trophy, as it is not presented to the winning captain – he gets a replica. So as well as being small and plain, it is somewhat hypothetical. But you can see it in the Lord's museum and it's well worth a visit, if only to say, "Wow! It's so small!"

they win easily, but then England fight back through the cool captaincy of Michael Vaughan and some great allround feats from Andrew Flintoff. A series of cliffhangers ends in a 2-1 win for England. Shane Warne takes 40 wickets and finishes on the losing side. See page 88.

2006–07 Ponting's revenge

Australia keep faith with their defeated captain, Ricky Ponting. He leads them on a mission: not just to win back the Ashes, but to destroy England. They succeed, winning 5-0. England, captained by Flintoff as Vaughan is injured, are hopeless. From the heights of 2005, they have gone all the way back to square one – or 1921.

YORKSHIRE v LANCASHIRE

Another great name. Any meeting between Yorkshire and Lancashire is called the Roses match, after the white rose of Yorkshire and the red rose of Lancashire. It all started on the battlefield, in the Wars of the Roses (1455–85). The first Roses match was in 1849 and according to Wikipedia there have been well over 600 of them – although that was counting 2nd XI games, which may have been stretching a point.

The matches attract big crowds, who are often bored senseless, as the teams are so desperate not to lose that they forget about trying to win. The classic example was 1926, when 78,217 people piled into Old Trafford, only to watch a mind-numbing, high-scoring draw in which the second innings never even arrived. But every so often, the pattern is broken, usually by an Aussie…

1924 Headingley
On a spicy pitch, a Yorkshire side packed with big names (Holmes, Sutcliffe, Rhodes) bowl Lancashire out for 113 and 74, so they need only 58 to win. They are all out for 33.

1927 Old Trafford
In a bid to liven things up after a few draws and one heavy defeat, Lancashire get their tearaway Australian fast bowler, Ted McDonald, to attempt an early version of Bodyline, aiming at the batsman with four men in a leg trap and no conventional slips. He takes 11 for 135 and Lancs win by eight wickets.

2001 Headingley
Darren Lehmann of Yorkshire and Australia hammers 252 off only 288 balls. Many old pros turn in their graves. Yorkshire go on to win the County Championship.

2004 Headingley
In a Roses Twenty20 match, Andrew Flintoff opens for Lancashire and blasts 85 off only 48 balls. But Lancs' innings falls away and then  Ian Harvey of Yorkshire and Australia goes one better with 108 off 59 balls. Yorks cruise home by eight wickets.

INDIA v PAKISTAN

These two used to be one – Pakistan began life only in 1947, when India became independent of Britain. They have a spiky political relationship, often clashing over the disputed territory of Kashmir. Sometimes it stops them playing cricket (they haven't met in a Test since December 2007); other times it stops them playing good cricket.

When they have managed to play each other, the matches have been Roses-like – too cagey to be entertaining. In the 1980s and 1990s, there were 15 draws in 16 Tests, but lately there have been only five in 15. In 2003–04, India won a Test in Pakistan for the first time and went on to a famous series victory. Many Indian fans who went to watch were astonished to find a warm welcome and to see that the two nations had far more in common than they had been led to believe.

1952–53 Delhi
 Vinoo Mankad, a slow left-armer (and opening batsman), settles the first Test between the two sides by taking 8 for 52 and 5 for 79. India win by an innings.

1952–53 Lucknow
Pakistan take instant revenge as the starring role switches to Fazal Mahmood, a seamer who was Pakistan's first great bowler. He takes 5 for 52 and 7 for 42.

1979–80 Madras
Kapil Dev, India's greatest allrounder, has an incredible match against a powerful Pakistan side. He takes 4 for 90, then wallops 84, then takes 7 for 56.

2003–04 Multan
Virender Sehwag hits 309 off only 375 balls – the first triple century for India. Unlike many huge scores, it leads to victory as Anil Kumble takes 6 for 72.

2005–06 Karachi
After two Tests in a three-Test series, it's 0-0 as the teams revert to their drawing habit. Pakistan change all that with a fantastic team effort. After collapsing to 39 for 6, they recover to 245 through a sustained wag of the tail. They restrict India to 238 and then their top seven make up for the first innings by all passing 50, which is extremely rare. They declare on 599 for 7 and win by 341 runs.

EXTREME

THE TiED TEST

Brisbane, December 1960. In an era of sleepy cricket, the captains of Australia and West Indies, Richie Benaud and Frank Worrell, made a pact that they would try to entertain. West Indies won the toss in the first Test and rattled up 359 for 7 on the opening day with Garry Sobers stroking 132. When they were all out for 453 off only 100.6 overs, Australia replied in the same vein with 505 off 130.3 overs. Sobers conceded almost as many as he had scored – 115.

West Indies then made 284 as Alan Davidson, a rather cool left-arm seamer, took 6 wickets to make 11 in the match. Australia needed only 233 to win, but low targets can be tricky and time was tight. Wes Hall, a great fast bowler smarting from being hit for 140 in the first innings, ripped through the top order. Australia collapsed to 92 for 6, and a leading commentator, Alan McGilvray, left at tea to catch a flight home. But Davidson was determined to make it his match. He hit 80 and at the other end Benaud reached 50. At 226 for 6, Australia needed only seven more runs with four wickets left. They couldn't lose – but they could panic. Davidson was run out, beaten by a brilliant throw from Joe Solomon.

Two balls later, at the end of the over, it was 5.54pm and there was time for only one more over. Australia needed six runs with three wickets left. And these were eight-ball overs, so the run-rate was quite manageable. But the bowler was Hall, fast, scary and charged-up. He hit Wally Grout, the Australian wicketkeeper, in the midriff. Grout doubled up in pain, but Benaud had set off for the run and they both scrambled in for a leg bye. Five needed off seven. Then Hall dropped short, Benaud's eyes lit up, he went for a pull and edged to the keeper. Hall bowled a dot ball, then Grout was so desperate to regain the strike, he ran a bye to the keeper. Four

needed off four. Grout top-edged a pull. It was in the air so long that people said four players could have caught it. Hall raced over to claim it himself – and dropped it.

The batsmen had run one so it was three off three. Hall bowled yet another bouncer: Ian Meckiff, an Australian fast bowler, swished, connected, ran two and went for the third to win the match, but Grout was run out by a scorching throw in to the keeper from Conrad Hunte. Australia were 232 for 9: one run needed, one wicket left, two balls to go. Their No 11, Lindsay Kline, who had been in bed with tonsillitis, came in to face the music. "If you bowl a no-ball now," Worrell told Hall, "don't go back to Barbados." Hall delivered the ball from a foot behind the line, to be on the safe side. Kline poked the ball towards midwicket, where Joe Solomon was waiting. He dashed in, aimed for the stumps and hit. Meckiff became the third man to be **run out** in the space of eight balls. The West Indians celebrated as if they had won, but the scores were level: it was the first tied Test.

THE TiMELESS TEST

Durban, March 1939. There were many timeless Tests but this, the last of them, is the one that has been remembered – partly because, in the end, it wasn't timeless. England were touring South Africa and were 1-0 up in a five-Test series with one to play. So it was agreed that the last one should be timeless. The groundsman prepared a suitably flat pitch and South Africa made 530 off 200 overs. England, captained by the legendary Wally Hammond, replied with a disappointing 316. South Africa piled up another 481 to get past 1000 for the match, so England needed 696 to win. By

now, a week had gone by – six days' play and one rest day.

England, with a mountain to climb, put on their hiking boots and got going. **Bill Edrich**, who had played eight Tests and done nothing, found his feet with 219 and added 280 for the second wicket with Paul Gibb. The eighth day was lost to rain, but on

the ninth England bored on to 496 for 3. Now they needed just 200 more. They managed 158, to reach 654 for 5, by tea.

But then it rained again and, after 43¼ hours' play, the game was called off – because England's boat was leaving. They missed out on completing the greatest run chase of all time. Wouldn't they have been better off missing the boat?

MATCHES

THE MOST DRAMATIC COMEBACK

Calcutta, March 2000. Australia, desperate to win a series in India for the first time in 31 years, are 1-0 up with two to play. They cruise to 214 for 2, but Harbhajan Singh, the offspinner known as The Turbanator, takes a very starry hat-trick (Ricky Ponting, Adam Gilchrist and Shane Warne) and pegs them back to 269 for 8. The Australian captain, Steve Waugh, makes a battling 110 and adds 133 with Jason Gillespie, so the Aussies still manage 445. They then bowl clinically and get India out for 171, with only one man passing 30 – the No 6, V.V.S. Laxman, who makes a swashbuckling 59. India follow on

and, at 115 for 3, they are staring down the barrel of an innings defeat and a series loss.

Their captain, Sourav Ganguly, boldly promotes Laxman to No 3, swapping him with the more defensive Rahul Dravid. Laxman adds 117 with Ganguly (48) and finishes the third day on 109 not out, with Dravid just getting going. The two of them put together an epic partnership, batting through the whole of the fourth day to take India from 254 for 4 to 589. Laxman amasses a sparkling 281, a new record for a Test score by an Indian; Dravid makes a more sober 180, and their stand

is a monumental 376. India are in charge now.

Ganguly declares on 657 for 7, setting Australia 383 to win. Harbhajan twirls his way to another six wickets, Gilchrist gets a king pair (out first ball both times) and India win easily, by 171 runs. In the final Test, Harbhajan takes even more wickets (15) and spins India to a great series win. Laxman's parents, who wanted him to be a doctor rather a cricketer, realise that he may have made the right decision.

▼ Day to remember
V.V.S. Laxman left and Rahul Dravid leave the field at the end of the fourth day, having batted through all three sessions.

◄ Last word
Harbhajan Singh gets the final wicket of Glenn McGrath lbw and India win the match after following on, 274 behind.

THE HIGHEST-SCORING ONE-DAYER

Johannesburg, March 2006. Australia and South Africa, old one-day foes, are 2-2 in the series with one match to go. For years, 300 has been a very good score in a one-day international. Australia win the toss on a spanking pitch and pile up an outrageous 434 for 4. Their captain, Ricky Ponting, hammers 164 off only 105 balls with nine sixes, while Mike Hussey, normally an accumulator, bashes 81 off 51 balls. Together they add 158 off only 15.4 overs. Jacques Kallis goes for 70 off his

six overs. The only question is whether South Africa will lose by 100, 200 or 300 runs.

But they have nothing to lose and it shows. "Come on guys," Kallis tells them, "It's a 450 wicket. They're 15 short!" Graeme Smith and **Herschelle Gibbs** rattle along at nine an over. Smith makes 90 off 55 balls, while Gibbs matches Ponting with 175 off 111. Wickets fall regularly but never in quick succession. When Gibbs is out, another old hand, Mark Boucher, runs the show and sees

South Africa home to 438 for 9 with a ball to spare. There have been 872 runs in the day, smashing the old record of 693. Mick Lewis, an Aussie seamer, finishes with the most embarrassing figures in one-day international history: 0 for 113 off his ten overs. "It's not like I bowled a heap of pies," Lewis says. "I actually bowled quite well."

AUSTRALIA	18:58	S AFRICA		TOTAL	438
■ LEE	7.5 68 1	SMITH	90	WICKETS	9
└ BRACKEN	10 67 5	DIPPENAAR	1		
CLARK	6 54 0	GIBBS	175	OVERS	49
LEWIS	10 113 0	deVILLIERS	14	BATSMAN ■	
SYMONDS	9 75 2	KALLIS	20	BATSMAN ■	
CLARKE	7 49 1	■BOUCHER	50	SC	S
Keeper: GILCHRIST		KEMP	13	RUNS TO	S
		UD NATH	35	OVERS L	
EXTRAS	BALLS LEFT	TO WIN	NACUS 12	RATE AC	8.8
20	1		1	RATE RE	

WISDEN
FROM A TINY FAST BOWLER TO A FAT YELLOW BOOK

The boy was short, slight and very good at sport. Nowadays, he would probably have ended up as a jockey. But this was back in the 1820s. He was born in Brighton in Sussex, one of the few places where cricket had caught on. His father, a successful carpenter, died young, and perhaps that left the boy more determined to make his mark. To help support his six brothers and sisters, he found work as a pot-boy at a pub – what we would now call a barman – and earned sixpence an hour (2½p) as a long-stop at James Lillywhite's cricket practices. The pub was owned by the Sussex wicketkeeper, Tom Box, who taught the boy to play cricket. He was so good at it that, on his 12th birthday, he played for a team called Eleven Youths of Brighton. Height was not so important for bowlers in those days because the arm was not allowed to be raised above the shoulder. So John Wisden, who weighed only 7 stone and was somewhere between 5ft 4 and 5ft 6, became the most shrimp-like of all the famous fast bowlers.

He didn't just bowl fast: he bowled straight. He played for Sussex at 18 and took six wickets in his first bowl for them. In 1850, aged 23, he played for the South against the North at Lord's, and in the second innings he took 10 wickets, all bowled. One of his victims was Tom Box. This is still the only time that anyone has ever got all 10, all bowled, in a first-class innings. Historically, any bowling average under 20 is exceptional; Wisden's average was a third of that, 6.66. He loved taking wickets and in 1850, in only 38 matches, he took 340 of them. His deliveries were described as "very fast and ripping". He became known as the Little Wonder.

John Wisden could bat, too: he played with a straight bat, was strong on the leg side, and in 1855, he made 148 for Sussex against Yorkshire, the only century scored in the whole first-class season. Fuller Pilch, another great player, rated him the best allrounder of his day. And as well as an

eye for a ball, Wisden had an eye for business. In 1849 he and another star player, George Parr, levelled a field in Leamington Spa, Warwickshire, to stage cricket matches, and in 1850 he started selling sports equipment there. In 1855 he went into partnership with a friend and fellow player, Fred Lillywhite, running a sports outfitter in central London. The shop sold something else too, which seems fairly strange now: tobacco.

The mid-19th century was a great time to be a cricketer. The game was growing rapidly and, thanks to the arrival of the railways, sportsmen were able to travel. Wisden appeared for the All-England XI, which played matches up and down the country, and then, when he tired of being treated arrogantly by the captain, he helped found the United England XI, of which he was joint secretary. Wisden was known for treating people well, and even started a benevolent fund to help cricketers who were struggling to make ends meet.

In 1859, he was one of the organisers of the first England tour overseas – to America and Canada, of all places. He went on it as a player and helped the English team win all eight of their matches. But touring can put a strain on relationships and something seems to have happened between him and his friend Fred on this trip, as their joint venture came to an end soon afterwards.

Wisden, bowling medium-pace by now, was still taking plenty of wickets, but, like many ageing bowlers, he was playing through the pain. He had rheumatism – constant pain in his bones and joints – and it was made worse by a sprain picked up playing racquets, which caused him to miss the whole 1860 season. In 1863, aged 36, he gave up the game. The decision is usually put down to the rheumatism, but he had a new project: launching a cricket yearbook.

He called it *The Cricketer's Almanack* (the apostrophe moved later) and it first appeared in 1864, price one shilling (5p). It was a funny little book, only 112 pages long, with a fair amount of padding – it even included random facts like the dates of the English Civil War and the rules of other games, such as quoiting. It wasn't the first cricket annual: Wisden's old friend Fred Lillywhite had been publishing his *Guide to Cricketers* once or twice a year since 1849, and since 1851 this had included a review of the previous season. But Lillywhite's book had been controversial because it included comments, some of them negative, on the leading players. Wisden decided not to do that, and that may have been one reason why his *Almanack* took off – which is ironic, as it later became famous for expressing fearless opinions.

John Wisden is said to have "suffered greatly" late in his life, as many sportsmen do. He died of cancer in 1884, at the age of only 57, and was buried in Brompton Cemetery in London.

He had no children, but his brainchild was destined to grow and grow. In 1889, the *Almanack* started naming its Cricketers of the Year (see panel, right). In 1891, a new editor was appointed – Sydney Pardon, who was in charge for 35 years and became one of the fathers of modern sportswriting. The book began to express opinions and to have an influence as well as recording the previous year's cricket. Pardon started the Notes by the Editor (see bottom right).

The *Almanack* kept on appearing through both world wars, and one battered copy of the 1939 edition was passed round endlessly in prisoner-of-war camps in the jungle in Thailand, much to the bemusement of the Japanese guards. At one camp, it was in such demand that borrowers were limited to 12 hours. This copy, which belonged to the cricket writer E.W. Swanton, was stamped by the prison authorities "Not subversive". It was so heavily thumbed that it fell apart and had to be re-bound by two prisoners using rice paste as glue. It is now in the Lord's museum.

Wisden has long been a collector's item. Rare editions, from the very early years or from the wars, are worth thousands of pounds on their own, and complete sets are much sought after. If you want one, you will need a load of cash and some long shelves, as there have been 144 editions and lately they have tended to be around 1700 pages long. In 2005, a set of the first 52 *Wisdens* was sold for £150,000 – but they had another famous name attached. They had once belonged to W.G. Grace, who crossed out some of the scores next to his name and replaced them with bigger ones.

In 1963, John Wisden and Co. celebrated its centenary in publishing by launching the Wisden Trophy, to be awarded to the winners of Test series between England and West Indies. *Wisden* is the world's oldest continuously published sports annual. In cricket, it is an institution with two distinct roles, acting as the game's chronicle and its conscience. It is also a surprisingly good read – see page 122 for tips on where to begin.

To find out more about *Wisden* and to see if you might qualify for the Young Wisden Schools Cricketer of the Year award, go to www.wisden.com.

SOME WISDEN TRADITIONS

The Five Cricketers of the Year

The editor always chooses the Five Cricketers of the Year, a tradition that dates back to 1889. Nobody can be chosen twice, and the choices are biased towards the English summer.

The Leading Cricketer in the World

Since 2004, the *Almanack* has named the world's leading player in the previous year. India's Virender Sehwag won it in both 2009 and 2010.

The cover

The famous yellow jacket first appeared in 1938. Before that, it was sometimes salmon pink. The two men in top hats, a woodcut by the artist Eric Ravilious, also made their debut in 1938. The first photograph appeared on the cover in 2003. It was a black-and-white shot of Michael Vaughan, of England, who scored seven Test hundreds in a year.

Notes by the Editor

Started by Sydney Pardon in 1901, the notes are the first thing in each edition. They express strong views: when they take issue with the game's bosses, it's a bit like having someone give your head-teacher a good telling-off.

501

● ● ● (not out) the highest individual score ever made in a first-class match, by Brian Lara, for Warwickshire v Durham at Edgbaston in 1994. It was an astonishing feat, especially as Lara had set a new Test record of 375 only two months before. The 501 contained a record 72 boundaries – 62 fours and 10 sixes. But the match still petered out into a draw. A big score can be a big bore.

400

● ● ● (not out) the highest individual score in a Test, also by Brian Lara. You wait ages for a record-breaking score, then several come along at once. Garry Sobers' record of 365 not out for West Indies v Pakistan in 1957–58 stood for 36 years. Then Lara pinched it with 375 for West Indies v England at St John's, Antigua in 1993–94. Within ten years, the record had fallen into Australian hands, when Matthew Hayden made 380 at Perth in 2003–04 – but as it was against Zimbabwe, a weak team further weakened by terrible political problems, nobody outside Australia got very excited. A few months later, Lara grabbed the record back, again in Antigua, again against England, by becoming the first man to reach 400. Vast scores usually require certain conditions – a flat pitch, a small ground or fast outfield, and feeble or unmotivated bowlers (both Lara's Test records came in dead matches, with the series already settled). But they are still quite something. There's a reason why Lara breaks records and most batsmen don't: he is a fast scorer with an enormous appetite (for runs).

19

● ● ● the most wickets ever taken by one bowler in a Test or first-class match, by Jim Laker, for England against Australia at Old Trafford, Manchester, in 1956. In theory somebody could take 20 in a match, but nobody ever has. Laker, an offspinner with a silky action, had a lot of help from the pitch, which was sticky at first, then dusty. The groundsman, Bert Flack, was under instructions to prepare a turning pitch, and he certainly obliged. Some of the Australian batsmen felt that they should have gone down in the scorebook as "bowled Flack". But it was still a staggering achievement by Laker, especially as there was a very capable spinner wheeling away at the other end – the slow left-armer Tony Lock. Poor old Lock took just one wicket. "Well bowled, you bastard," he said to Laker as yet another wicket fell. "Now give me the bloody ball!"

how the record has grown over 100 years

287	**R.E. Foster**	Eng v Aus, Sydney, 1903–04
325	**Andrew Sandham**	Eng v WI, Kingston, 1929–30
334	**Don Bradman**	Aus v Eng, Leeds, 1930
336	not out **Wally Hammond**	Eng v NZ, Auckland, 1932–33
364	**Len Hutton**	Eng v Aus, The Oval, 1938
365	not out **Garry Sobers**	WI v Pak, Kingston, 1957–58
375	**Brian Lara**	WI v Eng, St John's, 1993–94
380	**Matthew Hayden**	Aus v Zim, Perth, 2003–04
400	not out **Brian Lara**	WI v Eng, St John's, 2003–04

the magic

952

● ● ● **(for six declared, off 271 overs)** the highest team score in a Test, by **Sri Lanka** v India, at the Premadasa Stadium, Colombo, in 1997. India batted first and made 537 for 8 declared. The declaration came late on the second day, which is a normal thing to do – you pile up enough runs to have a chance of an innings victory, and then ask your opponents, who are dog-tired from two long days in the field, to bat for an hour or so. Sri Lanka finished that day on 39 for 1. The next day they didn't lose a single wicket, cruising to 322 for 1. They didn't lose a wicket the next day either, reaching 587 for 1. By now there was only one day left. Instead of trying to win, Sri Lanka just batted on and on, adding another 365. The term "bore draw" has never been more appropriate. They say records are made to be broken, but let's hope this one never is.

800

● ● ● the most wickets taken in a Test career, by **Muttiah Muralitharan** of Sri Lanka between 1992 and 2010. Australia's champion legspinner Shane Warne held the previous record for 3½ years, but Murali – who reached 800 by taking eight wickets in his final Test, against India at Galle in July 2010 – surpassed Warne's tally of 708 in December 2007, almost a year after Warne retired.

99.94

● ● ● the highest batting average of any Test batsman who has played more than a few games, achieved by **Don Bradman** of Australia, between 1928–29 and 1948. Of those to have played 50 Tests or more, only the England opener Herbert Sutcliffe, who played between the two world wars, averaged even 60. There's a rule of thumb for batting averages which goes like this:

40 a good player
45 a very good player
50 a great player
55 a phenomenal player
99 an unbelievable player

how the record has grown over 100 years
(and the year each player broke it)

118 **Johnny Briggs,** England, slow left-arm, in 33 Tests (1899)	**355** **Dennis Lillee,** Australia, pace, in 70 Tests (1981)
189 **SF Barnes,** England, seam, in 27 Tests (1914)	**383** **Ian Botham,** England, swing, in 102 Tests (1986)
216 **Clarrie Grimmett,** Australia, legspin, in 37 Tests (1936)	**431** **Richard Hadlee,** New Zealand, seam, in 86 Tests (1988)
236 **Alec Bedser,** England, seam, in 51 Tests (1953)	**434** **Kapil Dev,** India, swing, in 131 Tests (1992)
252 **Brian Statham*,** England, seam, in 70 Tests (1963)	**519** **Courtney Walsh,** West Indies, pace, in 132 Tests (2000)
307 **Fred Trueman,** England, pace, in 67 Tests (1963)	**527** **Muttiah Muralitharan,** Sri Lanka, offspin, in 90 Tests (2004)
309 **Lance Gibbs,** West Indies, offspin, in 79 Tests (1976)	**708** **Shane Warne**,** Australia, legspin, in 145 Tests (2004)

* Statham held the record for a month before it was grabbed by his own opening partner.
** Murali held the record for five months before Warne overtook him. By the time Warne retired, Murali had 674 wickets from 110 Tests. Source: mainly BBC.co.uk

numbers

All records as at October 25, 2010. For updates, go to the records section on Cricinfo – www.cricinfo.com.

2.28

● ● ● the lowest batting average of any Test cricketer who has played at least 50 matches, by **Chris Martin** of New Zealand. If batsmen could go in at No 12, that's where Martin would be. A respected seam bowler with 181 Test wickets, Martin used to cycle to net sessions as a youngster, which meant he couldn't take a bat with him. That's his excuse, anyway – and he's always stuck to it. But whatever the reason, his stats are eye-wateringly bad. In 81 Test innings spread across 10 years, he has managed to score a grand total of 89 runs. When he made an undefeated 12 against Bangladesh at Dunedin in January 2008, it was the first – and so far only – time he had reached double-figures. In fact, they turned out to be his only Test runs for 16 months. He has been dismissed 28 times for a duck, and failed to score on a further 24 occasions. And he makes the next worst batsman in the list – India's Bhagwat Chandrasekhar, who averaged 4.07 – look like Don Bradman. As they said of Bradman himself, we may never see his like again.

◀ Nought again
Chris Martin is out for another duck, this time against England at Old Trafford.

6

● ● ● the lowest team score in a first-class match, made by a team called **the Bs** against England at Lord's in 1810. One man was absent, and the rest may as well have been. The lowest since 1900 is 12 all out by Northamptonshire v Gloucestershire at Gloucester in 1907 (batsmen all present … and incorrect). The lowest in the 21st century is 19 all out by Matabeleland v Mashonaland, Harare, 2000–01. They may have succumbed to boredom as much as anything else: Zimbabwe's first-class competition contains five teams (now called, rather unimaginatively, Easterns, Westerns, Northerns, Southerns and Centrals), and for many years didn't even contain as many as that. So they have seen a lot of each other. It would be nice to think the Mashonaland supporters – if there *were* any – sang "Oh dear, what can the Matabe?"

▶ Top score
Bert Sutcliffe's 11 was the highest of the innings.

26

● ● ● the lowest team score in a Test – by **New Zealand** v England, Auckland, 1954–55. New Zealand batted first and made 200, which wasn't bad for them at the time: after 25 years of trying, they had yet to win a Test match. They then bowled England out for 246 and were probably entertaining hopes of that elusive first victory when they reached 6 for none. But then they collapsed like a house of cards in a high wind. England, playing under Len Hutton for the last time, were so ruthlessly efficient they didn't even concede any extras. The New Zealand captain, a former fighter pilot called Geoff "Boney" Rabone, was lbw to Brian Staham for seven, although he thought he had edged the ball. "It was very unfortunate," he said later. "We might have made 30 if I hadn't been given out." Curiously, the five lowest Test scores were all made against England. And all rather a long time ago.

the tragic

35

● ● ● the lowest team score in a one-day international, by **Zimbabwe** against Sri Lanka at Harare in 2004. Lucky they were playing at home – otherwise it could have been really disastrous. Nobody reached double figures: the highest score was 7 by Dion Ebrahim, equal with Extras. The innings occupied 18 overs and was over inside an hour and a half. Sri Lanka knocked off the runs in 39 minutes for the loss of one wicket. The previous record, also set against Sri Lanka, was 36 by Canada in the 2003 World Cup.

▼**Same old**
Courtney Walsh registers one of his 43 ducks, lbw to South Africa's Shaun Pollock.

43

● ● ● the number of ducks made in Test cricket by **Courtney Walsh** of West Indies, more than anyone else. A duck is so called because 0 once reminded someone of a duck's egg – and the name stuck. And egg is what it leaves on the batsman's face. Not that it bothered Walsh too much. He took 519 wickets in 132 Tests for West Indies between 1984 and 2000, and generally enjoyed his batting too much to worry about scoring runs. Next in the list comes Glenn McGrath (35 ducks – and the only seamer to take more Test wickets than Walsh: 563); Shane Warne (34, but a far better batsman than his presence here suggests); Muttiah Muralitharan (33); and our friend from the opposite page, Chris Martin (28). But there are some surprising names on the list of duck-makers too. Both Sri Lanka's diligent opener Marvan Atapattu and Australia's all-time legend Steve Waugh registered 22 Test ducks, while England's former opener and captain Mike Atherton made 20, mainly because he spent most of his career facing some of cricket's greatest opening bowlers: Walsh's mate Curtly Ambrose inflicted four ducks on Atherton, McGrath three, and the South African duo of Allan Donald and Shaun Pollock two each. Opening the batting can be a tricky business at times.

▲**It's all over** Farveez Maharoof (3 for 3) dismisses Zimbabwe's last man Tinashe Panyangara.

All records as at October 25, 2010. For updates, go to the records section on Cricinfo – www.cricinfo.com.

STATISTICS

HOW THEY WORK AND HOW THEY WORK

Cricket loves its stats. Averages get flashed up on the television screen and are much quoted by the pundits. So it's worth knowing a bit about them.

How averages work

A batting average is calculated like this: the total number of runs the batsman has made, divided by the number of times he has been out. So if he makes **30, 60, 0 and 10**, his average is **25 (100 ÷ 4)**. But if one of those scores was not out, his average would be **33.33 (100 ÷ 3)**. And if two of them were not out, he would have an average of **50**, even though he had only passed 50 once.

A batting average is usually presented like this:

	mat	inns	NO	runs	HS	ave	100/50
Brian Lara	131	232	6	11,953	400*	**52.88**	34/48

The abbreviations stand for **matches, innings, not-outs, highest score, average** and **hundreds and fifties**. The fifties don't include the hundreds, and the asterisk means that the 400 was not out.

A bowling average is calculated like this: the total number of runs the bowler has conceded, divided by the number of wickets he has taken. So if you take **3 for 60**, your average is **20**. If you then take **0 for 30**, **2 for 70** and **3 for 80**, you'll have a total of **8 for 240**, and your average will be **30**. The lower, the better: for Test bowlers, an average of 20 is phenomenal, 25 great, 30 good, and 35 OK as long as they make runs as well.

A bowling average is usually presented like this:

	mat	balls	runs	wkts	ave	5/10w
Brett Lee	76	16,351	9554	310	**30.81**	10/0

The abbreviations stand for **matches, wickets, average** and **five-wicket innings and ten-wicket matches.**

With both batting and bowling, you need to be clear whether the average is for a career, a series, a season or a period, and whether it is for Test cricket or first-class, one-day internationals or all professional one-day games (List A, as they're known). Averages are usually given to two decimal places (99.94), although goodness knows why: even Bradman didn't have the ability to score 0.94 of a run.

What's good about them

Averages are clear-cut, easy to work out for yourself, and they tend to even out over time. Look at how **Graeme Smith**, the South African captain, did in England in 2003:

Test	score	total	ave so far
1st	277	277	**277**
	85	362	**181**
2nd	259	621	**207**
3rd	35	656	**164**
	5	661	**132.20**
4th	2	663	**110.50**
	14	677	**96.71**
5th	18	695	**86.87**
	19	714	**79.33**

In the first two Tests, he was a superhero. But after that, the England bowlers worked him out, going round the wicket to cramp him on his off stump, just as they would with Adam Gilchrist in the Ashes two years later. Smith picked up two single-figure scores, as opening batsmen are always liable to, facing a new ball and fresh bowlers. And his average, so huge early on, went down with every innings – although it still ended up very high. So it reflected his series pretty well.

▲ **Heading for 277** Smith sweeps past Alec Stewart.

Strike rates

Averages are not the only statistical measure. There are also strike rates, and again, there is one for batting and one for bowling.

A batsman's strike rate is the number of runs he makes per hundred balls, so high is good. Here are the Test strike rates for five current players:

	mat	runs	balls	SR	note
Shahid Afridi (P)	27	1716	1973	**86.97**	fastest scorer ever
Virender Sehwag (I)	89	7152	8741	**81.82**	frightening for an opener
Tillekeratne Dilshan (SL)	63	3906	5951	**65.63**	became an opener in July 09
Ross Taylor (NZ)	25	1941	3103	**62.55**	world's fastest middle-order batsman
Rahul Dravid (I)	144	11,602	27,355	**42.41**	cautious but effective

Fast scorers help win matches by giving their bowlers more time to take 20 wickets. But sometimes the slowcoaches are vital too, holding up an end, preventing collapse and tiring the opposition out. Dravid wins matches in his own way.

Bowlers' strike rate

A bowler's strike rate is the number of balls he needs for each wicket, so low is good. This is an excellent measure because great bowlers are wicket-takers. Here are the best of all time in Tests among those with 200 wickets:

	mat	balls	wkts	SR	note
Dale Steyn (SA)	41	8273	211	**39.2**	fastest bowler currently playing
Waqar Younis (P)	87	16,224	373	**43.4**	king of the reverse-swinging toe-ball
Malcolm Marshall (WI)	81	17,584	376	**46.7**	master of pace and swing
Allan Donald (SA)	72	15,519	330	**47.0**	nicknamed White Lightning, struck often
Fred Trueman (E)	67	15,178	307	**49.4**	probably England's best fast bowler
Joel Garner (WI)	58	13,169	259	**50.8**	yorker ace, and Marshall's Bajan partner

Neither Shane Warne nor Murali features here. Spinners need more overs to take their wickets, so Murali is 22nd on the list with **55.0** and Warne 27th with **57.4**. And even the best bowlers need at least seven overs per wicket. Getting Test batsmen out isn't easy.

Bowlers' economy rate

This is the number of runs per over that the bowler concedes – crucial in one-day cricket. Again, low is good. Here are the best of all time in ODIs, among those with 200 wickets:

	mat	balls	runs	econ	note
Curtly Ambrose (WI)	176	9353	5429	**3.48**	tall and extremely accurate
Shaun Pollock (SA)	303	15,712	9631	**3.67**	swing and control with the new ball
Kapil Dev (I)	225	11,202	6945	**3.71**	India's best fast bowler, also a big-hitter
Courtney Walsh (WI)	205	10,822	6918	**3.83**	Curtly's partner, angling it in awkwardly
Glenn McGrath (A)	250	12,970	8391	**3.88**	unfailingly metronomic

What's not so good about them

Averages can be random. In 1953, Bill Johnston toured England with the Australians. He was a good fast bowler and a hopeless batsman, but he kept collecting not-outs – 17 of them in 18 innings. He scraped 102 runs, so his average was **102**. Which was amusing, but hardly accurate, as his average innings (completed or not) was **5.66**. Today's not out king is Jacques Kallis of South Africa, whose Test batting average in Zimbabwe is **503**.

Also, averages treat all runs or wickets as equal. "I'm not that into averages," Andrew Flintoff told me in 2005, "because you can make a hundred in a dead game and average 50 for the series, so they're not that representative. It's more about whether you have a good series – did you turn a game?" Which can be done with a gutsy 40, or a timely 2 for 20.

Cricket's love of averages forces players to cart their whole careers around, like emotional baggage. Flintoff was a top player who started poorly in Tests, and although that's ancient history now, it still ended up denting his figures. After 11 Tests, late in 2001, his batting average was **14** and his bowling average **58**. But he dragged that back, so that by end of his Test career in 2009, he averaged a far more respectable **31** with the bat and **32** with the ball.

THE ICC WORLD RATINGS

Since 1990, there has been a world rating system similar to that used in tennis or golf. Unlike averages, it's impossible to work out for yourself, as it's all done with a complicated algorithm that takes into account the total number of runs in the match and the quality of the opposition. But it is still interesting. Here are the ratings as they stood in mid-October 2010:

TEST BATSMEN		points
1	Sachin Tendulkar (I)	891
2	Kumar Sangakkara (SL)	874
3	Virender Sehwag (I)	819
4=	Shiv Chanderpaul (WI)	807
	Mahela Jayawardene (SL)	807
6	Jacques Kallis (SA)	791
7	Graeme Smith (SA)	787
8	V.V.S. Laxman (I)	767
9	Ross Taylor (NZ)	766
10	A.B. de Villiers (SA)	762

TEST BOWLERS		
1	Dale Steyn (SA)	887
2	Graeme Swann (E)	858
3	Mohammad Asif (P)	753
4=	Zaheer Khan (I)	744
	James Anderson (E)	744
6	Morne Morkel (SA)	739
7	Mitchell Johnson (A)	735
8	Harbhajan Singh (I)	679
9	Doug Bollinger (A)	659
10	Mohammad Amir (P)	658

All figures to October 14, 2010

HUNDREDS, FIVE-FORS,

Cricketers do love a round number. A hundred may be only a few runs better than a 90, but it means far more. You can see this by the way some players act when they get close – into the so-called nervous nineties. Their fluency dries up and they bat like beginners again. But if they make it to a hundred, joy is unconfined. It looks great on the scorecard, sticking out further than all the other scores. It brings a warm round of applause from the crowd and the chance for the batsman to wave his bat wildly. And it gets him on to the **honours board**, if there is one, never to be rubbed out.

The Lord's honours boards

There are honours boards in each dressing-room, and you can tell they mean a lot to the players because they are always talking about them. Everybody who gets a hundred or a five-for in a Lord's Test is up there. England's batsmen have been getting better: 37 of them have made the board since the start of 2000; in the previous nine years, only three managed it. But it's just as interesting to spot who isn't there. Shane Warne isn't; nor is Brian Lara, or Sachin Tendulkar. Visiting players may only play a Test or two at Lord's and not all are at their best.

Hundreds aren't everything – many a match has been won by a 70 or 80 – but you can tell a lot about a batsman by how often he makes one. Here are the most impressive examples:

A HUNDRED EVERY...

1.8 TESTS	Don Bradman (Aus)	29 in 52
2.2 TESTS	George Headley (WI)	10 in 22
2.9 TESTS	Clyde Walcott (WI)	15 in 44
3.3 TESTS	Graeme Pollock (SA)	7 in 23
3.4 TESTS	Matthew Hayden (Aus)	30 in 103
3.5 TESTS	Sachin Tendulkar (Ind)	49 in 171

To October, 2010. Figures rounded to one decimal place.

Doubles

When batsmen talk about booking in for bed and breakfast, it means they are not going to be satisfied with a mere century: they want to be around the next morning to turn it into a double. Yet only 296 of them have been made in 133 years of Tests. Australia lead the way with 62. Bangladesh haven't got one yet. The king of the 200 is Bradman, inevitably, with twelve, followed by Lara with nine. Ricky Ponting, undoubtedly a great batsman, only has four.

Triples

A triple hundred should be a very rare thing, and until recently, it *was* very rare. Only 11 were made in the first 113 years of Test cricket, up to 1990. Then the England captain Graham Gooch hit 333 against India at Lord's and started a fashion. In the 20 years since, there have been 12 more Test triples, including the four biggest scores ever made.

▼**Honoured** Stuart Broad gets his name on the Lord's board after his 169 against Pakistan in 2010.

Five-fors

The bowler's equivalent of a hundred is a five-wicket haul, known as a five-for. Five-fors are harder to come by than hundreds, but for some reason they go less celebrated. A bowler will tell you this is because bowlers are down-to-earth professionals who do the job without fuss, unlike those preening characters with a bat in their hand. The king of the Test five-for is **Muttiah Muralitharan**, who finished with a staggering 67. Next is Shane Warne with 37, and Richard Hadlee of New Zealand with 36. Murali took 10 wickets in a match 22 times, more than Warne and Hadlee put together. But Murali and Hadlee had the advantage of being their team's only great bowler. As Gooch once said of New Zealand: "It's the World XI at one end and Ilford 2nds at the other."

Warne had to share the wickets with another of the great destroyers – Glenn McGrath, who took 29 five-fors. He and Warne took 1001 wickets together in 104 Tests. They even retired from Tests together, on January 5, 2007.

SIXES AND HAT-TRICKS

Sixes
The biggest and the best

A six isn't just the biggest shot a batsman can play, it's often the best. It means taking a big risk, because he could be caught. He could be stumped too, since the shot often involves launching himself out of his crease. He could feel a bit of a fool. But then people who never risk making a fool of themselves don't go very far.

More than any other stroke, a six draws the crowd into the action. The ball is heading for them, and it is usually travelling in a great arc, which gives them time to spot it, follow it and enjoy the suspense. As the ball hangs in the air, time stands still. Is it going to be the best possible result for the batsman from one ball – six runs – or the worst – being caught? Is it going to hit someone in the crowd, or are they going to catch it, take a bow and get seen on telly by all their friends?

Six sixes in an over

Some batsmen have managed as many in six balls as Don Bradman managed in his entire career – though not (yet) in Test cricket. One day in 1969, the great West Indian allrounder Garry Sobers was playing for Nottinghamshire against Glamorgan at Cardiff. He was facing Malcolm Nash, a gentle left-armer. The over went like this: 6, 6, 6, 6, 6, 6. Sobers mostly played the pull shot, with a huge follow-through. You can see him do it, looking very smart with no helmet, on YouTube.

Sobers' feat was matched by Ravi Shastri, the Indian allrounder, in a domestic match in 1984–85, but nobody got very excited about that. It had never been done in international cricket until it happened twice in one year: Herschelle Gibbs of South Africa did it to Daan van Bunge, a legspinner from the Netherlands, in St Kitts at the 2007 World Cup. Six months later, during the World Twenty20, **Yuvraj Singh** of India repeated the feat off the bowling of England seamer Stuart Broad in Durban. A few weeks earlier, Yuvraj had been hit for five successive sixes in a one-day international at The Oval by Broad's team-mate Dimitri Mascarenhas. Revenge is not always best served cold.

Six-hitter supreme

Australia's wicketkeeper Adam Gilchrist finished his career with exactly 100 sixes – just over one for each Test he played in. At one point, he hit 16 in three successive Tests while making three hundreds against Pakistan and New Zealand in 2004–05. And the closest anyone has come to him is Brian Lara, with 88. New Zealand's Chris Cairns deserves a special mention, though: he hit 87, often from No 8, and scored about one-sixth of his 3,320 Test runs in sixes. England's greatest six-hitter is Andrew Flintoff, with 82, and of the 24 players to have hit at least 50 Test sixes, only six didn't play in the 2000s.

This trend for more six-hitting is partly because bats are heavier and boundaries shorter. But there has also been a change of attitude, with more batsmen taking risks. Don Bradman hit only six sixes in his Test career, Mike Atherton four, W.G. Grace one.

Hat-tricks

The bowlers' equivalent of a six, only rarer still, is a hat-trick – taking three wickets in three balls. The three balls can be interrupted by an over from the other end, or even a whole innings, but they have to be consecutive deliveries from the same bowler in the same match.

In Tests, a hat-trick comes along about once every four years. There have been 37 of them in 133 years of Test history. England have managed four in recent years, all by swing bowlers – Dominic Cork, Darren Gough, Matthew Hoggard and Ryan Sidebottom. Hat-tricks by spinners are extremely rare, but Shane Warne got one against England (and one of his victims was Gough). Wasim Akram of Pakistan, a magnificent, fast, snaky, reverse-swing bowler, took two Test hat-tricks (no one has taken three), and is also one of only three bowlers to have taken four wickets in five balls in a Test.

▶**Three and easy** Ryan Sidebottom removes Jacob Oram of New Zealand to complete England's most recent Test hat-trick, at Hamilton in March 2008.

HEROES

Ian Botham *Star allrounder and charity walker*

Very few series are named after one player, but the 1981 Ashes will always belong to Ian Botham. At first he was more of a loser. He made a pair (two ducks) at Lord's, his team went 1-0 down, and he resigned as England captain. When Mike Brearley, a father-figure to him, returned as captain, Botham found his strut. In the third Test at Headingley, he took six Aussie wickets, then top-scored with 50 before England, 227 adrift, were asked to follow on. At 135 for 7, a thrashing beckoned, so Botham decided to have fun, saying to his partner, the tail-ender Graham Dilley: "Let's give it some humpty." He slogged his way to 149 not out as Dilley made 56. Even so Australia only needed 130: perfectly gettable. But Australia panicked, Bob Willis – running in like a demented buffalo (with long legs and big hair) – took 8 for 43 and England won by 18 runs. Botham wasn't finished yet. In the next Test at Edgbaston he took 5 for 1 in 28 balls as Australia again choked with victory in sight. Then, at Old Trafford, he cracked 118 off 102 balls – and this time he wasn't slogging. England won 3-1, and the series became known as Botham's Ashes. He had his villainous moments too, getting banned for drugs at one point, but became a hero all over again by going on epic charity walks and raising millions for kids with leukaemia.

Douglas Jardine

Crafty and successful England captain

A captain's job is to win, right? And to come up with a plan that will defeat the opposition. Douglas Jardine, an England captain who happened to be Scottish, did that all right. It was 1932, England were going to Australia to try and regain the Ashes, and the young Don Bradman (see page 52) was already shaping up as the best batsman of all time. Jardine had to stop him. So he told his fast bowlers, Harold Larwood and Bill Voce, to bowl bouncers on leg stump, and posted a slip cordon on the leg side to catch the batsmen as they fended the ball off their throats (no helmets in those days). This was Bodyline. It almost caused a diplomatic incident, but it worked: England won 4-1. Bradman still averaged 56 – but by his superhuman standards, that was poor. Jardine had done what he set out to do, and had played within the laws. Wouldn't you have done the same?

AND VILLAINS

Thomas White

Early purveyor of gamesmanship

Question: what's the surest way of not being bowled? Answer: find a bat as wide as the stumps. It sounds ridiculous, but it was precisely the trick attempted by Thomas White during a village game in Hambledon in 1771. Even more ridiculously, there was nothing in the game's laws to prevent the ruse. That changed quickly: not long after, it was decreed that no bat could measure more than 4¼ inches across. Still, full marks for ingenuity.

Allen Stanford

Texan billionaire turned fraudster

When an offer sounds too good to be true, that's usually because it is. **Sir Allen Stanford** briefly looked like the saviour of English cricket when he dropped into Lord's in a sleek helicopter in the summer of 2008 and unveiled a large Perspex box crammed full with $50 notes totalling $20m (about £12.5m). The bulk of the money was on offer to the winners of a one-off game of Twenty20 at Stanford's private ground later that year in Antigua between an England XI and the Stanford Superstars – essentially a West Indies team. But the cash in the box was fake – and so, it proved, was Stanford, who a few months later was arrested for fraud worth up to $8bn.

Douglas Jardine

Heartless and unsporting England captain

Sport is supposed to be fun. There are rules, or laws as cricket calls them, but there's also the spirit of the game, which needs to be honoured. That's why you shake hands with your opponents at the end. Douglas Jardine wanted to win at all costs in Australia in 1932–33. Bodyline was a vicious policy that could have killed someone (no helmets in those days). He was snobbish too, bordering on racist – saying Australians were "uneducated" and "an unruly mob". When he swatted a fly, a heckler yelled: "Leave our flies alone, Jardine. They're the only friends you've got." When Australia's Bill Woodfull was hit just above the heart by Larwood, Jardine said: "Well bowled, Harold."

Gilbert Jessop

Clean-hitter from Victorian era known as "The Croucher"

Jessop was a Gloucestershire fast bowler, but he is best remembered for an innings that inspired England to victory over Australia at The Oval in 1902. His nickname derived from his strange stance at the crease – it looked as if he was sitting on the toilet – but there was nothing constipated about his batting that day as England chased 263. At one stage they were 48 for 5, but Jessop – all 5ft 7 and 11 stone of him – smashed 104 in 77 minutes. England won by one wicket. To put Jessop's innings in context, the average Test hundred takes about 3½ hours. Not bad going in any era.

Bernard Thomas

England physio who saved an opponent's life

Physios are like goalkeepers and umpires: you don't notice the good ones. But when Ewen Chatfield, a New Zealand No 11 on Test debut, edged a short ball from England's Peter Lever into his head in Auckland in 1974–75, Thomas was quickest to react. Chatfield, whose next memory was waking up in an ambulance, had swallowed his tongue. As he said years later: "It was a good job Bernard Thomas was there or I wouldn't be around today." The incident was a frightening one – but it hastened the introduction of helmets, so at least some good came of it.

Kerry Packer

Australian businessman who changed the game forever

To cricket administrators in the late 1970s, Kerry Packer, a big businessman, was not merely a villain but only a little less villainous than the devil himself. Yet to a generation of players he was more like a guardian angel. It all started when Packer wanted exclusive TV rights to cover Australian cricket on his own station, Channel 9. The Australian board said no, so Packer took the law into his own hands, signing up many of the world's star players and setting up his own tournament instead. He called it World Series Cricket, staged games under floodlights with white balls and black sightscreens, and dressed the players in coloured clothing (the West Indians wore a fetching shade of salmon pink) – all of which were new ideas at the time. And he made the players rich beyond their wildest dreams. The ICC banned Packer's players, only to lose in the high court when he challenged their ruling. And when WSC was disbanded in 1979, it was only because of a climb-down which finally gave Packer the TV rights he craved. These days, Packer is dead, but Channel 9 still covers Tests in Australia very well.

Rebel tourists

Just what apartheid South Africa wanted

For decades, life in South Africa was ruled by apartheid, which meant that only people with white skin could vote, or go to nice beaches, or play Test cricket. This was especially unjust as most South Africans were black. Many countries were outraged, and from 1970 they refused to play against South Africa. As the white South Africans were sports-mad, this hit them where it hurt. They hit back by offering foreign sportsmen big money to go on rebel tours. An England team went in 1981–82, and another one in 1989–90. One man, the offspinner John Emburey, went on both tours. In between, amazingly, he captained England. The second tour was led by another ex-captain, Mike Gatting, who dismissed protests as "just a bit of singing and dancing". Happily, the tour flopped, Nelson Mandela was released, and apartheid crumbled.

Hansie Cronje

South African captain embroiled in match-fixing

Hansie Cronje was like the head boy who had it all: popular, successful, good-looking and captain of the cricket team. But his world fell apart in 2000, when the Delhi police uncovered evidence that he had become involved in match-fixing. At first Cronje did what plenty of schoolboys would do: he panicked and denied everything. Then, pressed by his boss, he owned up to his crimes, and was banned for life, aged just 31. Two years later he was killed in a plane crash – a fallen idol in more ways than one. But he was still given a hero's funeral.

strange
BUT TRUE

One of the best bits in *Wisden* is the Index of Unusual Occurrences, introduced in 1996. Here are some choice examples – and a few from earlier times.

Brett Lee, the Australian fast bowler, used to play for a team called the Oak Flats Rats in Wollongong, New South Wales. In his first proper game, he took six wickets in the same over, all bowled.

In 1899, in a junior house match at Clifton College, a 13-year-old boy called A.E.J. Collins scored 628 not out. Collins, an orphan, treated the bowling with "lordly contempt", although the bowlers defeated him a few times: he was dropped on 80, 100, 140, 400 and 556. The drop on 80 may be the most expensive mistake ever made on a cricket field. Once Collins reached 400, word spread, and crowds came to watch, along with a correspondent for *The Times*, who kept getting his name wrong, calling him A.E.G. not A.E.J. The match was timeless and eventually, after six days, Collins's team, Clarke House, won by an innings and 688 runs. So, strictly speaking, they didn't need his runs. But they did need his wickets – he took 11. After school, he went into the Army, and he was killed in action early in the First World War. The field where the game was played is known as Collins's Piece, and 628 is still the highest score ever recorded in cricket.

In 2006, two brothers opened the batting in a one-day international – on different sides. The match was Ireland v England in Belfast. Ed Joyce, an Irishman, was making his England debut after qualifying through playing for Middlesex. His younger brother Dominick was playing for Ireland. Ed made 10, which was 10 more than Dominick. Two of their sisters, twins Isobel and Cecelia, and another brother, Gus, have also played for Ireland, while Ed has since gone full circle by making himself available for the country of his birth again.

Until March 2005, only one set of twins had played Test cricket – the Waugh brothers. Steve Waugh had played more Tests than anyone else (168); Mark Waugh, whose debut came when Steve was dropped, was ninth on the same list with 128 Tests. But then New Zealand picked James Marshall, whose twin, Hamish, was already in their team. And these two had something the Waughs didn't: they were identical. They were playing against Australia, whose captain, Ricky Ponting, said that if they batted together, he wouldn't be able to tell them apart. This was hardly surprising as their own father said he found it difficult, too, when the twins were wearing whites. James opened the batting, while Hamish was down at No 3, and sure enough, they found themselves batting together after half an hour of the match. They added 38 before Glenn McGrath removed James. But they made it easy for the Aussies to tell who was who: James wore an arm guard. Or was it Hamish?

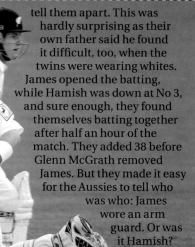

On May 16, 2007, a boy in Swansea turned 17, and his mum booked him a driving lesson as a present – but she had to cancel it because he was chosen to play for Glamorgan against Gloucestershire. The boy was James Harris, an allrounder who bowls medium-fast. He proceeded to take 12 wickets, breaking the record for the youngest person to take 10 wickets in a county championship match. He had to miss the next game, though, to sit his A-levels. "I've got to get my head in my books for the exams," he told reporters. "But then hopefully it will be cricket, cricket, cricket."

In a Twenty20 match at Edgbaston in 2004, Warwickshire's Neil Carter hit the ball high in the air. Somerset's Keith Dutch was bracing himself to catch it when the ground announcer, George Gavin, shouted "Wooooooooooh!" Dutch held on. Warwickshire apologised.

On their tour of India in 1951–52, England were fielding in a warm-up match at Poona when they were joined by a monkey, who wandered on to the field and stood at point, just to the left of cover. It was chased off by a member of the ground staff wielding a stick. Not to be deterred, the monkey reappeared the next day and went to stand at gully. The same member of the ground staff again chased it away. The story is told in *The Reduced History of Cricket*. "Disgusted at this harassment," say the authors, "the monkey jumped on the pavilion roof and refused to speak to the media at the end of play."

In a Second XI game against Derbyshire at The Oval in 2003, the Surrey openers, Scott Newman and Nadeem Shahid, reached 500 for no wicket in only 74 overs. The international umpire Billy Bowden, who was warming up before standing in a Test match, whipped out a camera and stopped play to take a picture of the two batsmen, grinning broadly, in front of the scoreboard. They were eventually parted at 552, whereupon Bowden handed the camera to the other umpire, Bob McLeod, and posed in front of the scoreboard himself, giving a thumbs-up.

During the First World War, British soldiers held a cricket match at Versailles, "in an enclosure between some houses out of observation from the enemy," according to the poet Robert Graves, who was one of the players. The match was Officers v Sergeants. "Our front line is three-quarters of a mile away," Graves wrote in his book *Goodbye To All That*. "I made top score, 24; the bat was a bit of a rafter, the ball a piece of rag tied with string; and the wicket a parrot cage with the clean, dry corpse of a parrot inside. Machine gun fire broke up the match." It is not known whether this was the inspiration for the dead-parrot sketch in Monty Python.

In a one-day game against Glamorgan at Headingley in 2003, Ryan Sidebottom of Yorkshire and England finished with the bizarre figures of 0.1–0–11–0. He started with two wides, then bowled a short ball which was hooked for six. After sending down three more wides, he retired with a tight hamstring. He later joined Nottinghamshire, won a Championship medal and received a surprise recall by England in May 2007.

On their tour of England in 2002, India picked a 17-year-old reserve wicketkeeper called Parthiv Patel. He was quite short and when he led the team out on to the stage at an awards ceremony, some people assumed he was the team mascot. Then the first-choice keeper got injured and Patel found himself in the Test team. The England and Wales Cricket Board had just brought in a rule that players under the age of 18 had to keep wicket in a helmet, unless they had a note from their mother or father giving permission for them not to. The board decided not to insist that Patel produce a note.

In 1994–95, the double world-record holder Brian Lara played in a charity match in Sydney and faced the bowling of an Australian Test allrounder called Zoe Goss. Visibly alarmed by the prospect of getting out to a woman, Lara played scratchily for a few minutes. Then he charged down the track, had a swing, edged the ball and was caught behind. In case the umpire hadn't heard the nick, the keeper stumped him as well. So Lara ended up getting out twice to a woman off the same ball.

Sources: *Wisden Cricketers' Almanack*; Cricinfo; the *Daily Telegraph*; *The Reduced History of Cricket* by Aubrey Ganguly and Justyn Barnes (Andre Deutsch, 2005); *A Social History of Cricket* by Derek Birley (Aurum, 1999). For more occurrences, turn to the back page of any recent *Wisden*.

FAMOUS QUOTES

Cricket – a game which the English, not being a spiritual people, have invented in order to give themselves some conception of eternity.

Lord Mancroft, politician

I tend to believe that cricket is the greatest thing that God ever created on earth.

Harold Pinter, playwright

This is great. When does it start?

Groucho Marx, comedian, after half an hour's play at Lord's

Of course it's frightfully dull! That's the whole point!

Character played by **Robert Morley** in **The Final Test**, a 1953 film about cricket

What do they know of cricket, who only cricket know?

C.L.R. James, author

It's hard work making batting look effortless.

David Gower, England batsman of the 1980s

These people haven't come to watch you bowl, they've come to watch me bat.

W.G. Grace, to a furious bowler, after he had been bowled first ball, and the umpire allegedly called "not out"

Ninety per cent of cricket is played in the mind.

Richard Hadlee, great New Zealand bowler

Captaincy is 90 per cent luck and 10 per cent skill. But don't try it without that 10 per cent.

Richie Benaud, a very good Australian captain and an even better commentator

He's got a degree in people, hasn't he?

Rodney Hogg, Australian fast bowler, on Mike Brearley, England's captain, in about 1979. Brearley later qualified as a psychotherapist

▲ **Psyching them up**
Brearley was a master at getting the best from his players, like Bob Willis at Headingley in 1981.

Warnie's idea of a balanced diet is a cheeseburger in each hand.

Ian Healy, Australian wicketkeeper, on Shane Warne

6 CELEBRATED SLEDGES

Sledging, as you know, is a mean, sad thing to do, but it sometimes redeems itself by being quite funny. Health warning: some of these tales may be apocryphal (a fancy word meaning not strictly true), but they are part of cricket's folklore.

During the Bodyline series of 1932–33, the England captain, **Douglas Jardine**, was batting. He complained to his Australian counterpart, **Bill Woodfull**, that a slip fielder had sworn at him. Woodfull solemnly addressed his team-mates: "All right, which one of you bastards called this bastard a bastard?"

When India toured Pakistan in 2003–04, Shoaib Akhtar (fast and often furious) was bowling to Virender Sehwag (brilliant but hot-headed). Shoaib kept firing in bouncers and Sehwag kept letting them go past him. Shoaib, exasperated, asked: "Why don't you hit one for a change?" Sehwag imperiously replied: "Are you bowling or begging?"

Matthew Fleming, an allrounder who went on to play one-day cricket for England, was making his county debut, for Kent, against Yorkshire. Fleming had an unusual background for a cricketer – he was a member of the banking family and the great-nephew of Ian Fleming who wrote the James Bond books. His first scoring shot was a six. So was his second. The wicketkeeper, the late **David Bairstow**, said: "I'd bat like that too if I had your money."

Ian Botham went in to bat against Australia in the early 1980s. **Rod Marsh**, a great wicketkeeper and conversationalist, asked him: "How's your wife and my kids?" Botham replied: "The wife's fine. The kids are retarded."

Ian Healy, another excellent Australian wicketkeeper, was in temporary charge of Australia in an Ashes Test while the captain was off the field. He moved a fielder to a position several yards from **Nasser Hussain's** bat, saying: "Let's have you right under Nasser's nose."

Jimmy Ormond, a seam bowler then playing for Leicestershire, was making his Test debut for England at The Oval in 2001. When he went in to bat, **Mark Waugh** said to him: "Mate, what are you doing out here? There's no way you're good enough to play Test cricket." Ormond replied: "Maybe not, but at least I'm the best player in my own family."

PLAYER SPEAK

You might say ...	They will say ...
pitch or wicket	*track or deck*
good shot	*shot*
edge	*nick*
sledging	*banter or verbals*
cricket bag	*coffin*
century	*hundred or ton*
score of 150+	*daddy hundred*
score of 100–120	*baby hundred*
do well	*come to the party*
outswing	*shape*
line and length	*good areas*
take control	*put your hand up*
tall order	*big ask*
turning pitch	*Bunsen (rhyming slang: Bunsen burner)*
five-for	*Michelle (Pfeiffer, film star)*
well bowled, Graeme	*bowling, Swanny*

GO

AND SEE A GAME

Watching on the telly is great, but for atmosphere, and a feel for the pace of the game, there's nothing like going to a big match. It can be a long day, but follow these tips to make sure it's an enjoyable one.

Cricket is quite an odd sport to go and watch. It lasts all day, unless it's a Twenty20 game. It stops for meals, and also (boo) for rain or bad light. And the action happens in a series of little flurries which can be hard to follow with the naked eye.

That's the bad news. The good news is:
- the whole scene is quite something, from the perfect grass to the groups of male fans who come dressed as nuns
- there's usually a great atmosphere, with singing, dancing and flag-waving
- you get a strong sense of how fast the ball travels
- one or two players will field near you
- there's plenty of space, and it's safe, so the grown-ups can be persuaded to let you go off by yourself or with a friend
- there are ice-creams to eat, bats to

drool over in the shop and famous faces to spot
- and if you do miss a crucial moment, there's always the replay on the big screen or the highlights on telly when you get home.

There are two dangers – getting burnt or bored. Deal with the first one by going Slip, Slap, Slop as they say in Australia (slip on a shirt, slap on a hat, slop on some sunscreen), and don't mess around because the damage that leads to skin cancer is usually done in childhood. Deal with the boredom by watching selectively and taking breaks (see below). And if you're not sure you can face a whole day, just go for the afternoon, or start with a Twenty20 game – they're fast-moving and great fun. Whatever you do, remember the point is to enjoy it.

5 TIPS FOR BIG GAMES AT LORD'S

1 go to the museum (behind the pavilion)
Admission for kids is only £1 and although it's quite old-fashioned, it's full of intriguing things, from W.G. Grace's boots (a bit grubby) to the Ashes (unbelievably tiny). Don't miss the film theatre at the back, or the sparrow in a glass case on the ground floor – it was stuffed after being killed by a ball in 1936.

2 check out the real-tennis court (behind the pavilion)
Real? More like surreal. A weird mixture of tennis and squash, with a sloping roof to bounce your serve off. During Tests, the viewing area turns into a champagne bar, but you can sneak in there for a gawp.

3 have a bacon sandwich and a smoothie (in the food court, behind the big screen)
The permanent bars don't serve great food, but the temporary stalls set up for big matches do. You can have an Indian, fish and chips, an Aussie pie, or, best of all, a fresh bacon sandwich. Squirt on some sauce, and wash it down with a smoothie from the little stall in the top right-hand corner. Then tell your parents that as you've been so healthy, you've clearly earned a visit to the old-style sweet stall behind the Tavern.

6 MOMENTS TO PAY ATTENTION

1 at the start
Each day is a new beginning. You never know how the pitch will play and who will get on top, so watch closely for the first half-hour.

2 when KP comes in
Some players just make things happen. Kevin Pietersen is one of them. Get ready to wave your 4 or 6 sign – especially if he is joined by Matt Prior or Graeme Swann.

3 straight after lunch, tea or drinks
A wicket often falls in the first over after a break, or the first ball after drinks.

4 after 80 overs in a Test
The bowlers can take a new ball, which acts like a can of Red Bull – the bowling gets quicker, wickets may fall, and often runs flow.

5 when the tail-enders come in
Bad batsmen are good to watch. Look out for some slogging, and see the fielders' heads go down, as if tail-end runs count double.

6 when Graeme Swann bowls
Offspinners are not supposed to be crowd-pleasers, but Swann has developed a weird knack of taking a wicket in the first over of a new spell. And if the batsman is a left-hander, look out for a potential lbw.

▲ **Spelled out** Swann quickly snares another left-hander, Imran Farhat of Pakistan.

3 MOMENTS TO GO FOR A WANDER

1 half an hour before lunch
When the players go off, the shops and stalls get ridiculously crowded. Go early and get back to your seat to eat your lunch, then you can watch the highlights of the morning on the big screen.

2 after 20 overs in a one-day international
In the 50-over game, the middle overs are the dullest. The field is spread, the bowlers are just trying to contain, and the batsmen milk them for singles. Go for a stroll, and ask someone to text you if the powerplay starts.

3 when Jimmy Anderson is batting
His batting has improved greatly since the days when he used to play for Burnley, and he's even graduated to the heady heights of No 10. But he takes his role as nightwatchman very seriously indeed, and his overall strike-rate is 35. Eminently missable.

THE BARMY ARMY
Some people like to watch cricket very quietly, wearing a jacket and tie, as if sitting in church. And some don't. If you see a fellow spectator singing a song, doing the conga, wearing a nun's outfit and carrying a tray of 24 beers, he's probably a member of the Barmy Army. The Barmies were founded in Australia in 1994–95, when England were so hopeless, you had to be barmy to spend a whole winter watching them. They get mixed reviews. Are they admirably dedicated, tireless and quite funny, or tediously repetitive, tiresome and witless? Go along and decide for yourself. Your opinion may depend on how close you are sitting to them. Meanwhile, for a collection of their chants, go to **www.barmyarmy.com**.

HOW TO GET TICKETS

1 Ask a member
Got an uncle or grandpa (or aunt or granny) who's a member at Lord's or one of the other Test grounds? Don't be shy about asking them to take you along. They'd love to. They may even turn into a small child before your eyes.

2 Get your parents to join the mailing list
Or even the England Supporters' Club. Details at www.ecb.co.uk.

3 Go along on the day
It's easier to get in than you might think. Often a few hundred tickets will be held back for sale on the day – turn up about 9am, queue up, get your tickets and then go for breakfast. Sometimes there are fans with spares to sell too. On the fifth day of a Test (usually a Monday in England), all the tickets are held back and they are often reduced. The snag is that the game can fizzle out, but still, you'll have been to a Test match.

DO
- take binoculars
- take water
- stroll round behind the stands
- take a mobile if you have one
- wear sunscreen
- applaud both sides
- take a tennis ball

DON'T
- move behind the bowler's arm
- ask who's winning
- shove your autograph book under a player's nose without saying anything
- snore too loudly
- laugh if someone drops a catch

4 take the rules with a pinch of salt (everywhere, within reason)
Lord's is a magical place, but it does have an awful lot of fussy rules. As you go to your seat, a notice says: "The use of portable telephones is not permitted." And then you notice that everyone is on their mobile anyway, making plans to meet up with friends or family. You also notice that there are adverts everywhere promoting mobile-phone companies – they even used to be on the England team shirts.

5 play Count The Ties (round the back of the stands)
If you do find yourself on the concourse in an interval, progress is painfully slow. Amuse yourself by seeing how many MCC ties (orange and yellow, known as egg-and-bacon) you spot coming the other way. On the Sunday of the West Indies Test in 2007, my daughter Laura scored 51, writes *Tim de Lisle*. Make the game more like cricket by scoring four for an MCC hat, six for a blazer, and 50 for a set of MCC pyjamas.

THE MEDIA

Cricket was a multimedia experience before the term even existed. Because it takes a long time and the action happens in short bursts, the game is perfectly suited to television and radio. It's also the best sport to read and write about, and it has taken to the internet like a duck to a school scorecard. But there's now so much media coverage that it can be hard to find the good stuff, so here are some pointers.

TELEVISION

Best live coverage
Sky. (Also the worst, since it is the only channel with any live rights.) Strong on quantity: they show all England's matches, plus plenty of county cricket. Also good at camerawork, interviews, and detective gizmos like Hawk-Eye, Snicko and HotSpot. Getting better at commentary and analysis, even if one or two of the numerous England captains on the team sound jaded and a touch bored. But there are notable exceptions: Mike Atherton is calm and shrewd, and Nasser Hussain insightful and intelligent. Look out for humour from the former England coach David Lloyd, known to the world as Bumble, and stats from the faceless but astonishingly thorough Benedict Bermange.

Best highlights
Five. Smartly packaged, with Mark Nicholas presenting, and beautifully timed – during home Tests (May to September) they're on at 7.15–8pm, perfect for family viewing.

RADIO

Best live coverage
Test Match Special (usually BBC Radio 4 long wave, sometimes 5 Live Sports Extra on DAB). Not just a commentary team but a national treasure, *TMS* has fans who don't even like cricket. The show has a special flavour, old-fashioned but full of character – even if it has tried to appeal to a slightly younger audience in recent years. There's genial jokiness from Jonathan Agnew, relaxed earnestness from Christopher Martin-Jenkins, wry humour from Vic Marks, quirky insight from Phil Tufnell, technical analysis from Geoff Boycott and delicious chocolate cake from Mrs Blenkinsop in Tunbridge Wells.

Best for news
BBC 5 Live (AM radio or DAB). Obsessed with football – they think Chelsea v Bolton matters more than England v India. But they do cover home Tests and one-dayers, usually with a solid update from Pat Murphy or Alison Mitchell about once every 15 minutes.

INTERNET

Best for scores, stats and history
www.cricinfo.com.
An amazing site. Their scorecards are fast, they do live averages, they always tell you the number of balls faced and their text commentary is sparky, if not as good as the *Guardian*'s. They also have StatsGuru, a searchable database of the whole history of international cricket, so you can check out Ian Bell's Test average against Bangladesh (a mere 158, having at one stage reached 488) or Jimmy Anderson's bowling average against Pakistan (13). Plus, they have good writers in India and around the world, fine columns like Ask Steven (you send in a question, he answers it), and an increasingly excellent news service.

Best for basic news
www.bbc.co.uk. Want to know who's in, who's out, who's injured and who's just resigned? The BBC site is the place to go – quick, efficient and easy to navigate. Plenty of lively comment too, but not so much authority.

Best for text commentary
www.guardian.co.uk. Not content with having several good writers in the paper, the *Guardian* has a couple more doing over-by-over coverage. Look out for Rob Smyth, who is a riot but really knows his stuff – and some good emails from readers.

Best newcomer
www.testmatchsofa.com.
A renegade, online version of *Test Match Special*, it was founded by a group of unemployed friends in time for the 2009 Ashes, and now boasts 200,000 unique listeners. It's off-the-wall, passionate, and broadcast from the sofa of one of the commentator's front rooms, but look out for the adult language.

NEWSPAPERS

Best all round daily

The Times. Mike Atherton is a busy man. In between commentating for Sky, he has to write match reports and columns as the paper's chief cricket correspondent, and he does it very well – in 2010, he was named Sports Journalist of the Year, a rare honour for a former player. He is well-supported by his deputy, the diligent Richard Hobson, and – on match days in England – by his predecessor, Christopher Martin-Jenkins (press-box doyen, appointed MCC President in 2010) and chief sports writer Simon Barnes (elegant writer, horse-lover and bird-spotter). You used to be able to read them free online. Now you'll need your parents to pay.

www.thetimes.co.uk

Best all round Sunday

Sunday Telegraph. Ever-decreasing newspaper budgets mean the Sunday papers now tend to share writers with their sister dailies, but the *Sunday Tel* has retained an authority of its own, thanks to Scyld Berry, the most experienced and wisest of the main correspondents, and the former Glamorgan captain Steve James, who is always engaging and never dull.

Best for comment

Daily Telegraph, which has authoritative reporting from its two main men, Derek Pringle and Nick Hoult, plus a string of readable and well-connected columnists. Geoff Boycott is blunt, hard-hitting, and usually right – even if he bangs on about his own career a bit. The former England captain Michael Vaughan pulls no punches, and Shane Warne – who played against Vaughan in two Ashes series – pulls even fewer. Simon Hughes, a Middlesex seamer who also provides analysis for Channel 5, is perceptive, and Simon Briggs, the paper's former deputy cricket correspondent, writes the occasional well-pitched feature.

www.telegraph.co.uk

Best for county cricket

Guardian. This may not be saying much now that even the upmarket papers have gone lukewarm on county cricket, but the games the *Guardian* covers, it covers properly, usually allotting 300–400 words to a day's play. David Hopps writes wittily, especially about his native Yorkshire, Andy Bull is a rising star, and Andy Wilson sniffs out news. The irreverent online county blog is increasingly popular, and well worth a visit.

www.guardian.co.uk

MAGAZINES

Best for writing and design

The Wisden Cricketer (monthly). Nothing to do with *Wisden Cricketers' Almanack* these days, it is edited by John Stern, who produces a smart, readable magazine with excellent interviews, photos and comment.

Best for a laugh

Spin (monthly). Hard to find, but worth seeking out: cheeky and imaginative, if a bit chippy.

Best for the players

All Out Cricket (monthly). Off-piste and lively. Edited by Andy Afford, who used to play in the same band as England offspinner Graeme Swann: Dr Comfort and the Lurid Revelations.

7 TYPES OF CRICKET ARTICLE

News What just happened

Comment What the writer thinks about it

Match report What happened in the match

Sidebar Article next to the match report, usually more colourful or opinionated

Column Regular comment from the same writer or player

Feature Thorough look at a team, player or trend

Profile Feature about one person, usually involving an interview

BROADCAST LIKE BENAUD

6 tips from the man himself

The greatest cricket commentator is widely reckoned to be Richie Benaud, the voice of cricket on British and Australian television for more than 40 years. Now in his late seventies, he is only working for Channel 9 in Australia, but he remains the Bradman of the microphone. Here are his tips:

1 Develop a distinctive style

2 Put your brain into gear before opening your mouth

3 Never say "we" if referring to a team

4 Concentrate fiercely at all times

5 Try to avoid allowing these past your lips:

"Of course..."
"As you can see on the screen..."
"You know..."
"I tell you what..."
"That's a tragedy..."
or *"a disaster..."* (The Titanic was a tragedy, the Ethiopian drought a disaster, and neither bears any relation to a dropped catch.)

6 Above all, don't take yourself too seriously, and have fun

Adapted from *Wisden Cricketers' Almanack* 2003

CRICKET BOOKS A FIRST XI

Cricket is famous for producing good books. It has also produced plenty of bad ones – players' autobiographies, especially, should be approached with extreme care – but here are 11 books that can be enjoyed by children as well as adults, and the age at which you might try them.*

These are just guidelines. Some people take to reading young, others don't, and it doesn't make much difference in the long run.

age 7

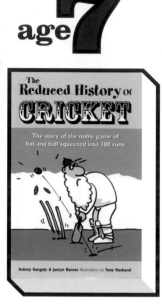

The Reduced History of Cricket
by Aubrey Ganguly and Justyn Barnes (Andre Deutsch, 2005)

Slim volume containing 100 entertaining stories and plenty of cartoons.

8

Playfair Cricket Annual
edited by Ian Marshall (Headline, every April)

Pocket-book of facts and figures on all the county players, plus scorecards from last year's Tests.

The Cricketers' Who's Who
edited by Michael Heatley (Green Umbrella, every April)

The details on every county player, from the exams he has passed to his views on the game.

9

The Wisden Guide to International Cricket
edited by Steven Lynch (John Wisden, every November)

Pithy profiles of all current international players, umpires and coaches.

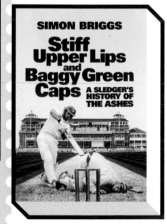

Stiff Upper Lips and Baggy Green Caps
by Simon Briggs (Quercus, 2006)

The story of the Ashes with all the rude bits left in, written by a bright journalist who is a sports feature writer on the *Daily Telegraph*.

10

One Hundred Greatest Cricketers

by John Woodcock (Macmillan, 1998)

Quick sketches of the all-time greats from an elegant writer who was *The Times*'s cricket correspondent for 33 years.

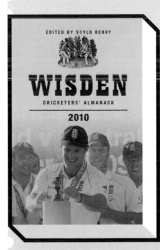

Wisden Cricketers' Almanack

edited by Scyld Berry (John Wisden, every April)

Punchy comment, chunky records, solid reports on all last year's internationals and county matches, and plenty of dry wit. Some kids find it hard going, but others lap it up – the editor of the 2010 edition, Scyld, started reading it when he was six. See panel, right.

11

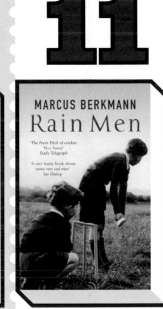

Rain Men

by Marcus Berkmann (Abacus, 1995)

The first and funnier of two books about the same cricket club, the Captain Scott Invitation XI – probably the worst team ever to inspire one book, let alone two. The other one is **Penguins Stopped Play** (2006), by Berkmann's former co-captain Harry Thompson, and it's pretty funny too.

On and Off the Field

by Ed Smith (Penguin, 2004)

The diary of a good player's best season – 2003, when Ed Smith made so many runs for Kent, he played three Tests for England in an exciting series against South Africa. Honest and highly intelligent.

12

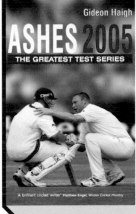

Ashes 2005: the Full Story of the Test Series

by Gideon Haigh (Aurum, 2005)

Most memorable of the many books about a classic series, written by an outstanding Anglo-Australian cricket writer.

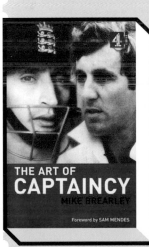

The Art of Captaincy

by Mike Brearley (Hodder, 1985)

The best book about the most complex of all cricket's arts, expertly explained by one of England's most successful captains. Probably the only cricket book to have inspired an Oscar-winning film director (see page 68).

HOW TO READ WISDEN

Wisden is like a museum: it can be a bit daunting, but there's plenty of fun to be had if you know where to look. Here are five tips:

1 Start at the back with the **Index of Unusual Occurrences**, which gives you an at-a-glance guide to some of the wackier stories. When you see an entry like "Live TV coverage of home Test starts at 4am", it's hard not to find out more.

2 Next, head for the **England players** section, which is a sort of school report on how all they fared in international cricket in the previous year.

3 Then find your **county** (arranged alphabetically) and remind yourself how well or badly they did last year.

4 Don't be afraid to **dip in at random**. There's always something interesting, especially in the boxes, which tend to be lighter than the main text. And it's amazing how often you go in to look up one thing and end up somewhere quite different.

5 Try the **articles** at the front, such as Andrew Strauss's account of how England won the Ashes in 2009. A lot of people think *Wisden* is all stats, but once you find the articles, you'll know better.

HAVE A GO YOURSELF

STAGE ONE PARK CRICKET

1 Persuade someone to play with you. Two is the bare minimum, three is fine, four or five is ideal. If grown-ups try to protest that they're no good at the game, gently point out that you're not exactly Kevin Pietersen either.

2 Get two tennis balls, preferably old (not too bouncy) and a cheap wooden bat (not plastic – they're noisy and useless). One of the balls is a spare. Take some water too. Stumps are optional: you can use other things for a wicket, like a thin tree, a shopping bag or a small child (well, the first two anyway). The second wicket can be a sweater. If there are only two of you, use inanimate objects as fielders – clothes, backpacks, etc. They won't be much worse than your friends.

3 Go to the park, unless you have a very big garden. Choose an area, about 20 metres square, that has short grass, no dog mess, and no irritable-looking people. Angle the pitch so that the sun isn't in the batsman's or bowler's eyes.

4 Agree on the rules beforehand. My preferred answers are in brackets.
- **the boundaries** (that line of trees over there)
- **whether you can be out first ball** (no)
- **whether it's tip and run** (yes, once the batsman has 10)
- **whether it's one-hand-one-bounce** (yes; half out)
- **who is deciding lbws** (a grown-up, if they are competent to; if not, don't bother with it)
- **whether you have to say "walking" or "in" to show you don't want a second run** (yes – "walking" – it's clearer)
- **when the batsman has to retire** (at 20)
- **how many innings each player is going to get** (start with one and make sure everyone has the same number; stomping off in a huff after you've batted is a grave crime)
- **whether to doctor the ball.** A ball that is half-taped will swing, so try that once you're more confident, and you may end up bowling for Pakistan

5 Decide who's batting first. If everyone wants to, toss for it. Announce which team or player you're going to be. Play like them if you can. If you can't, follow the basics…

Batting

Keep calm. Stand side-on. Grip the bat with two hands, wrong hand on top. Move your feet forward or back. Watch the ball right onto the bat. If the ball is heading for the stumps, keep it out. If not, whack it. Don't hit everything to leg.

Bowling

Take a short run-up. Keep your arm straight. Aim for accuracy first. Get the length right – the ball should bounce once before it reaches the batsman and head for the top of the stumps. Then the line – ideally off stump, certainly within the batsman's reach. Add spin or swing later.

Fielding

Pay attention. Get your body behind the ball as well as your hands. If you're bored, try harder. If that doesn't work, negotiate an earlier finish. Don't just sit down or stomp off.

Everyone

Try hard but not too hard. Games are only fun if you take them reasonably seriously, but if you take them too seriously, they're no fun at all.

Do say

Great shot. Good ball. My turn to get it.

Don't say

You're rubbish. My average is 46.25. Shane Warne does it, so it must be allowed.

Beach variations

Find a strip of firm sand. Work out which way the tide is going. Give six if the ball is hit straight into the sea; six and out if it's lost.

STAGE TWO FINDING A CLUB

If you keep making 20 in the park, or taking wickets, you're ready for a step up. And here you're in luck. No generation in sporting history has had as much encouragement to have a go. The government wants you to. The England and Wales Cricket Board wants you to. Several charities want you to. You're in demand.

● **If you're in England or Wales, you can find your nearest club at: www.play-cricket.com**

● **If you're in Scotland, try: www.cricketscotland.com**

● **If you're in Ireland, get a parent to ring the Irish Cricket Union in Dublin on (01) 845 0710, or go to www.cricketeurope4.net**

STAGE THREE PLAYING AT SCHOOL

If your school plays cricket, you're in luck. Sadly, most schools in Britain don't. But there are big efforts going on to make it easier for them. If your school doesn't play cricket, ask a teacher if you can. Ask them to get hold of a Kwik cricket set to get things going, and tell them there is a charity, Chance To Shine, set up to encourage cricket in state schools. It is trying to raise £25m, which the government says it will match. Its aim is to reach ten million state-school children in England and Wales by 2015, with a coach going in for four hours a week in the summer term, and courses in the holidays as well.
www.chancetoshine.org

STAGE FOUR GETTING SOME COACHING

Cricket is quite complicated, so you'll be better at it if you have some coaching. It's not cheap but you can ask for it as a present. Try to home in on any cricket-loving uncle or grandparent – perhaps there's one who gave you this book. They will be keen to help and may even go with you to get a bit of a refresher course themselves. A creaky, aching 50-year-old makes a reasonable match for a sprightly 12-year-old.

If you live near a county cricket club, ask your mum or dad to ring them (or ring yourself – phone calls are easier than you might think) and find out if nets can be booked. Book an hour if you can, and take along three friends, then you can bat for 15 minutes, bowl for 40 and spend five minutes getting changed and trying to work the vending machine. It's good exercise and good fun, especially in the middle of winter.

Anyone in reach of London can book a net at the MCC Indoor School at Lord's by ringing 020 7616 8612. You can choose to have a coach, a bowling machine (if you're 12+) or both. It's expensive – £44 per hour without a coach, £66 with – but good value, especially if you can split the cost. The nets are top-class and the coaches are gentle but effective.
www.lords.org

REMEMBER ...

These stages can happen in any order. Some people first sample the game at school, others at club open days. The point is to get on and do it.

DO TRY THIS AT HOME

You can play in the corridor with a mini-bat and a ping-pong ball, but it soon gets frustrating. A better idea is to persuade a generous parent to give you a Crazy Catch. This is a rebound net, invented in New Zealand, which sends the ball back at you at unexpected angles. You have to take it outside to use a cricket ball, but there's a lot of fun to be had indoors with a tennis ball. You can play alone, unlike most forms of cricket, or with someone else; all ages can play together. Your catching will improve dramatically. Should you ever find yourself writing a cricket book, you'll find it's the perfect way to relax after a morning bashing away at the keyboard.
www.crazycatch.com

This index is selective, but aims to point you to anything more than a passing reference. For definitions of cricket terms, see page 26; for the main fielding positions, see page 66

THANKYOU

Tim de Lisle writes: When you work for Wisden, you find yourself standing on the shoulders of giants. It's especially true of this book, which started life about 14 years ago as an idea developed by Matthew Engel and Christopher Lane, then editor-in-chief and publisher of the *Almanack*, now consultant editor and consultant publisher. I'm grateful to them for having the idea, and for not doing it themselves.

This book ended up going its own way, the main difference being that it became more visual. For that, most of the credit goes to Nigel Davies, who designed all the inside pages. Back in 1997, Nigel arrived at *Wisden Cricket Monthly* from the world of Manga comics. He took some persuading to stay (thank you, John Brown), but he is still there as art director of *The Wisden Cricketer*, after surviving two changes of editor, two changes of owner, one change of name and five changes of address. He is the king of cricket designers, creative, prolific, and tireless.

While the concept came from Wisden, the execution has come from A&C Black, who were the *Almanack*'s distributors when this book was first published in 2007, and are now its owners. Nigel and I are grateful to Robert Foss, our first editor there, and to Charlotte Atyeo, the current sports publisher; to Jill Coleman for her trenchant leadership; to James Watson for his work on the cover; and to Naomi Webb for the publicity.

Special thanks go to my agent, Araminta Whitley, for her relaxed expertise over 22 years; to James Bunce, who did the repro with great skill and good humour; and to two former Wisden colleagues, Simon Briggs (of the *Telegraph*) and Steven Lynch (of Ask Steven fame), who read a lot of pages with tactful acumen. Any errors that remain are my fault, not theirs. And very special thanks to Lawrence, for not just updating the book but improving it. He has brought wit and wisdom to the task, and great composure – he's the player every team needs, who gets the job done without any fuss.

Big thanks to the seven sounding boards I used – Daniel de Lisle, Laura de Lisle, Tanya Aldred, Dileep Premachandran, Josie Robson, Bobby and Sam Butler-Sloss; and to those who helped with specific pages – Clare Skinner, Philip Brown, Rory Brown, Billy Bowden, Nathan Ross, Mark Ramprakash and the Blogg family, Sue, Nigel and their son Hugo, the 12-year-old umpire. (Sue and Nigel, remember: as it says in the Spirit of Cricket, the umpire's decision is final.)

The main sources used were the phenomenal Cricinfo.com, BBC.co.uk, *Wisden Cricketers' Almanack* and Wikipedia. I also drew on *What Is a Googly?* by Rob Eastaway, *One Hundred Greatest Cricketers* by John Woodcock, *Arm-Ball to Zooter* by my co-author Lawrence Booth, *A Social History of Cricket* by Derek Birley, *A Century of Great Cricket Quotes* by David Hopps, *All About Cricket* by Brian Johnston, *Freddie Flintoff: England's Hero* by Tanya Aldred, and *Barclays World of Cricket*, edited by E.W. Swanton et al. For inspiration, the main source was *Pick Me Up*, the superb neo-encyclopedia by David Roberts and Jeremy Leslie. The idea of telling a story at regular intervals on pages that look like a different book came from *The Dangerous Book for Boys* by Conn and Hal Iggulden.

Behind every cricket fan lies a tolerant family. I've been lucky and had two such families. My parents, Everard and Mary Rose, gave endless loving support on this and every other front. They took me to matches, bought me kit and books, and, along with my sister, Rosie, found themselves listening to rather more cricket conversation than they might have wished.

These days, my cricket habit is inflicted on my wife, Amanda, our son Daniel and our daughter Laura, who all put up with this project without losing their cool or their warmth. But the central figure in my cricket life has been my brother, Charlie, who introduced me to the game, played it with me in our ropey old net, made interesting points about it, led the way into cricket writing, and treated me more sportingly than any younger brother had a right to expect. This book is dedicated to him.

Lawrence Booth writes: When Tim de Lisle invited me to update this book, it felt like a chance to come home. Tim was editor of *Wisden Cricket Monthly* when I turned up, fresh-faced, at the magazine for a work-experience stint in the summer of 1998. Work experience usually means a lot of photocpying and making the tea, but the fact that Tim gave me more interesting things to do, and some tips on doing them, helped me to turn cricket-writing into a career. To Tim go my thanks for firing a passion and for trusting me – in an inversion of the natural order – to have a crack at his prose instead.

This was no straightforward task, but the process was made much easier by the brilliance of the book's designer, Nigel Davies, and the calm encouragement of our editor at A&C Black, Charlotte Atyeo. Thanks also to Becky Senior for her painstaking proofreading, and to the England cricketers Charlotte Edwards and Claire Taylor for their contributions to the new spread on the women's game.